adopting
h♥pe

With contributions from Anne Stark,
Kate Stark Knight, Mary Ellen Stark
McWilliams, and many others.

FAMILIUS

Copyright © 2018 by Lorri Antosz Benson
All rights reserved.

Published by Familius LLC, www.familius.com

Familius books are available at special discounts for bulk purchases, whether for
sales promotions or for family or corporate use. For more information, contact
Familius Sales at 559-876-2170 or email orders@familius.com.

Some names and identifying details have been changed to protect the privacy
of individuals. Although the author and publisher have made every effort to
ensure that the information in this book was correct at press time, the author and
publisher do not assume and hereby disclaim any liability to any party for any
loss, damage, or disruption caused by errors or omissions, whether such errors or
omissions result from negligence, accident, or any other cause.

Library of Congress Cataloging-in-Publication Data
2018937155
Print ISBN 9781641700368
Ebook ISBN 9781641700870

Printed in the United States of America

Edited by Leah Welker
Cover design by David Miles
Book design by inlinebooks

10 9 8 7 6 5 4 3 2 1

First Edition

LORRI ANTOSZ BENSON

adopting h♥pe

Stories and Real-Life Advice from Birthparents, Adoptive Parents, and Adoptees

AN ESSENTIAL RESOURCE FOR PARENTS WHO ARE

Surviving the agonizing wait to become parents,

Preparing to bring your child home,

Telling your child "the story,"

Making your child feel loved.

Dedicated to

The "Sistas," my four daughters:
Taryn, Taylor, Halli, and Kate.
Your tremendous abilities to love,
accept, celebrate, and embrace
each other are one of my
greatest gifts in life.

CONTENTS

NOT ALONE ANYMORE

Ana Rose O'Halloran

Ana, age thirty-five, is the executive director of a nonprofit theatre in Los Angeles. She and her husband, Grant, have been married for five years and adopted their first child, Blaine, in June 2017.

I have always known I wanted to be a mom. So, when I met Grant, it was upsetting to hear he didn't want children. I still remember us looking at each other awkwardly for the rest of our date. We had been dating about a month, and it was apparent to everyone, including me, that we were going to get married. However, Grant not wanting children was a deal breaker for me. Two days later, he called me and told me that he hadn't stopped thinking about our conversation. He told me he couldn't see a future without me and that if having children meant we could be together, then he wanted them too.

Grant and I are planners—to the extreme. Around the time that we met, he was in the process of buying a house. It ended up being the first house we lived in together, and while it was great for a couple starting out, we knew it wouldn't be big enough for us to start a family. We had our plan: get married, renovate our current house, buy a bigger house, and then start our family. So, after we got married we spent the next year completing renovations. Near the end of the renovations, we agreed the timing was right to start our family. This was the beginning of a three-year period of heartbreak after heartbreak.

For the first few months, I shrugged it off every time I realized that I wasn't pregnant. I tried to act as if it were not a big deal, because I knew that stress could affect the possibilities for the next month. I tried to look happy, and not jealous, as friend after friend told me they were going to have a baby. After the first six months, I started reading books and articles, and it seemed everyone's advice for couples our age was to wait one year before going to a doctor. So, I became more diligent, taking my temperature every morning and tracking my ovulation. When that still didn't work, Grant and I agreed to see a fertility doctor. Based on everything we read, it seemed easier to run tests on Grant first, so we did.

We both assumed it was an issue with me. So, we were quite shocked when the doctor informed us that it was an issue with Grant. He suggested Grant be put on a fertility drug to try to increase our chances of getting pregnant. We followed the advice, but we were met with the same disappointment each month when we realized we still weren't pregnant. The doctor then suggested I get tested too because he wasn't sure why this wasn't solving the problem.

I was scheduled for an HSG test. Luckily, I was really busy at work and didn't look online to see what this meant. I probably would have backed out if I had. The pain from this test was so intense that I almost passed out in the doctor's office. I still remember crying to my mom on the phone, heading home afterward instead of to work where I had planned to go, questioning how I would ever have a baby if I couldn't even take the pain of this test. Then the other line started ringing, and it was the nurse, who informed me that the test showed I had something called a bicornuate uterus. She said while this didn't prevent me from getting pregnant, it significantly increased my risks of having a miscarriage if I did. I was devastated. I drove myself home, pulled the covers over my head, and sobbed my eyes out in bed for several hours until Grant came home.

We decided to go back to the doctor and come up with a new plan. The doctor let us know that after retesting Grant, the fertility drug had actually had the opposite effect that he had hoped. He recommended that we try IVF and that we both go on fertility drugs to increase our chances before it was too late. Neither of us was very excited by the idea of being on the fertility drugs at the same time, and theoretical conversations we'd had of worst-case scenarios became a reality, crashing down on us.

We needed to decide how we wanted to move forward with starting our family. We had previously discussed adoption as an option, but more in the "if we have more than one baby, it might be nice to adopt" way. We talked for hours. We ruled out surrogacy, finding a sperm donor, and IVF as options for us. I cried more deeply than I have ever cried in my life during these conversations. I felt like part of my heart was dying, but by the end of the last discussion, we had our plan. We knew we wanted to move forward with adoption to create the family that we both so desperately wanted.

In some ways, I think we were lucky that our infertility journey took so long. During the adoption process, we kept being told that in order to successfully adopt, it was important that we fully mourn the loss of our biological children. I had already done that each time we received bad news from the doctor and, ultimately, on that last day, as I cried for my biological children who would never exist.

Grant and I got to work coming up with our plan for the adoption. We discussed so many things about our future child—gender, race, age, medical background, and geographic preference. We decided to hire an adoption attorney to help us rather than going to an agency because we felt that was the better fit for us. We decided we didn't care if we had a boy or girl. We didn't care what race the baby was; we knew we wanted a newborn and that we wanted to adopt domestically. One of our biggest conversations was about the type of contact we wanted with our child's birthparents. I told Grant that I only wanted a closed adoption. My reasoning was that everyone I knew who was adopted didn't know their birthparents and seemed fine, and the thought of an open adoption just made me feel too vulnerable somehow.

Shortly before Christmas, we had our first home study visit. As part of this process, we were required to take classes online and read books. They made recommendations but also allowed us to pick our own books to read. That week, I happened to be at a bookstore picking out some books for our nieces and nephew for Christmas gifts and as I turned to leave, I noticed a section right behind me about adoption. I stopped to see what books were there and noticed one about a birthmother's experience with her own adoption, *To Have and Not to Hold*.

I read Lorri Antosz Benson's story in one day. Grant kept giving me sideways glances because I was crying the entire time, but this time I was crying because I felt like part of my heart was opening up. Lorri's account of her own story combined with the letters she received from her daughter's adoptive mother melted away all of my insecurities about an open adoption. While I knew that this story was theirs and wouldn't be the same for me, I thought that if those two women could find such a deep respect for each other, then I could for my child's birthmother, too. I told Grant I had changed my mind. I made him read the book, and we let our attorney know about our decision.

Soon, our attorney started presenting us with opportunities. Each time we had to decide if we wanted to be presented to the birthparents. It was really hard to say no to some situations that weren't the right fit for us, because we had waited so long, and several times Grant had to convince me that we should say no.

Then it happened. Of course, I didn't know it at that moment, because we had agreed to be presented several times already, only to be disappointed when we were told the mother didn't pick us. This time our attorney called us to let us know that this mom wanted to meet us and only us.

I was so nervous for the first meeting. Our attorney told us to approach it like a first date, which was exactly how it felt. Except it was a first date that we had to drive six hours to get to, so I had plenty of time to worry. Would she still think we were the right people when she met us? Would she change her mind? We spent over two hours with her at breakfast, and then I knew. I told Grant as we got into our car to leave, "I think this is our baby. I can just tell it's meant to be."

The next eight weeks were an emotional roller-coaster. I would go through so many emotions almost simultaneously—I would be overjoyed, overwhelmed, anxious, repeat. We decided to tell our family and close friends, but we worried that the adoption might fall through somehow, so we didn't tell anyone else. It was the most intense secret I have ever kept. Being planners, this was another really tough time for us. We had no control over what was happening with our baby, and our lawyer finally had to remind us that while this was our baby, this wasn't our pregnancy. She told us if we didn't give up control and just "go with it," we might sabotage this situation. So, we tried to focus on other things so our worry wouldn't consume us.

We kept being told that our birthmother wanted us there when the baby was born. So, Grant and I decided to go up early to make sure we were nearby. This gave us a chance to meet the birthfather too. I went through all the same emotions and fears that I had before we met the birthmother, but again, as soon as we met him, we knew everything would be fine. After a couple of days, they finally decided to induce labor. There we were, all together in the delivery room for fifteen hours. Grant had come up with a bunch of questions for the birthparents, things he wanted to tell our son about them someday. While I was a little embarrassed about it, it ended up being really fun and helped pass the time. We all took turns answering the questions and learning about each other's favorite musicians, where we grew up, and our hobbies.

At 5:19 a.m. our son Blaine was born. Our birthmother had told us that she didn't want to hold him when he was born. In fact, she insisted that the nurses give him directly to me. Our birthfather, on the other hand, wanted to see him. I made sure he knew we wanted him to hold Blaine if he wanted. When they started escorting us down the hall to the room our facilitator had helped arrange for us, I told the birthfather to come with us. It was the best and most surreal moment of my life, looking down at my son staring back at me. I composed myself and asked his birthfather if he wanted to hold him, and he did. Then Grant held him. I kept thinking about how lucky Blaine was that so many people loved him so much already.

The next twenty-four hours were equally amazing and hard. I kept thinking about how intense my feelings of joy were, and then how Blaine's birthparents must be experiencing the same intensity of sadness just a few feet away down the hall. They left the hospital pretty quickly, but Blaine's birthfather came to see him again before he left. I asked if he wanted to hold him again, and he did. Grant left with him to head to the parking garage because we had small gifts for them both. I sat in the hospital room thinking about how trivial the gifts felt in this situation, but when he came back to the room, Grant said they liked them. We saw them again the next day after we were released from the hospital. To our surprise, his birthmom agreed to come, even though she had originally told us she didn't want to see him.

I got really nervous as we headed to meet them. I just kept thinking that they were going to change their minds when they saw him again. They walked in, and we chatted a little. After a few minutes, I asked his birthmom if she wanted to hold him, but she didn't. After a while, it was clear we had their blessing to leave. I think they just wanted one last reassurance that they had made the right decision. I gave them both hugs and told them how grateful we were that they had chosen us and how much we loved Blaine. His birthmom whispered back that we were her angels. We started our drive home, me crying in the backseat with Blaine, as we headed to start our life together.

It has only been two months since Blaine was born. I think about his birthparents every single day. As I hold him, I see their faces. When I tell him I love him, I think about how much they love him too. As I spend my days with him, I think about them spending their days without him. Blaine is so lucky: he has four parents who will forever love him intensely. I know we probably won't see them for a while, but I can't wait for Blaine to see them again in the future. Then, he will be able to experience their love for him firsthand like I have throughout this difficult and beautiful process.

When Grant and I were going through the adoption process, we found it to be a surprisingly lonely journey. I think that's why I was so drawn to Lorri's first adoption book, *To Have and Not to Hold*. Being able to read her firsthand account made me feel more connected to the adoption community and gave me a new perspective about how our future birth-mother might be feeling about the process. That's what I hope this book does for you.

I believe strongly in the power of storytelling. Being able to read and relate to other people through their stories gives us all the opportunity to gain empathy for others and recognize our own place in that story. Each of these adoption stories—just like Lorri's and mine—is unique, but after reading them, I hope you will feel less alone (and maybe even learn something new) while you go through your own adoption journey.

PART ONE

There's More
to Our Story

CHAPTER ONE

WHO'S AND WHY'S

Lorri Antosz Benson

Lorri is the author of Adopting Hope, *along with her first book about adoption,* To Have and Not to Hold. *She is married to Steve, she has three grown daughters, is the birthmother of Kate, and a grandmother of five. For her full bio, please see the end of the book or her website (www.LorriAntoszBenson.com).*

So often, the stories we hear in the media about adoption involve a famous name: a singer or athlete or movie star. *People* magazine is filled with stories of this one who adopted three children from Africa, or that one who grew up as an adopted child. While they all have an amazing story to tell, I have discovered that it's the average person who has the stories and experiences that could be the basis for a screenplay or country song. The people who wait, without the benefit of money or influence, to be chosen as parents. The birthmothers and birthfathers who agonize over the idea of giving up their child and then live with a dream of someday seeing that child. The adopted children who walk a fine line, balancing their "need to know" with their desire to not hurt their wonderful parents. I've discovered everyday heroes, and even saints, while putting this book together. And their stories hold so many universal truths, knowledge, and experience! I've discovered a treasure trove of information for anyone on an adoption path.

When I wrote my previous book about adoption, *To Have and Not to Hold*, my main objective was to tell an extraordinary story. I knew the account of my accidental pregnancy and all that followed had the elements of a spellbinding novel: sorrow, joy, love, tragedy, loss, relationships, passion, and, most importantly, the happy ending.

If you haven't read it, in short, I was twenty-four, at the start of my career in television, and had just gotten my big break, working as an associate producer for Phil Donahue. I was in the early stages of a relationship when I found myself very accidentally pregnant. After agonizing for nine months over a decision of how I could possibly raise my baby alone, in a city with no family or support system, and with a twenty-four seven job, I made the heartbreaking decision to place my daughter for adoption. All the details of this, and the years that followed, are in *To Have and Not to Hold*; suffice it to say, my daughter Kate initiated the opening of our adoption, which resulted in the blessed, blended family that we enjoy today. We were lucky, and we have had a fairy-tale ending, and I am quick to say that I know that is not always the case.

I did, however, feel like a positive adoption story was worth telling in general. I also hoped *To Have and Not to Hold* would get a few messages across to any readers with adoption stories of their own.

One was for adoptive parents. I felt certain that the parents of my birthdaughter, Kate, had done a remarkable job in their part of our story. Besides raising her exactly according to my hopes and dreams, they also supported her "need to know" in the most compassionate, selfless way. They put her curious desires ahead of any parental anxiety they may have felt. And when a miraculous connection took place, they welcomed not only me, the birthmother, but my husband and family as well, giving their daughter the chance to forge relationships with unknown sisters and another father figure.

I felt that reading about Anne and Temple's compassionate and loving approach, which yielded such beautiful results, could be an inspiration for adoptive parents who feared a relationship between their child and a birthmother or birthfather. Understandably, a great many parents would prefer to keep their family *their* family. I completely get the trepidation and concern that a mother or father would feel if there was even a chance of threatening the stability of a nuclear family. It's a tough risk to take, but in our case, Anne and Temple's gamble enhanced the lives of all concerned. It took nothing away from their relationship with their daughter, and instead it brought together people who seemed meant to be family. At the same time, they deepened their own bonds with each other and with their children.

I also wanted to get a message out to potential birthmothers. Making the choice to place a child for adoption is courageous, horribly difficult, and life changing, but it can turn out to be a blessing for all involved. It can turn out to be the right choice, and while it's a choice that certainly benefits the adoptive couple, and hopefully the child, it can also work out for the birthparents. I wanted to tell pregnant women that adoption is a viable option, one that can be done. So many women say they could never give up their baby. Is it easy? Certainly not . . . and probably right up there with the most difficult decisions one can make. But it can be done, and in my mind, it's better than some of the other choices. Let me be clear: obviously, I support mothers keeping their children. I have three daughters I raised with my husband. But if circumstances are so difficult that it's not possible to give a child the attention and support needed, then yes, I advocate adoption.

Finally, I also had a message for adopted children. You were not rejected. You were not unloved. I wanted to tell this story so you could see that it is a tremendous love that gives a woman the heroic strength to choose the best path for her child. In writing *To Have and Not to Hold*, I hoped to reach those of you who struggled with the idea that you weren't wanted.

I realize that our story is not everyone's story. And that is how *Adopting Hope* came to be. My publisher, Christopher Robbins, and I wanted to create a follow-up to *To Have and Not to Hold* that would address the fact that each adoption is unique. Adoption is complicated. Some are fairy tales, some are just real life, and sometimes things don't work out how they were planned. I started out wanting this book to be a positive testament to adoption. I figured we'd get amazing, upbeat stories from all over the country, stories that could provide encouraging words of wisdom to people entering the adoption world, whether as adoptive parents, potential birthparents, or maturing adoptees. And then I started talking to people.

The more I researched, the more stories I found, the more I realized that it was imperative to have all kinds of examples illustrated in a resource meant to be helpful. You can learn just as much from relationships that suffered as you can from thriving ones. Many lessons are learned during challenges, setbacks, and struggles. In fact, I think it's fair to say that life's biggest times of growth are during the valleys, not the peaks. For that reason, I expanded the scope of the book to include stories from lots of viewpoints, and with varying end results. I want *Adopting Hope* to be a resource for people who want answers. It's for people who don't want to feel alone. It's for those who are interested in learning from others' experiences. It's also for anyone who loves reading great stories . . . There are about forty of them for you!

And so it begins. **Part one** of this book is the full circle that *To Have and Not to Hold* started. It is the continuation of our story from the perspective of my birthdaughter, Kate, her adoptive mother, Anne, and her sister, Mary Ellen, who, though also adopted, has chosen not to contact her birthparents. It contains valuable suggestions and advice from people who, in my possibly biased opinion, did everything right.

Part two will feature stories from birthparents, with their unique take on what works and doesn't work, followed by **part three**, which will offer the viewpoint of adoptive parents. Finally, in **part four**, you will hear from the adoptees. These are the ones whose lives were arguably most affected. These are the children the birthparents agonized over, the babies so desperately wanted by their adoptive parents.

One theme that resonated over and over in the stories I collected was the idea of destiny. All along, I've been amazed by the "meant to be" flavor of our story. There was an irrefutable feeling that somehow Kate's family and mine were supposed to be together; that Anne and I were destined to share a remarkable friendship; that Kate and her sister Mary Ellen were meant to be sisters with my girls. I thought that was just us, but time and time again, people told me they had a feeling of destiny. So many adoptive parents described knowing when their child was placed in their arms, even in cases when other adoptions had fallen through. And even in stories that didn't necessarily have happy endings, many feel that fate was part of their adoption story.

So many of these voices from across the continent have stories that could fill their own books. Adoption stories tend to have twists and turns that could rival any best-selling novel, and these are no exception. In a very few cases, the writers' names and identifying details have been changed to protect people in their lives. For almost all, however, every detail is true, and certainly in all chapters the suggestions, lessons learned, and words of wisdom are genuine and from the heart. I hope their stories move you, educate you, make you laugh, make you cry, and, most of all, I hope they are helpful to you as you make your way on your own, very personal, adoption journey.

CHAPTER TWO

THE MORE LOVE,
THE BETTER

Anne Stark

Anne, an attorney, is the adoptive mother of my birthdaughter, Kate. She raised Kate and her other adopted daughter, Mary Ellen, with her husband, Temple, in Dallas, Texas. Tragically, Temple passed away in 2007 from early-onset Alzheimer's disease.

When Lorri asked me to be a part of her next book on adoption, I was up for the challenge. I may not be a writer, but I am an adoptive mother with a very happy adoption story, and I never shy away from sharing this happiness. Our story is one of a close, family-centered existence, and this has everything and nothing to do with adoption. It's just how we are.

My brother and I were raised by my parents in a loving home. I knew well before I married Temple that I wanted to have children because I felt a strong urge to provide the same loving environment that my parents had given me. Temple was an only child, raised in a similar way. He was also adopted, and his easy attitude and matter-of-fact sensibility about adoption helped me to see it as a very natural and positive state of being. After we had been married about a year, we expected to be able to conceive a child—without having given any real thought to the prospect that it might not happen. After about eight years of doctor's appointments, tests, and one surgery, we finally had a doctor in Philadelphia tell us it was a virtual impossibility for me to become pregnant. During that same time period, we had decided to move forward with adoption. But because of our moves around the country with the military, our graduate studies, and our first jobs (ten different addresses in the first eight years of marriage), we were unable to stay on local adoption agency lists.

But for Temple's tenacity, I might not be writing these lines. While we were in Philadelphia, we located an agency in Chicago, The Cradle, that did adoptions for couples on the East Coast. During Temple's first phone call with The Cradle, they indicated they were not taking any new applications at that time. He spent the next year making friends with anyone who answered the phone at The Cradle, always letting them know we were very anxious for them to let us start the process. Temple was a powerfully persuasive man, and he finally got the word that we could start an application.

That was our jackpot. We sent in our paperwork, did our interview in Chicago, and had a home study in Philadelphia. Our caseworker indicated it could take as long as a year after we were approved in June 1981. I was in law school and about to start my third year in the fall, so my prayers for a baby included the caveat that it would be better not to get the call during finals.

As it happened, at noon on December 4, Temple got the call at his office and immediately reached me at the law school the first day of the reading period for finals. He asked me if I remembered what I was doing on November 8, and after I made several exasperating attempts to find out why he wanted to know that, he finally said, "That's the day your daughter was born." We had no nursery, no crib, and no diapers because we never could bring ourselves to set up a baby's room, afraid it wouldn't happen. That Saturday was a whirlwind of buying baby stuff and setting it all up, and then off to Chicago on Sunday. Our sweet, wonderful Kate "bombed" into our lives on Monday morning, December 7, Pearl Harbor Day, in Evanston, Illinois. When we returned to Philadelphia that night, we found a house decorated by law school buddies with little pink ribbons everywhere! It was the most exciting day of our young married lives, and the next morning, all we could do was gaze with incredulity at this little being who was finally our child.

For the next three years, Kate was the center of our universe. Like all new parents, we were clueless, but we were also quick learners. We wanted to share her with our parents and also wanted her to have the benefit of grandparents close by. From a career standpoint, when Kate was a year old, it made sense to move back home to Texas. Before doing so, we called The Cradle to be certain that we could arrange a second adoption in Texas; we had always wanted more than one child, and now the desire was even stronger since we wanted Kate to have a sibling. The Cradle was kind enough to go out of their jurisdiction. Mary Ellen was born on November 12, 1984, and became our Christmas baby—with the phone call happening on December 20. Kate actually was the one who took the call!

I had not received any letters from Lorri since Kate was six months old. During our waiting period for Mary Ellen, when the records opened, I received a letter from Lorri explaining that The Cradle's policies had kept us from exchanging letters and information for those three years. I sent The Cradle my permission so communication between Lorri and I could continue after our records closed again following Mary Ellen's adoption.

Being parents was the most natural thing in the world for Temple and me. Being adoptive parents is no different in any appreciable way than having borne your children naturally. I never think about the girls being anything other than our daughters, even though I was always mindful of their birthmothers and so thankful for their gifts to us. As we raised our girls, Lorri and I exchanged updates and eventually pictures of our families. For me, these packages were exciting and fascinating. Temple had never felt the need to search out his birthparents, but he was curious about siblings. He always supported both my curiosity and, later, Kate's desire to know her birthparents. My only hesitation over the years was wanting to make sure Kate was old enough to understand and mature enough to not use her store of information to hurt her sister, whose birthmother's updates were not as frequent.

When Kate was sixteen, she decided she wanted to meet Lorri and her family, and I shared her inquisitiveness. After all our letters over the years, I already felt like I knew Lorri, and I knew her love for Kate was genuine. Temple and I believed with all our hearts that the more love a child feels from all sources, the better. Although the outcome was uncertain, I felt the potential benefits more than outweighed any risks. That gamble paid off in spades when Kate and I arrived in Florida for a weekend to end all weekends. From the first moment we met Lorri and Steve, all of us felt the immediate and natural connection. The sisters bonded instantly, and as we sat on the sofa together the first morning of our visit, Lorri and I talked nonstop about Kate's first days with Lorri and her first weeks with Temple and me. We shed many a tear together. Steve was the most accommodating and wonderful husband of a birthmother that could be imagined—he simply made it all very normal and fun. It was only a matter of time before Temple and Mary Ellen were brought into this new "normal," and although neither of them chose that path for themselves (and in fact, thirteen-year-old Mary Ellen thought that it was just plain "weird"), they opened their hearts and welcomed all the Bensons into our family.

The rest is history, as they say, and well documented in Lorri's book, *To Have and Not to Hold*. I've spent some time thinking about what lessons I've learned along the way and what helpful advice I might be able to give.

These are my thoughts about what concerns and considerations were key in our adoption story with Kate and Mary Ellen. As I was ruminating on this subject, it seemed that all topics usually led back to the very simple premise that if you put yourself in the other person's shoes—the shoes of the birthchild or birthparent—and earnestly try to grasp his or her perspective, you will in all likelihood come up with a good plan to deal with the random issues that crop up and will foster truly wonderful relationships.

These thoughts may not always jive with adoptions that are open from the very beginning. Our adoptions were closed at the time we brought our babies home. Kate's was gradually opened, and Mary Ellen has chosen not to take that step.

1. THE ADOPTIVE PARENTS' MINDSET

Before adoption—prior to getting "the phone call"—an adoptive parent needs to *be prepared*. That means much more than just getting the room and the house ready. There has to be a concrete cognitive realization that you are becoming a parent. Harder to do without a pregnancy, but the commitment has to be exactly the same. The child who is adopted has to know and believe at a fundamental level that he or she is *your* child and that you are his or her mom or dad. The only way that happens is for the commitment to be mentally in place long before you bring the little bundle home. It's hard to describe how that develops, but it is the key element of adoptive parenting—to assume your role fully and without any reservation or differentiation because the child was born to another. It's akin to the couple who has a longstanding relationship but has not committed to marriage. Once engaged, they experience a new level of commitment and dedication to one another. It's the same feeling for adoptive parents, except that the commitment and dedication to being a parent has to take place while you are in limbo, waiting for a phone call, and before you even lay eyes on your child.

After adoption, you are parenting as the child's "real" mom or dad. After several sleepless nights, the baby's teething, the baby's first ear infection, and so on, it's very real. But your child will at some point become aware of the existence of other parents—the birthparents. So, without lessening your carefully nurtured commitment, you have to realize that the child has another dimension in his or her life—and that dimension is another type of parent that has an undeniable tie, one which will likely be explored at least partially or even fully in years to come. That dimension should never feel like a threat; it cannot take away your parenthood. Children of committed adoptive parents will always know that those adoptive parents are the people who raised them and are their parents in the fullest sense of the word. Having a relationship with a birthparent will not diminish that relationship unless you let it.

2. DISCLOSURE

And now for telling The Story. How do you tell a child he or she is "adopted"? The best telling is one that spreads over time, with no beginning that the child can recall. Our situation was greatly benefited by the fact that my husband was an adopted child—and one who felt like that fact was not a very big deal at all. He was completely comfortable with his status and felt no different than any of his friends concerning his parents. So, I asked his mom how that happened: How did she make him feel so comfortable? How did she tell him? She said that from the time he was two weeks old and first placed in her arms, she told him "the story." Hers was different from the one we told Kate and Mary Ellen, because it was hers. Ours was basically how we wanted so much to have a baby and were not able to, but we were able to contact a place called The Cradle and were so lucky and blessed to have them help us find them so we could be their mom and dad. Although some adoptive parents embroider the basics with the tale of "we chose you," (and even we may have said that occasionally), that is not really exactly what happens in most instances. In our case, The Cradle chose a small pool of adoptive parents based on their evaluation, the birthparents' input, and our input. Finally, Lorri chose us from five profiles she read. So, we thought that the story should be told with the true facts in a very simple way, always ending with the fact that we were so happy we were able to be her mom and dad.

A six-month-old, two-year old, or four-year-old will likely not put together the fact that they have birthparents, so we chose to focus on our relationship with our children in the early telling, not really thinking that awareness of the birthparents would happen as early as it did. We were waiting for the right time for the first discussion of the birds and the bees! But when Kate was six years old, she told a neighbor's child she was adopted, and the neighbor's child explained that there was a woman out there that grew Kate in her tummy. I don't know when that awareness hit Mary Ellen—but as with all things, younger siblings learn earlier about a lot of things, usually from their older siblings.

It seems as if it is asking way too much of a little boy or girl in kindergarten or elementary school to fully comprehend why children are given to adoptive parents without feeling some sense of rejection. That was our foremost concern—staving off feelings of rejection. So, our focus when those questions arose about the birthparents was always to emphasize the goodness and love that prompted the adoption: the need for her to have a mom and dad that could care for her and provide the very best home for her. Simply saying that it was not possible for the birthparents to fill that need seemed to be a very acceptable rationale for younger children, without going into any long story about the circumstances that existed.

As the children aged, those discussions did focus more on the birthparents and the reasons for the adoption, but we generally let those conversations flow from their need to know and not on any time schedule we laid down. And again, the emphasis was always not to say "Your birthmother gave you up for adoption," but to say "Your birthparents gave us the greatest gift: a gift of love, and it was you."

There is a completely natural curiosity for every adopted child to wonder about birthparents: what they look like, what type of personality they have, what they do, and so on. To try to interfere with that interest or cut it off is unwise. We took our cues from Kate and Mary Ellen; when they wanted information, we gave them what they asked for, not more, not less. I believe that gave them control over a very personal aspect of their life—that dimension that only they could feel. Being in control hopefully made it less threatening or painful.

3. OPEN OR CLOSED?

The trend during the time when we adopted was for agency adoptions to be closed until both the child and birthparent consented to opening up the adoption. The child's consent could not be given until the age of majority unless provided by consent of the adoptive parents as guardians. I understand that now the trend is for adoptions to be open from the time of placement.

Our experience with starting out on a closed basis was a good experience—for us. I can't determine whether it would have benefited either of our children to have had a completely open adoption. All I can say is that the time prior to the opening (which was about sixteen years for Kate) gave us the time and space to fully develop our parent—mom and dad—status. Perhaps that long period of being the only parents known to our children gave us the confidence to help Kate open her adoption and our willingness to help Mary Ellen do the same, without any fears about that process. We always welcomed that prospect and were hopeful that we might get to meet the birthparents, mostly because of our profound sense of gratitude. But the bottom line should really be about the child's prerogative and his or hers only. The relationships adoptive children have with their birthparents are fundamentally *their* relationships to develop or not. I don't believe that decision should be made for the child. Nor should there be pressure on a child one way or the other. This is perhaps a line of thinking that is alien to today's adoption process, but in watching Kate's and Mary Ellen's decisions and knowing other adoptive children who have opened their adoptions, it has become very clear to me that it is an extremely personal decision and one that should be based primarily on the needs and desires of the adoptee.

There are great rewards to be had in opening an adoption, and it should be a joyful experience for all involved. I know that is not possible in many circumstances, but Kate's story was book-worthy in its success—a happy ending for her and for both families. We have all benefited from the joining of two families through Kate's adoption, and I sincerely believe that is possible *if* the parties involved always seek to understand the feelings and perceptions of the other parties in the process and focus on the best interests of the child.

4. RANDOM EXPERIENCES WITH ADOPTION

As the girls grew up, there were so many times that their adoptive status cropped up without warning. The most typical was the stranger at the grocery store who said to Kate or Mary Ellen (both at various times, many times): "You look so much like your mother."

At first, I think I just smiled knowingly at my child and went on. But eventually, we would laugh, and one of us would say, "Well, that's weird because I am [or she is] adopted."

Then the clerk or person in line would sheepishly smile and exclaim, "*Really?*"

For some folks who were born a century ago or don't know much about adoption, there is a certain stigma to being adopted that makes it seem as if the child were somehow different. That thinking is always so alien to me. So, the more I could broadcast that these very normal children with a very normal relationship with Mom and Dad *were* adopted, the better. As a result, I was always very open about that fact. I think that contributed in some measure to the girls feeling like it was a normal process, too—nothing out of the ordinary. I seem to recall that the first few times that happened with strangers, I may have made the girls feel a little uncomfortable, but repetition worked: that discomfort disappeared quickly.

Another random thing that *will* happen is the inevitable argument retaliation: when your adopted child tells you in the midst of a terrible fight, "You are *not* my mother!" That retort has to roll off you like water off a duck's back because it is said only to hurt you in the moment and not because it is heartfelt. In my children's minds, that was the worst thing they could say to me to get "even" with me when they were their most angry. I recall Kate saying that one time; I don't even recall if Mary Ellen ever pulled it out, because I wouldn't have taken it as a serious statement.

There are so many fun happenstances in getting to know your child's birthparents, not the least of which is finding out about the inherited traits and mulling over nurture versus nature. The best example was riding with Kate at her college graduation as she drove our Suburban madly through the streets of Austin. She was mouthing at every driver or honking her disdain at them, and I turned to Steve and asked if Lorri was like that when she drives. He laughed out loud, and we both had a good chuckle over the similarities. The fact that Kate was setting up and playacting TV news shows at age six or seven (she being the director, of course), long before the time she knew her birthmother was a TV producer, is pretty amazing.

My final random thought is about you, Lorri! I have told you this before, but it brings so much in perspective to say it again. On December 10, 1981, when we were on the airplane flying home from Chicago with Kate, I tried to read your two letters: the one for Kate and the one for us. I started bawling and couldn't finish them; it took me several days to open them again and finally read them. That day on the airplane, she lay sleeping on the tray table (so we wouldn't wake her up) in a cloud of blankets, peaceful for most of the flight. I had been positively giddy with joy the entire day and was feeling so much happiness at finally becoming a mother. But Temple seemed a little downcast considering the circumstances. I asked him what was wrong, and he said that it was hard for him to fully enjoy the moment when he knew that there was someone out there feeling such pain in giving us this baby— that our joy was so completely the result of someone else's loss and sadness. That brought you home to me for that moment and for many more in the future.

CHAPTER THREE

ON BEING ADOPTED

Kate Stark Knight

Kate, Lorri's birthdaughter and Anne's adopted daughter, is thirty-six and lives in Dallas, Texas. She is the director of the GroundFloor program at United Way of Dallas. She has been married to Alex for six years and has two children.

I never remember a time that I didn't know I was adopted. There was never a conversation during which I "found out." Being adopted has always been part of my identity, but never in a negative way. For me, it just meant that I found my family a little differently than other kids and that I had two mommies. Honestly, the birthfather part of the equation wasn't nearly as strong as the birthmother part—and I don't really know why.

I have strong early memories of curling up between my parents, cozy on their big bed, and examining the single 8.5 × 11 sheet of paper containing facts about my birthparents. With my birthmother on one side of the page and my birthfather on the other, we talked about how I got my eye color from my birthfather and maybe my interest in entertainment from my TV producer birthmother. The page included "hobbies" and "interests," and I remember smiling at the idea that I liked skiing like my birthmother, and wondering if I might be good at tennis like her, too. This activity was a repeated pastime, anytime a twinge of curiosity built up. My parents were always willing to take the time to talk about these thoughts and questions— in fact, they seemed to share my curiosity and excitement!

The impression that I always got from my parents about my adoption was one of pure gratitude. They so desperately wanted to be parents and have a baby. They tried for so long to conceive and then for so long to adopt. When I finally came along, they were grateful for the opportunity, and I don't think that feeling ever subsided. My father, an incredibly empathetic person, was also adopted. He understood my curiosity, but as a parent, he also understood the amazing sacrifice my birthmother made in giving me up. The way my parents talked about my birthmother and my adoption made me picture someone who loved me very, very much and was incredibly brave. Someone who loved me so much that she wanted a wonderful life for me, a life that she knew my parents could provide. Later I would find out how true that was: my birthmother was incredibly selfless and truly made her decision out of love for me.

I believe that the combination of these things—adoption being an open part of our family's make-up, my parents' sharing my interest and curiosity about my birthparents, and the way my parents characterized my birthmother—all made for a very positive feeling toward being adopted. It was a non-issue that, if anything, made me feel special and more loved.

My parents would say things like, "You are special. We got to choose you." And that made me feel so good. Of course, I was curious and had questions, but I felt incredibly secure in my family and confident in my parents' love for me. They were my parents, and that was that. I think a large part of what made me feel so secure was that our family was always rock-solid. My parents' marriage was exemplary—there was never a question that my mom and dad were an awesome team. Also, my grandparents on both sides were present and very involved in our lives. My sister and I were the only grandchildren (my dad was an only child and my mom's brother did not have children), so we grew up with an abundance of love and attention from our family members. I believe that this solid family foundation gave me much of the security and confidence needed to be comfortable with the idea of having birthparents without feeling like I was "missing" something.

Personally, I think the way my mom handled sharing her correspondence with my birthmother was absolutely perfect. My mom and birthmother had written to each other anonymously my entire life, but that was not a relationship that my mom ever forced on me. While I always knew I was adopted, and I took great joy in imagining these people that created me based off the facts on that bio-stat sheet, I didn't learn of the letters until I was about twelve. My mom waited until she felt like I was mature enough to absorb that fact and until I began asking more and more questions. At that point, I remember her telling me about the letters. She said, "If you ever want to read them, they are in an envelope in the bottom drawer of my closet. You don't have to read them, but if you decide you want to, you know where they are, and you can go get them any time." It was such a no-pressure way of opening that door for me.

It took a long time for me to want to read them. It felt like a big step. But one day I was home alone and just felt ready. I remember going to my mom's closet and finding the envelope. It felt hot in my hand—I just couldn't image what I would find in there. I took the envelope and went out to the sofa in the den. Sitting cross-legged, I opened the letters one by one, and I cried and cried. They weren't sad tears. I smiled a lot, but I just felt overwhelmed with emotion. My mom came home later that afternoon and found me there. She asked me what was wrong. I just held up the envelope, and she wrapped me up in a big hug. She cried a little too. She said she felt so lucky that my birthmother was such an amazing, generous woman to share me with her—and that she loved me very, very much. Even then, discovering this birthmother person did not make me question who was my mother—not even a little. But it did feel a little like solving a piece of a mystery.

When I was fourteen, I spent the summer babysitting for a family on the East Coast. When my parents came to visit late in the summer, my mom brought with her a packet that had come in the mail from my birthmother. It had been a while since she had received a letter from her, and this one was different—it included a photograph of my birthmother's three daughters. My half-sisters. I was *fascinated* to look at the faces of my sisters. I share a strong similarity to my middle sister, Taylor. Looking at the picture, for the first time I felt the strong urge to know these people. That was probably the first time I knew I would meet my birthmother one day.

The decision to open my adoption felt sort of inevitable. More of a "when," not "if." When I was sixteen, I told my mom that I was ready to open the adoption. I'm not sure what exactly triggered that—it wasn't a specific event. I was just ready. We started first by learning each other's names. Reading the name "Lorri Benson" was so cool. I thought, *OK, now I know.* For the next several months, we began to email. Those were the days of AOL; how exciting it was to hear "You've got mail" and have the message be from this long-mysterious birthmother. It was thrilling to be able to ask all kinds of random questions that I didn't even know had been pent up. We had always talked a lot about "nature versus nurture" in our house, and I do believe that there are many, many "nurture" characteristics that I developed, but undoubtedly there are some things that are just "in you." Now there are funny stories about how similar Lorri and I are—particularly about driving and the "producing" life. It was just very cool to learn where some of those things about myself came from. Also, teenage years are such self-focused years. Looking back, opening the adoption in my teen years gave me another person that was directing attention to *me* and who I was—and that felt good too. That might sound self-centered, but I didn't realize it at the time; it's only now, as I reflect on this, that it occurs to me that the timing might have been beneficial to my teenage development as well.

Throughout this process, I felt nothing but support and encouragement from my parents. *That*, I think, was paramount to the success of our blended families. I know that family friends weren't always 100 percent supportive, and some even questioned my parents, but my mom and dad never wavered. And if my grandparents did, they didn't allow me to see it. My sister thought I was crazy, but my entire family welcomed my newfound family with open arms. There was never a question; Lorri and her family just became an extension of mine, and I've never for one second felt any resentment, disappointment, fear, or distaste from my mom. Early on, it was mostly excitement! Everyone seemed excited to meet this person. I eagerly shared news from our emails.

Eventually we decided to talk on the phone, but Lorri said that she would "never intrude on my life." I would have to make the first move. I remember sitting on my bed with the phone in hand—dialing and hanging up dozens of times over the course of a few weeks. When I finally got the courage to let the phone ring, Lorri's husband answered and went to get her. I could hear the smile in his voice. I don't even remember what we talked about, but I remember it felt easy.

It's not to say that every aspect of my adoption story has been easy. As straightforward as things always went with Lorri, things with my birthfather weren't quite as smooth. Lorri let him know that we had opened the adoption and gave him my phone number. As things were unfolding with the Benson family, I was also communicating with my birthfather, albeit much less frequently or deeply. A year or so after I first met Lorri, and after spending quite a bit of time with her and her family on my own, a situation came up where my birthfather was flying through DFW. Many of my early meetings with Lorri and her family took place at various airports on layovers, so it didn't seem strange in those pre–9/11 days when he suggested I come meet him at the airport. For whatever reason, it didn't feel like that big of a deal. I, of course, told my parents the plan, but I didn't ask them to come with me, and they didn't insist. There is only one thing in this whole adoption saga that I remember my mom saying she regretted: not coming with me to the airport.

I met my birthfather that day. He was a very nice man. But there was so much emotion there—it was not easy and straightforward, which I understand completely, particularly now. So many years later, I know so much more about the events around my birth—heck, there is a book about it! I get why things were awkward. But then, I was seventeen, and I left the airport and cried the entire drive home. I wasn't hurt, or sad really. I was confused; it just wasn't smooth and easy like it had been with Lorri. I learned later that when my birthfather boarded his connecting flight, he also cried. There is just so much emotion tied to this sort of thing. All the emotion that went into the original situation that created the adoption scenario in the first place . . . and then the emotion of meeting and learning about this other person. A lot can go wrong. I think it's essential to surround yourself with strong, unwavering support every step of the way.

Over the next several years, I navigated what my relationship could and should be with both my birthmother and birthfather. Amazingly, both my birthparents attended my college graduation. Both my birthparents and their spouses attended my wedding reception! I have met all of my half-siblings (three half-sisters from my birthmother and a half-sister and a half-brother from my birthfather). I am not particularly close to my birthfather and his family, but we are comfortable, and we stay in touch. It means a lot to me to have that connection—to know that if I ever had questions I could reach out for an answer.

My birthmother's family, however, is a different story. We are all extremely close. They are a part of my life, and we call, text, and see each other regularly. My sisters dote on my kiddos, and I am included on family group texts. My husband considers himself as having two mothers-in-law! We are one crazy, weird, perfect blended family.

Finally, I want to be sure to say a word about Lorri's husband. In the scheme of people who did things "right," he needs a lot of credit. It would have been easy for him to not invest himself in me, this child from "before," but he chose to jump right in. Steve has been the biggest cheerleader of our blended family from the beginning. There were many years when Steve would work two days each month in the city where I was living. I treasure the memories of our monthly dinners. I lost my dad in 2007. I am so incredibly thankful that I have another father figure in Steve to be a part of my life.

CHAPTER FOUR

IT'S NOT MY TIME

Mary Ellen Stark McWilliams

Mary Ellen is Kate's younger sister and Anne's second adoptive daughter. She is married to Daniel, has two children, and also lives in Dallas, Texas. She is a party manager for a nonprofit, The Birthday Party Project. She has chosen not to search for her birthparents or open her adoption in any way, although Anne has had contact with her birthmother.

My adoption story is not a simple one. My adoption has been both open and closed, one in which my mother has been in contact with my birthmother since my birth, but I have chosen not to meet her. For me, this has allowed me to feel connected to her without ever directly having contact with her.

Growing up, my mother always informed me when my birthmother would contact her or when my mom would make contact. It was typically around my birthday. While I was always receptive to hearing about their contact, I never had a desire to directly connect with her myself. In my case, I had no reason to connect with her because my mother filled that role; I got everything I needed out of a mom from her! To have a relationship with my birthmother didn't seem necessary to me. The idea was just confusing, and the thought of trying just seemed like opening a Pandora's box.

When Katie decided to meet Lorri and her family, I was thirteen. I absolutely couldn't understand that decision. When my mom called me from the Benson's home to tell me how the reunion was going, all I could think to say, over and over, was, "Isn't it weird?" When Katie brought the Bensons into our family, it stopped being weird and started to feel normal. This worked for Katie, and we all welcomed her birth family into the fold. But it didn't change how I felt about my personal situation. It still felt way too weird for me.

When I was a teenager, I became curious about what my birthmother looked like, and I wanted to learn about my birth family's medical history.

My mom reached out to her, and she sent some photos of herself and my birthfather and medical history. I also learned a few things about her: she was short like me, and she seemed active, based on a photo of her hiking. I also learned she liked to rearrange her furniture and had also dealt with self-esteem and depression issues before. This information was particularly fascinating to me, because for the first time I learned how similar we seemed to be! For a while, I thought a lot about what it would be like to know her and to learn from her, seeing how we dealt with similar issues. I never took the next step, though, in reaching out to her.

She and my mom continued to connect, and when I was getting married, my birthmother asked to meet me and come to my wedding! I freaked! I also got mad. She had never been to any other major event in my life—how dare she now invite herself to my wedding? This really shook me up. I also did not want her coming to my wedding because meeting her was an event in and of itself, and we were not going to do that the day of my wedding! So, my mom delivered the news to her.

I had a lot of guilt around that decision. I didn't want to hurt her or upset her. But the truth was I couldn't honor that event and the event of my wedding at the same time. And I wasn't ready to meet her.

It wasn't until about seven years later that someone else in my family made contact with her. This time it was my husband, Daniel. When my first child was born, he tested positive on his newborn screening for a rare, life-threatening disease, one that could be managed but nonetheless was dangerous if we didn't feed him every three hours! The disease was genetic, and we were both curious if anyone in my birth family had it. Daniel reached out to her on Facebook, and they became friends and exchanged messages. Thankfully, no one in her family had it, and further testing eventually revealed that our son was only a carrier for the disease.

Through Facebook, though, a different connection began. Now that they're friends, I've been able to see more photos of her. She has even commented on family photos that Daniel posts! I find myself mixed about all of this: how weird it is that she and my husband are Facebook friends, how weird it is that she sees photos of our lives and our children's lives—some intimate moments, too! But yet we haven't even met! I clearly still am not able to process this, as I can only find the word "weird" to describe it all.

So here we are thirty-three years later. I now have a family of my own, and she now has one of her own: she is married and has an eleven-year-old son. I've noticed that communication between her and my mom has lessened over the years. I can't help but think it's because of me . . . as if she's giving up because I have yet to reach out to her on my own. This is when I feel so sad I cry. I want her to know how forever grateful I am to her for giving me life. *Life!* I wouldn't be here if it wasn't for her!

She did something so incredibly brave and big for me, I can't even mentally grasp it! The greatness of that sacrifice makes it too overwhelming for me to process. I want her in my life, but I cannot understand what the relationship would look like, and that's hard for me. I honor this woman so much, but if I do not need her as a mom, in the traditional sense of the word, what would she be? Like an aunt? A cousin? No! She can't be that. But then what? And that's when I get stuck.

If I were to tell a biological parent why their child hasn't reached out to them yet, I would say it's because it's too big for them to handle! They don't know how to fit you into their life because they already have a mom. But because you mean so much to them, they struggle trying to understand how to make your relationship just as special. They have so many mixed emotions around the matter—all of the time.

But always know this: they think the world of you. They honor you. They love you. And they thank you every day for giving them their life!

PART
TWO

Birthparents

CHAPTER FIVE

HOW TO GET THROUGH THE HARDEST EXPERIENCE OF YOUR LIFE

Jessica Hale

Jessica is currently a stay-at-home mother to her two-and-a-half-year-old daughter. She and her husband live in Tampa, Florida, and have been married for eight years.

As a birthmother, I can confidently say that giving a child up for adoption is the most difficult thing one may ever endure. The emotional, psychological, and physical pain that a birthmother experiences before, during, and after the adoption is a level of grief that is difficult to put into words.

It hurts. Your heart aches. Your body longs to hold your baby. Your love, so fierce, for the child that you carried makes you feel you are losing your mind because you want him back so badly. It's excruciating. You will question your decision. You will want to change your mind. But before you go off the deep end, it is extremely important to remind yourself why you made the decision in the first place and to know that grieving is not only inevitable, it is completely normal. It is important to remember that your baby, although not in your arms, is safe, loved, and cared for deeply by a family that wanted him or her so badly. You can move on. You will grieve often, and life may never ever be the same, but you can find a new normal, and you will be OK. It will not be easy, no matter what, but if you prepare yourself, the transition from pregnancy to life without your child can be a bit smoother. Looking back, a few things helped, a few things hurt . . . OK, a lot of things hurt, but there are definitely some words of wisdom I would like to share with birthmothers contemplating adoption for their baby.

I released my son for adoption fourteen years ago. When first finding out I was pregnant, it was a complete and utter shock. I had stopped taking the pill because of an article in *Cosmopolitan* that talked about how taking the pill could increase the risk of breast cancer. I wasn't in a relationship at the time, so I decided to stop taking it to avoid chancing any unnecessary risks later in life. A few weeks later, I met my son's birthfather through a mutual friend, and our relationship progressed rather quickly. I had just graduated from college and was taking the summer off before starting graduate school in the fall. I had no job, no health insurance, and no clue what to do with myself, much less a baby. When I told the man I was dating about the positive pregnancy test, he let me in on a huge part of his life that he had kept a secret from me: he was married and had a child with his wife. Devastation overtook me. I felt completely deceived, vulnerable, and worthless. My world crumbled around me. I was not in love with him and would not have married him, but knowing that everything we had up to that point had been a lie really changed things. At that moment, I no longer wanted communication with him, and I decided if I was to raise the baby growing inside me, I could quit graduate school, find a job, and raise him on my own. Such a scenario would be easier said than done.

This began the longest nine-month journey of my entire life. I went ahead and started graduate school while trying to assess what to do with the baby that was rapidly developing inside me. I contemplated abortion. At the time, it was honestly the only thing that made sense. But abortion was against the way I was raised, and when it came down to it, it was something I couldn't do. I have never gotten into the politics of abortion and have never considered myself to be pro-life or pro-choice. However, I knew it was not the right thing for me. There was a feeling deep down, a little voice that whispered to me that the baby I was carrying deserved a chance at life, so that was what he was granted.

While pregnant, I used to cry all the time . . . oh, and puke too. Yep, I cried and puked. That pretty much summed up the entire nine months of my pregnancy. I was very ill and vomited most of the day. I was sick in every sense of the word. I worried that I was emotionally destroying the baby inside me. How could he possibly turn out normal when all I could do was stress out and be sad all the time? Was I giving him a good start to life by being so upset? Worrying about his well-being gave me even more to stress and worry about.

If I had to go back and do it all over again, I would have given myself more love. It felt as if the entire world was against me, so it was very difficult to love myself in that situation, but stuff happens. It's life. You have to play the cards you are dealt, so to speak. I know it's extremely difficult when you have everyone questioning your plan and your decisions. Why didn't you just get an abortion? Why didn't you use protection? How could you sleep with a man you didn't even love? How could you be so careless? Do you really think you will be able to give your baby away? These are tough questions that can make you feel like you aren't even human any longer.

But at some point, you grow thick skin; you learn to ignore the chatter, the opinions, the righteous attitudes, and even the snarky remarks. You do it for yourself. You do it for your baby. It's called survival. Taking care of yourself is taking care of your child. Take long walks, go on a picnic with friends, dance to your favorite music, go to the zoo or a pet store if you love animals, take an art class if you like art, or bake if it is something you enjoy. If you are spiritual, you can meditate, pray, recite positive mantras, take a prenatal yoga class, or get a massage. Do something for you. Whatever it is that fills you up inside, do it.

Being a hormonal mess is one way to describe pregnancy. Being pregnant unintentionally and contemplating giving your son or daughter up for adoption is not just another ballgame, it's like an entirely different solar system of feelings that you didn't even know existed. It's a range of emotions that you cannot fathom unless you are actually faced with them.

My advice on how to cope is to start a journal. I started writing journals to help process all of the thoughts that constantly swirled in my mind. I had one journal for appointments, meetings, phone numbers, addresses, and things that needed to be done—an organizer of sorts. The other journal was for my deepest thoughts and concerns. It was my diary, and it became my best friend. I told that diary everything I was experiencing. It never judged or gave advice, but it made me feel like a new person every single time I wrote.

I also began seeing a therapist. I had money saved from graduation that was quickly dwindling, and I had bills to pay. However, the decision to see a therapist weekly was absolutely the best investment I have ever made for my mental and emotional health. It was not easy. There were times when I would walk out of therapy and want to just give up on life because it all seemed so overwhelming, but each day was an inch forward in the right direction. It was a baby step up a gigantic mountain that had to be climbed.

There was no choice but to move forward, and my therapist helped me do that.

Listen to your gut. The first lawyer I went to see about potentially relinquishing my baby really made me mad. He was close to where I lived, which was convenient, but I felt pressure from him and his staff. It angered me that someone I didn't know was trying to convince me to make the biggest decision of my entire life based solely on his opinion after a fifteen-minute meeting. I left and knew in my heart that I would not be meeting with him again. The next day, when I received a follow-up call, I politely but firmly asked to not be contacted again.

You have to be a voice for not only yourself but also the little being that is growing inside you; that is your job, whether or not you are giving the baby up for adoption. You are the mother, and you have to speak up during this important time of your life. The next week, I found a lawyer with whom I clicked. He was friendly and professional, and I knew he was on my side. Having that trust was crucial during the process.

Don't be afraid to meet adoptive parents. It doesn't mean that you have to go through with the adoption or that you are giving someone false hope if you decide not to go through with it. It can actually give you some clarity, and the earlier you choose parents for your child, the more time you will have to get to know them before the baby comes. Interview them; meet them for coffee and dinner. Speak with them on the phone. Write down questions you have for them in your journal so you can ask them the next time you meet. Don't drag potential adoptive parents along if you know deep down you are not going to go through with the adoption, but get to know them if you think you are; it's the only time you have to make sure you are making the best choice.

Adoption can be a wonderful thing. As deeply painful of an experience as it is for the birthmother, there is also a sense of relief once it's all over. I had a really difficult time deciding whether or not to go through with it. I drove myself nearly mad trying to decide. However, I knew that I wanted my son to be raised in a two-parent home with a father figure. That was the one thing I continued to go back to. I have always believed that the influence of having two parents is monumental to a child's development. I'm not saying for a second that a child raised by a single mother or father can't thrive; there is no question that is a possibility. However, a stable two-parent home was extremely important to me and was one thing I was completely unable to give him at the time.

The parents I chose had been married eleven years and had been trying to get pregnant the whole time. I fell in love with them. Everything about them felt right. I wanted to keep my son, and I wanted to never let him go, but I knew without a doubt that he would be absolutely loved, cared for, and cherished by the parents I chose. Once it was all over, I no longer had to worry about what to do. Giving birth was rebirth. I was a changed person with a new outlook on life. I overcame so many trials and challenges, and I am the person I am today because of all the experiences that shaped me.

A final suggestion for both birthparents *and* adoptive parents would be to have some sort of ceremony afterward. This could take place in the chapel at the hospital, in your hospital room with your spiritual advisor, or once you return home in a place of worship or a sacred place that is close to your heart. It is a very special time that can help you come to terms with what has taken place in your life, and for birthparents, it can help begin the grieving process in a healthy way.

After signing all the documents to officially give my son his new life, I met the adoptive parents in the chapel at the hospital. The chaplain read Bible verses and said a prayer with us. He then left us alone to say our goodbyes. My son was not allowed to attend the ceremony however, as I was legally not allowed to see him again once all the paperwork had been signed. I have heard of ceremonies in which the birthmother actually hands the baby over to the arms of the adoptive mother. With each situation being entirely different, something like this may or may not work for whatever reason. It may be that you end up doing a ceremony completely separate at a later date, but I believe it is an important thing to do for birthparents and adoptive parents, whether they decide to do it alone or together.

No matter your situation or what decision you make, pregnancy is a time to take care of yourself and a time to be kind to yourself. If it is an unplanned pregnancy, that may be difficult for you to do, but it will make all the difference. It is so easy to contemplate the "what-ifs" and the "if-onlys" until you are blue in the face, but those thoughts will only destroy your peace. Accept where you are and work toward a solution for the situation at hand. You can't go back, but you can certainly move forward.

I can guarantee one thing. If you find yourself in this situation, no matter what you decide for your child's future, one thing is sure: you will never ever be the same. You will grow by leaps and bounds. You will get knocked down, but you will also get back up. You will love again, and you will feel happiness again. Your heart will break, but it will also mend. Be there for yourself. Good luck, momma.

It has been fourteen years since the adoption took place. I feel blessed to receive letters and pictures a few times a year from the couple that adopted my son. Also, we met once, seven years ago, for dinner. I can't quite put into words what it was like to see my son with his adopted parents for the first time; it was an emotional reunion, to say the least. As soon as we sat down to dinner, however, all nervous energy subsided as I was quickly reminded how kind and warmhearted the two people I had chosen to care for my son are. I have not seen him in person again since but feel content with the pictures and letters I receive. I continue to feel so much gratitude in my heart for his parents for being so open and loving toward me, and I'm so thankful to them for loving him as their own. Knowing he is happy and safe means everything.

My husband and I have been married for eight years, and we have a two-year-old daughter. We don't have any plans to have another child, but I always say, smiling, "Those things are up to the Universe to decide."

I have been working on a memoir about my story in hopes to one day have it published. Reading Lorri's book *To Have and Not to Hold* and contributing to this book have given me even more inspiration.

My final message to all moms: May you return to happiness each time you grieve, may you persevere in the midst of life's most difficult challenges, and may you practice resilience with a heart of compassion.

CHAPTER SIX

NO REGRETS

Evie De Mendoza

Evie is thirty-eight years old, from Northern California, and grew up the middle child of five girls. Since placing her daughter for adoption in 2002, she has since married and has just given birth to her first child with her husband: a daughter. She lives in Santa Monica. Her father, Danny Lake, also placed a daughter for adoption when he was a teen. His story is in Chapter Seven.

My name is Evie, and I am a birthmom. Coincidentally, I am the daughter of a man who was a birthfather when he was young. I chose adoption for my daughter in my first trimester, within about a week of learning that I was pregnant. However, that was actually not the first option that crossed my mind.

It was the summer before my senior year of college in 2001. I was working full-time and supporting myself. I had just barely turned twenty-one and was enjoying the new privileges that came with it! I was not in a relationship with the birthfather. In fact, he had told me that he couldn't see himself having a serious relationship with me because I wanted to "wait until I was married." Despite my better judgment, I played with fire, and after not feeling well for several weeks, I finally went to the doctor, and I found out that I was pregnant. I was angry and scared. I kept calling all the Planned Parenthood offices to try to come in, but it was after hours.

I went back home and shared the news with my roommate. As fate would have it, she had actually been meeting with a post-abortion counselor every week, and her appointment happened to be that evening. She suggested I come with her and just talk to the counselor, and so I did. I shared my story, and she asked, "So, what would you like to do?" Despite my conservative Christian, pro-life upbringing, I replied, "I want to know how long I have to have an abortion." She answered my question, and then she asked me if I knew what happened in an abortion. I replied, "Um, I think so," and then she went on to matter-of-factly yet graphically explain what the process would be at that stage of my pregnancy and what would happen to the baby's body. There was nothing persuasive about her approach, but it was *that* conversation that made me realize that there was no way I could proceed with an abortion.

She asked me if I had considered adoption, and I hadn't, but I had just turned twenty-one and certainly wasn't ready to be a parent, and that sounded like a better route than abortion. I went back to the birthfather and shared with him that I was pregnant. He was shocked as well and even questioned if the baby was his. Fortunately, he supported my decision to go through the adoption process.

The ball was in my court to select parents for this baby. I was barely an adult! I didn't know anything about parenting or what qualities to look for! So, I came up with a list of five things that were important to me.

1. They would be of my same faith
2. A stay-at-home mom (A luxury many mothers and children don't have, but why not give that to this baby?)
3. No other children (I wanted this baby to have 100 percent of the parents' attention)
4. Financially stable
5. Of the same nationality (I wanted the baby to blend in with the family)

I started my search, working with an international adoption agency, and started receiving "résumés" of families from all across the country who wanted to adopt. The families didn't know what my criteria were, however, and I wasn't finding any that matched all five points. I became nervous and discouraged and wondered if I was being too picky. My mom reassured me that I was not and that God would be faithful. It still makes me teary-eyed when I think back on that conversation.

Sure enough, one day I was trying to reach an old friend; I dialed 411 and found a number listed under her name! This fact was crazy because I'm pretty sure she lived with her parents. I called, we chatted, and I shared the story about my pregnancy and that I was looking for parents to adopt my baby. She asked if she could call me right back, which she did after talking to our college-group youth pastor. He had a friend who had been looking to adopt, and several other situations had fallen through. They connected me to this couple, and in September of 2001, I met the perfect parents to adopt my baby. They matched everything I was looking for, and more!

They had been working with Bethany Adoption Agency, a private organization, so we continued the adoption process through them. The adoptive parents also preferred an open adoption, which is the path we pursued. During my pregnancy, I chose not to see the ultrasounds or find out the gender so that it would be easier for me to stay detached.

Fast forward to January 13: I went into labor at 5 a.m. and gave birth to a beautiful little girl! The moment I held her in my arms for the very first time is indescribable, and I was *so* very grateful that her adoptive parents had wanted an open adoption. As she grew up, I continued visiting her. I watched her develop into the beautiful young woman that she is. Blessed with multiple talents, she has had and continues to have incredible opportunities to perform wherever there's a spotlight. I visit her about once a year and get pictures and updates from her adoptive parents, although that has slowed down recently.

Her adoptive mom also connected with my mom on social media. I was hesitant to do the same for a while, mostly to protect my heart from any unexpected posts. I finally connected with her adoptive mom as well after my mom kept sharing pictures with me of my daughter and updates she saw. I decided I would rather see them firsthand. Yes, there have been a few "ouch" moments, as I expected. But I remind myself that my "lens" is very different from everyone else in her life; they are not seeing her through my eyes as her birthmom.

I am now in my late thirties, happily married, and my husband and I are the parents of a brand new baby girl! I am very much ready to be a mommy and cannot wait for what is in store for our future. I have several pieces of wisdom from my experience that I would like to share with others.

My advice for birthparents is to play a role in selecting the adoptive parents. So many people have a misconception of how adoption works and don't realize the birthparents do have a say in selecting the adoptive parents. My advice for both the adoptive parents and the birthparents is to strongly consider open adoption instead of closed adoption. This is a benefit to the child and was a blessing to me as well.

Also, when my daughter was a little girl, her parents explained her adoption to her as a happy story and that she "grew in Evie's tummy." They shared a story about how they came to the hospital when she was born and were so excited to bring her back home with them. She was able to understand very young what my connection to her was, so it wasn't an awkward conversation later, when she grew up. I highly recommend telling the story right from the beginning.

When my dad was a teen, he and his girlfriend placed a baby in a closed adoption, and just in the past few years he came into contact with his daughter, and that's also been a really neat experience. He can relate to the sad, unexpected moments I've experienced. Although his adoption story didn't influence me (my sole reason for choosing adoption was the counselor's graphic description of the abortion procedure), I've thought about his situation versus mine. He often asks me if I wish I had made a different decision and parented instead. And honestly, the answer is no. I wasn't ready to be a parent at the age of twenty-one, and my daughter has had so many experiences and privileges with the most loving family. It was the best decision I could have made.

I am grateful that I have an open adoption, something that was not common in my dad's generation. He's been blessed to have the opportunity to meet his daughter later in his life, and I'm sure that has filled a missing piece of his heart. For me, I just hope that I am able to have a closer relationship with my birthdaughter down the road, but I'll allow her to initiate. I recently reached out to my daughter's adoptive mom and shared my heart for the first time in a long time. When my daughter was a toddler, I shared my thoughts and feelings with her more often. I think at that time the focus was more on coping with my emotions.

Now my daughter is a young adult, and I would like to have more of a friendship with her, maybe pen pals or something. Lately when I call, she is away from home, busy with theater and rehearsals, so I usually just have brief conversations with her mom. In a few years, she'll be off to college. I may never really see her, let alone hear from her. I also wonder if that desire will be somewhat fulfilled now that I'm a mommy; there are a lot of unknowns that will play out as life unfolds.

My adoption choice has brought blessings that I could have never imagined.

- Example 1: When I have conversations with complete strangers and the topic of my adoption comes up (usually when they've asked if I had any children), it sometimes opens a meaningful, engaging conversation. This has also happened with women who were pregnant and scared or others who were considering adoption.

+ Example 2: I have volunteered for organizations and have had the opportunity to meet young girls who were pregnant and considering abortion because they were afraid of what their parents would do if they found out. I've been able to encourage them and mentor them along the way.

+ Example 3: I've been able to watch my daughter grow up into such an incredibly beautiful and talented young woman. I love being able to share her pictures with people in my life and even seeing some of my traits in her.

Since our adoption is open, our adoption triad has met, although her birthfather only met her in person one time as a toddler. They do keep in touch via email. I try to have a visit when I travel back home to see my parents since they live close to the adoptive family.

One thing I would mention as an aside concerns the term *give* or *gave up* as a description for what a birthmother does with her baby. To me, those terms lead to the negative perception of "giving your child away," which I think is part of the misconception many have with adoption. People don't understand *how* a mother could "give her child away" to another family. We *place* our child in the best possible life situation to give him or her the best possible chance, and we do it out of love.

Being a birthmother is a journey. There will be unexpected thoughts, feelings, and emotions along the way. In recent years, when I was ready to be a mother, it was more difficult to watch my daughter grow up and to not be her mommy. I didn't expect to have those feelings. My suggestion would be to find people or a person in whom you can confide, with whom you can be vulnerable, cry, or be sad when you are having a hard time. Those moments are a testimony of the sacrifice of being a birthmother. Giving birth to my beautiful daughter and being able to have a relationship with her as her birthmother has been more rewarding than I could have ever imagined.

CHAPTER SEVEN

SO MUCH JOY

Danny Lake

Danny Lake is a sixty-four-year-old father of six daughters (including the birth-daughter he placed for adoption). One of his daughters, Evie, is the contributor in Chapter Six. He is a private investigator from California and has been happily married for forty-three years.

My name is Danny Lake. Back in 1966, at age thirteen, I began working at a butcher shop in Pomona, California. I got the job because of a girl named Laura who I met over the summer. Her parents owned the business. By 1969 we were boyfriend and girlfriend, and we were in love. I continued working for her parents. At the start of my junior year, her sophomore year, Laura told me she thought she was pregnant. For three months, we kept this a secret until one night we felt we had to tell her parents. They were devastated. I was just a football player, and Laura was smart and college-bound, so she decided to have the baby and place her for adoption. I was against it, and so was my strong-minded German mom. I felt we could make it work. I remember in June of the following year, at the hospital, Laura's father sitting in the waiting room with me, smoking a cigar and just staring at me. When the baby girl was born, I was allowed to go into the room and hold this precious life. I could not understand giving this baby up. My heart ached. But I knew the best thing for her was to have mature parents who were desperate for her and able to care for her. After two days in the hospital, my little baby was gone. I had no idea who had her or what city she had gone to. I was told very little about the adoptive parents—only that one of them was a schoolteacher.

From that time on, I wondered about this little girl. It seemed as though not a day went by in which I wasn't wondering where she might be. I had so little information to go on. Was she even still alive?

I went on with my life, and in 1974, I married a wonderful woman. Together we had five beautiful daughters. I told my daughters they had an older sister out there somewhere. It seems I was always talking about her. When twenty years had passed, I wondered what her adult life was like: Was she involved with drugs, or was she successful, well adjusted, and happy? Numerous scenarios ran through my mind. I was working as a private investigator at the time and did an investigation into her whereabouts with no luck. I even contacted her birthmom, who told me never to contact her again.

In 2009, my daughter Anna was in law school. She asked me, "Dad, what would you think if I found our sister?" I was nervous when she asked this because with all the advances in technology, I thought it could happen. One week later, Anna called me and said excitedly, "*Dad . . . I found her.*"

I'm getting tears just writing about this. I was excited, nervous, afraid, happy—so many emotions. Anna attempted to call her several times. Finally, a woman picked up. My daughter said to her, "Hi, my name is Anna Lake, and I think you might be my sister." She went on to ask, "Were you born on June 6, 1969, at Park Avenue Hospital, and were you adopted?"

"Yes," the woman responded. After a brief conversation, they decided to have the woman, Paula, call me. My daughter called me and told me. I was scared to death. (More crying as I'm writing this.) After what seemed like forever, the phone rang, and we began to talk. It was amazing, and wonderful. I just kept falling more and more in love with her. We decided that she was going to come to my house and meet me and my wife and a couple of our girls. After the phone call, I was on my knees thanking God and crying. It seems like I was crying for days, tears of such joy.

In the meantime, I had located the birthmother, now living in another state, so Paula could contact her, which she did. The first words out of her birthmother's mouth were, "That time of my life was the worst. I have been in therapy ever since that time." She went on to say, "I wish I had had an abortion."

Paula was devastated. She thought all her life it would be her birth-father to say something like that. Her adoptive mom had told her at an early age that she was adopted, so she had understandably gone through most of her life with only vague predictions of what her birthparents might have been like. For instance, when she had pictured her birth-mother, she had imagined a beautiful actress or something similar.

Her birthmother gave Paula a medical history so she would at least have that. Paula had shared with me that growing up she was unable to complete medical information due to her lack of knowledge about her birthparents.

One interesting and wonderful thing is the strange coincidences we've learned about each other. For instance, I played semi-pro football in Ontario, California, for two years, and we practiced on a field at Chaffy High School. I found out that Paula lived in a house directly across the street from the field and that her mother was a teacher at the school. She says she remembers football players practicing on the field. I had no idea she was so close. Small world.

To make a long story short, meeting Paula was awesome. She fits right in with my other daughters. In fact, Paula thinks she's funny, just like the other ones. She teases me about how I kicked her to the curb. Ha!

The truth is, I have no regrets. When I found her, I cried for days. I was so nervous to meet her. I love her so much, but her upbringing is what I would have wanted for her. Her parents could not have been better parents. They loved her and nurtured her to become the wonderful woman she is today. I know without a doubt adoption was the best decision for her, and I couldn't love her more if I had raised her myself. I could go on and on about how wonderful this has been for everyone involved, except the birthmom, but that is my story, and I love Paula with all my heart. She is so special to me.

When my daughter Evie came to me and her mother with the news that, at twenty-one, she was pregnant, it was like déjà vu. Evie knew my experience with Paula and how it was the best option since the birthmother and I were still in high school. We discussed all that would be involved with Evie raising her baby herself, and she eventually chose adoption. Later, while Evie's daughter was growing up, I wondered if Evie questioned what she had done. She was getting older and had not had another child. I felt in my heart that I had influenced her to make the decision she did. I felt somewhat guilty. I even discussed this with Evie, who reassured me this was not the case. But my question still lingers, and I think my experience made it easier for her to make that decision. I would not advise her differently, though, even after reuniting with Paula. Evie's daughter is a precious little girl who has the most loving parents.

In general, I'm not convinced that open adoption is the best way to go. I think it's not fair to the adoptive parents. But in this case, it is comforting to know Evie's baby has the greatest parents possible, ones that love her and nurture her.

WORDS OF ADVICE

If you are pregnant and don't know what to do, at least talk to an adoption agency. The life I adopted out is such a wonderful person and not a mass of tissue.

As for giving my child up for adoption forty years ago and not having any idea if Paula was alive, dead, on drugs, or anything else: I talked with all my daughters about what I was feeling and the questions I had. I recommend always communicating what you're going through.

The overriding emotion I feel now is the satisfaction that it was the right thing to do at the time. Sometimes what you want to do is not always the right answer. When I used to look back, I always thought I should have raised her. My mom and sisters thought the same thing. But the reality is that Paula has very loving parents and a good life. That's what's important. I was a child myself then. Things worked out the way they were supposed to work out. No regrets.

I also suggest that, as a birthparent, you keep the ball in the child's court. Let their family be the priority, and take your cues from them. Paula doesn't say, "Keep the distance," but I've made a conscious effort not to disrupt their lives. I feel it's best for her adoptive mom, who I've sensed has some jealousy over this. Paula's sons have met me. The youngest told Paula's mother, "You're not my real grandmother." This crushed Paula and her adoptive mom. I have limited physical contact now. I did attend one of my grandson's high school football games. She introduced me to everyone she knew as her birthdad. Or "Baby Daddy," as we like to joke. I see Paula maybe two times a year, but we text, email, and call throughout the year. It melts my heart each time.

CHAPTER EIGHT

IT'S NEVER TOO LATE

Judy Craig

Judy Craig lives in Ohio. She is married with two grown sons and is the birthmother of Nanci Done-Nemeth, whose story is featured in Chapter Thirty. Nanci's adoptive mother's story is in Chapter Twenty-Four. This is the only triad besides Lorri's featured in the book.

I was just twenty-two, recently divorced, with an eighteen-month-old child, and living with my parents when I found out I was pregnant again, and it was embarrassing and scary for me. I was not financially or emotionally ready for another child. In this time of turmoil, my parents were a big help in deciding what I should do. I jumped at the suggestion that I go live with my grandparents in Florida to have the baby. I was so embarrassed that I did not want anyone to know, and I knew keeping the child was not the answer for me.

I was fortunate that the hospital I went to had already been told that I was placing the child for adoption, because when I went into labor, I passed out. I refused to see the child afterward because I knew I would not be able to go through with the adoption if I did. At that point, I just wanted to put everything behind me. I left the hospital and left Florida immediately. I moved back to my parents and tried to get on with my life. I tried to forget. I never told anyone, not even my current husband. Over the years, it became easier to not remember anything or think about it.

It was a complete shock, but a wonderful one, when forty-four years later, I received a call from an attorney asking if I would consider seeing my daughter. They told me all about her, and I immediately said yes. Thank the Lord I was ready in my heart for this. I told my husband my story, and he was wonderfully supportive. My daughter now calls him dad since the biological father did not want any contact. She came to our town and stayed with us for two weeks, meeting all my family. We bonded as soon as we met. I noticed instantly the resemblance to her older brother, who also bonded with her immediately. It took a lot of explaining after all these years, but everyone was very encouraging.

One of our most special and memorable experiences was our visit to my mother, who was in an assisted-living facility and had Alzheimer's. The day my daughter came to visit, she looked long and hard at her. I explained to her who my daughter was, not knowing if she understood or not, and her response was "Judy, you got your baby back." That wonderful and unbelievable moment would end up being one of her last lucid ones. So much healing began that day.

One of the reasons my daughter had sought me out was because she needed medical information on my family, since she had medical issues. I think it's critical that those involved in any capacity in an adoption (i.e., those at the hospital, the lawyers, the courts, the nurses, the adoption agencies, etc.) request *all* family medical history and pertinent information at the time of birth. In her case, it was very necessary and could have assisted her greatly over the years with her serious health-related issues.

I also believe that even in a closed adoption, the child should be able to contact the birthparents through an attorney when they are age eighteen. It's safest for all if there is an intermediary person in the event the birthparent does not want contact or needs time to process being found. In my case, the timing was right, and I very much wanted this reunion.

I was incredibly fortunate to go to my daughter's hometown and meet and spend some wonderful time with her adoptive mother, Helen. I have the utmost respect for Helen. She is an absolute jewel. I marvel at her since she was a single mother when she adopted, and she did an incredible job raising a wonderful child. We remain in contact to this day.

My daughter never seemed to resent me. She was gracious, kind, loving, and forgiving. She simply needed to know the circumstances of her birth. Finding and reuniting with my daughter was the best thing that ever happened to me!

CHAPTER NINE

A PERFECT PARTNERSHIP

Heather Newport

Heather is forty-three, and her birthdaughter, Megan, is twenty-two. She is a business owner from Southern California who has had the pleasure of raising two stepsons and a daughter and realizes she has been blessed beyond her measure.

When I think about our story, it is just that: ours. I guess that's one thing that stands out when I hear other adoption stories. This isn't my story. *Our* story is about Francene, Greg, Megan, and me.

When I found out I was pregnant, I knew there was no way in hell I was giving her up. Then my mom's best friend adopted a baby through Bethany Christian Services, and she came to see me and convinced me to talk to them. At four months along, I met with one of their counselors, Linda, to work through the process. One thing that she said that spoke to me was, "You know, every girl grows up thinking what life will be: fall in love, get married, have children, grow old with the ones you love . . . and you're not the only one who had a chink in the plans."

Francene, the adoptive mom, also had the same dreams and plans. While I got pregnant at nineteen, she found out she could not have children at seventeen. She had an ovarian cyst rupture, and she had to tell all prospective men that she could not have kids. Brutal. When Linda told me that, it made me realize that there were *two* hurting women who could potentially become whole again.

One of my favorite moments in my life was when I met Greg and Francene Fisher for the first time. We met at about six or seven months, and I loved them instantly. I do think that knowing her backstory had something to do with it. My counselor and I met them at a restaurant, and

I brought a bouquet of roses for them: three red and one white to symbolize the three parents and the unborn child. Our daughter now has a tattoo of that bouquet on her leg.

I chose not to know the sex of the child, but I invited Francene along to my prenatal appointments. I do believe that sharing the experience had much to do with our current relationship. I understood that she was missing out on something we as women grow up expecting to experience. Pregnancy, morning sickness, growth of the belly, baby showers, feeling a baby kick inside you . . . it was amazing and sad to me that Francene was never going to experience that. As difficult as it was for me, at least I got that!

The time she and I had to bond, knowing we shared a love for the baby inside me, was like no other bond. I invited her and her husband, Greg, to be there for the birth. (I'm bawling now, twenty-two years later, as I write this.) I wanted them to be able to say that they had seen their child come into the world. I wanted Francene to be as much a part of their child's birth as possible. They brought in their first adopted child, two-year-old Courtney, to touch my belly. They told her, "This is who we're getting your brother or sister from, just like we got you from Julie."

I thought that was important, explaining adoption from such a young age. No surprises.

So, Greg and Francene stood by me, and Francene held my hand while Megan was born. Two moms, watching their daughter brought into this world. Loved by two different families. One sad, one happy. Or both sad, both happy, on some level.

Megan was beautiful. Perfect. Loved by so many. It was a huge family affair. Most of the Fishers were there, my family, and all my friends came to see her, hold her. My perfect memory from that day is when she looked up at me, recognizing my voice. I wanted so much for her. I wanted a dad, a mom, siblings, a cohesive life that I just could not provide. I cannot forget the nurse taking Megan away. It still hurts, but I do not regret one single moment.

We held a baby dedication in the hospital room with our pastor, Greg (not the adoptive father). I believe it helped to transition Megan's care from me to the Fishers, and I would recommend something like this for everyone. Pastor Greg said something that I've never forgotten: "We are all here to care for our children for a certain time. Heather cared for Megan as best she could for nine months and has to give her up now. Greg and Francene are here to care for her for eighteen years, and then they must give her up."

Wow! Parenting is about loving them enough to let them go! Adoption or blood . . . we must all raise our children with the intent of letting them go. That was at the same time sad and powerful. And true.

Another favorite memory is meeting Megan at age three. Before her cognitive skills had developed enough to put together who I was, we were able to meet for a short time and play together. It meant so much to me to see her, touch her, and know for certain the wonderful care and love she was getting.

At fifteen, Megan decided she wanted to meet me. All children are different. Her sister was much more private with her adoption, while Meg always bragged about having two moms. I think it's extremely important to go along with how the child feels. My two biggest fears were that my daughter would think that she wasn't wanted, and that she wouldn't want contact with me.

I credit Francene, her mom, with us coming together. What an amazing woman. She kept contact with me, sending stories and pictures. I cried with every letter, email, picture . . . while knowing that Francene was loving her and caring for her every minute. Megan and her mom discussed our meeting at length over time, and they decided together that she was ready.

When we finally met, I was just as happy to see Francene as I was Megan. That night was incredible, another favorite moment in life. I brought the same bouquet to the restaurant and sat across from her in awe. I remember that I didn't want to step on Francene's "mom toes," as much as I wanted to envelope my daughter with all the love I hadn't been able to give her the last fifteen years. My main goal was to let her know that she was incredibly loved. Not unwanted. That was the reasoning behind my choice. Megan said she knew. Her mom had told her and shared my letters with her. That was huge to me. Again, I credit Francene.

It's a fine line. Giving birth isn't the same as caring for your daughter; her bumps, her bruises, her dealing with bullies, homework, ups, downs . . . and then to have her want to meet her "mom"?! But Francene and I have a connection. Maybe because of the prenatal appointments? Maybe because she was there with me at Megan's birth? Maybe because we share an intense love of the same daughter? Maybe because we are a bigger and happier family? Maybe because we appreciate the people in our family, because family isn't about blood. It's about choice.

I have met most of Megan's family now, and she has met a large portion of mine. It has been, for the most part, incredible. I have been shown so much love and appreciation from her family, and I feel like much of my family has been grateful to meet her. I remember on that first meeting when she was fifteen, Megan was most interested in tangible things we had in common. Freckles on the same fingers, big ears, same eyes—a connection to a person blood-related. As years have passed, and our relationship has progressed, we've seen personality similarities between her, my daughter Maddie, and myself.

Giving Megan up for adoption was the most painful and fulfilling thing I've ever done. With much gratitude to the Fishers, though, I've gained a family, not lost one. I will be forever grateful to them for giving our daughter the life I could not provide and being gracious enough to include me in theirs. I think it's come with a healthy respect on both sides and an understanding that it's all about Meg.

What it means to me to be a birthparent is difficult to describe. It has meant many sad Mother's Days, August 5ths (her birthday), heart-wrenching moments when I would see babies with their mothers. There have been nights of crying and desperately wanting to hold her again. But it has also meant the amazing joining of two families for the love of one girl. It has meant a chance to tell people my story in hopes of helping others experience the joy of adoption. It has meant being able to talk to other scared, pregnant girls about their choices. And it's been the chance to reconnect and develop a relationship with our daughter, and that has meant the world to me.

Through my experience, I have suggestions that I hope will be helpful to readers.

I am thankful I worked with the adoption agency Bethany Christian Services. They provided one-on-one counseling, which I believe is critical to anyone going through this experience. They helped me choose adoption for Megan and helped me pick the right family for her. The amount of counseling I received prior to making my decision was enormously helpful in my adoption process. We discussed all avenues, minus abortion, to ensure that I was making the right decision for me and my child. I was 100 percent sure of my decision before beginning the process of choosing a family.

I believe that having Francene join me in prenatal visits helped us, the two moms, connect on a deeper level. This was a journey we were taking together. This was a child we all loved, and developing our relationship before Megan's birth made a positive impact on how we would interact after her birth. It also allowed Francene to be a part of Megan's life that she never thought she'd be able to experience as an adoptive mom. These were experiences she'd be able to share with our daughter throughout the years.

I think that having a private room at the hospital helped immensely; the staff was very aware and accommodating of our unique situation. In conjunction with that, it allowed all my friends and family to be able to visit Megan and me, knowing my time with her was limited. Having them there and able to meet her allowed them to see and perhaps be more sympathetic to the emotional roller coaster I'd be on for the next few years.

Again, I believe that the counseling before and after Megan's birth truly helped prepare me for what was to come. Do not be afraid to seek help! I've always been a tough woman who can make it through anything. As much as I was prepared, it still cut me to my core, and seeking help from nonjudgmental professionals assisted me greatly in dealing with the severe emotional ups and downs.

One thing I always thought important was when I chose adoption, I wrote down all my genealogy, medical, and personal history, and my decision-making process on choosing adoption so that if Megan ever wanted to meet me, it was because she wanted to meet *me*! I didn't want her searching me out because she needed to know why or where or who. I wanted her to have all the information possible, so that the choice to meet me or not would be entirely up to her inclination.

There are plenty of adoption assumptions that I would like to challenge! The first one that comes to mind is about the grieving process. When I was having a particularly hard day several months after Megan was born, a friend said, "Hey, it's been months now. You should be over it by now and move on." I almost punched him right in the nose! No one can tell you to move on, and you really shouldn't expect that you will fully move on. Although I have never once regretted my decision, giving your child up for adoption creates a hole that is never filled. Twenty-two years later, there are still some painful moments, and that reality needs to be recognized and accepted. I had several miscarriages when I was ready to be a mom, and at those times, the pain was doubled in thinking I might have given away my only chance to be a mother!

Other people, some of my family members included, believe that the close relationship between the Fishers and myself is odd. They feel that I should back away, that I am interfering or stepping on their toes. They believe I should quietly disappear. We disagree. Every family situation is different, and I have always had it in mind that the Fishers are her parents. That being said, I think we all agree that our coming together has been beneficial, not just for Megan but for her parents and me also.

And *never* tell a birthmom on Mother's Day that she's not really a mom. We are! Maybe I was a bit naïve, but I was not prepared for how many people did not understand or were judgmental of birthparents. It's part of the reason I share my story with everyone I meet, and why I believe Lorri's books are important!

I am honest. There are positive impacts of adoption as well as negative. On the positive side, I have a friend, Francene, who I can call, cry with, celebrate with, even seek parenting advice from. A couple weeks ago, our daughter was in a car accident, and Francene called to let me know. Megan was okay, but she lives far away, and we were able to support each other. We also got together to celebrate Megan's birthday while she was away.

It has had a positive impact on the daughter I am raising now. She and Megan have also been able to develop a close relationship and understand that family is what and who you make it.

Of course, there's been sorrow and grief for me to handle, but I wasn't the only one impacted. Adoption can also negatively affect the birthparent's family. I don't think I truly understood how hard it was for my immediate family to "give away" a family member. Being so young and intrinsically self-centered, I was more focused on my own situation and how it affected me. I did not understand until later that, while seen as a positive choice, my pregnancy and Megan's adoption were extremely difficult for those close to me. My unborn child was referred to as "illegitimate," which irked me to no end, and I had family members who would not associate with me at church for the shame of it all. Both reactions were hurtful to me, yet I did not understand the pain and struggles they were experiencing that would cause them to behave that way.

While the process was painful to me, still I did not understand their pain and struggle. Megan was their first grandchild, their niece, their friend's daughter who they felt they would never know. I remember my mom standing next to me throughout Megan's birth with a look of both joy and extreme sadness, partly from watching her daughter go through a difficult process but also the uncertainty of her first granddaughter being handed off to strangers. I found out later that my grandma had asked a male friend of mine to take us on so Megan could be kept in the family. Some chose not to see us in the hospital, some did. Some have shown excitement and acceptance in meeting her now, and some have not. I believe that those family members who have not do so only because of a lack of understanding and an uncertainty as to the "protocol" of adoption. This is another reason I believe in this book—to show that the process is not just about the adoption trinity but for all those close to it!

My final "word of wisdom" would be to find people who have gone through this. Seek out advice, but understand that every situation is different. I wish I had known another birthmom going through this. So many are ashamed of being birthmoms that they don't tell anyone. I've met several because I *am* open. There's a serious stigma that goes with "giving away" a child, and guilt, shame, embarrassment, and terrible pain often accompany that incredibly selfless choice! It is awfully sad when a woman who has chosen abortion is more easily accepted and regarded than a woman who has chosen adoption for her child! The lack of understanding of adoption is immense, and I have tried to help change that for years.

I think that Megan, Francene, and I are exceptionally close. I truly wish that all adoption stories could be this amazing. I am hoping that my story, among others, can help alleviate the fears, undo the misconceptions, and assist others in turning something painful into something beautiful.

CHAPTER TEN

FORGIVENESS AND BLESSINGS

George Fadok

George is a retired Navy captain and currently a Navy JROTC instructor at Fredericksburg High in Fredericksburg, Texas. He and his wife, Dianne, have a nineteen-year-old daughter, Catherine, and he has two daughters, Kristen and Lindsay, and a son, George, from his first marriage, as well as his birthdaughter, Jill.

Fictional literary works are always accurate in their accounting of events, because a work of fiction represents those events (i.e., the storyline or plot), and even the world itself in which those events occur, solely from the viewpoint of the author. Conversely, any oral or written recollection of actual events is inherently inaccurate, shaped by the perspective and memory of each of the tellers of that story. The stories told by each participant or witness about events that actually occurred will naturally have both commonalities and differences. If my recollection of the following events is different from theirs, I offer an apology to all who witnessed or remember those events from a different point of view. There are some details regarding the past forty-something years that I don't mention, as my intent is to avoid opening old wounds and causing any pain.

I was twenty years old, unmarried, and in the delivery room when my daughter Jill was born; it was August 9, 1976. I did not see her on the day she was born. A carefully placed sheet blocked the view of the birth itself, but I was there. I am Jill's natural father, a term I favor over "birth" or "biological." This was the mid-seventies, and in Arizona, according to various websites, most adoptive parents favored a "closed" versus an "open" adoption. In simple terms, a closed adoption is one in which legally there can be no contact between the natural mother or father of the adopted child and the adoptive parents and child after the birth of the baby. I did not fully understand the terms at the time, so it is only by looking back that I can identify the process of a closed adoption. I remember signing some paperwork, a consent for adoption perhaps, sometime shortly after Jill's birth. It may have been seventy-two hours after her birth as the current law states, and it may also have been in a law office, but I don't remember the details. Additionally, at that time, most private counsels, friends, religious leaders, social workers, and so on advised no contact with a child you were placing in an adoptive family. They said to do the right thing for the child and move forward with your life.

From that point on, I believed I would never see or know who Jill was or how her life turned out. I did not know her name and did not know her adoptive family. I did occasionally wonder who this baby girl was and how she turned out, wishing and praying for a positive outcome. But convinced of the correctness of my decision, these thoughts mostly remained private. I would not find out her name for eighteen years.

The decision to give this baby to adoptive parents was complex, as are most important decisions in life. And this was an important decision to me. It was also easily the most difficult one I have ever had to make. One alternative given serious consideration was to marry her natural mother, but my thoughts and feelings were that the baby would have a better life with an established family. Loving this baby wasn't part of the decisional equation: I would have greatly loved any child I brought into my home, so of course I would have loved Jill with all my heart!

Ironically, Jill's natural mother and I did end up getting married, and we had three more children before divorcing after many years. My second wife and I also have a daughter, who just graduated from high school. I have been blessed with and have raised four children, and I hope I have satisfied each of their own individual needs, as well as the collective needs of a family, for a loving father.

Jill's natural mother had often expressed a desire to meet and know Jill upon her reaching majority age, but although interested in the outcome of this child's life, I maintained a belief that any reunion would have a potentially disruptive effect on the families of everyone involved, especially on the three children I was raising at the time.

Eighteen years passed after the adoption, and Jill's natural mother sought her out. By sheer coincidence, or God's plan if you are a believer, a connection existed between Jill's adoptive father and her natural mother's mother

(Jill's natural maternal grandmother) the day she was born; amazingly, they were both employees of the same organization. Jill's grandmother figured it out almost immediately but said nothing until she was of age. So, a path to her natural daughter already existed, and once she turned eighteen, Jill's natural mother found her.

Soon thereafter, I learned of Jill and a little bit about her. Some of the emotions I remember feeling were fear, trepidation, nervousness, emotional pain, and anger—anger not with Jill, but with the situation that was unfolding. I was now raising three teenagers and was concerned with how they would react. I was afraid of yet another potential disruption in their lives, lives already complicated by our recent divorce, which resulted in a bifurcated then blended family.

I was offered a chance to meet Jill, and I was full of anxiety and quite scared. What would I say to her? How would we respond to each other? I was very uncomfortable, not because of Jill herself but because of the history, and because of my conceivably antiquated assumptions, and perhaps because of my own shortcomings. Since Jill's natural mother had already made contact, my three children knew Jill by then and talked excitedly and positively about her. She was, for them, a full-blooded sister, and their relationships were developing accordingly.

When she appeared at the door, I saw she was a beautiful girl; she still is. We greeted briefly in the front entry at the place where she was staying, and I was relieved when it was over. I was thirty-eight years old, and for one of the few times in my life, I did not know what to do, or what should or would happen next. I still had strong concerns regarding the effect this could have on the children I was raising. Twentieth-century families can be complicated, and so, many years passed before I saw Jill again. Subconsciously perhaps, I made a decision (or reaffirmed what I had thought from the day she was born) to let her live her life and make the choice on what our relationship would be in the future.

The next time I saw Jill, I think it was at the wedding of one of my other daughters. She was a married woman by then, with a child of her own. I met her husband as well, and I could sense (and I was told by those who knew him) that he was a good man. Time proved this to be correct. Jill and I would see each other at family events, weddings, baptisms, and the like, over the next few years. Our contact was always cordial: "Hello, how are you doing" a kiss on the cheek, and perhaps a brief hug. But I always left never knowing whether or not, or under what circumstances, I would see her again. The last time a visit with Jill left me with these feelings of uncertainty was in July 2015, as we, along with extended family, celebrated the baptism of my youngest granddaughter.

Two weeks after the baptism, Jill sent me an email. It was the first time I can recollect that she or I had done something like this. When I read the email, I sensed, correctly or not, that the words and thoughts came right from her heart and soul. It was a beautiful and thoughtful message, and it contained what I interpreted as a request. A request to try to know and love each other in a deeper and more meaningful way. A communication between a daughter and a father. Maybe I got that wrong, but that's how I felt; and it was good, heavenly I think, to feel that way.

In the email, Jill recalled a conversation she had with her son during the weekend of the baptism. She said it was a challenging conversation for a parent to have with a nine-year-old boy, a boy who enjoyed the reception and the people but who also wondered about these people he saw at the family gathering. He wondered where he was in this twenty-first century family tree and about the relationships of which he was now becoming more aware.

I wanted my response to be perfect and hoped the words would adequately express my joy and thankfulness for Jill's message. There was so much to say after thirty-nine years; how would we begin? I sent a reply simply stating that I loved her and looked forward to getting to know her better and loving her more. I never once thought I would respond in any other way.

In the next few emails, we talked about how we would communicate, both of us agreeing that a personal visit would offer the richest exchange, but since we are physically separated by almost a thousand miles, that would have to wait, at least a while. Email was the preferred method, and so we began sharing small tidbits of our lives and feelings. I extended an invitation to Jill and her family to visit soon, and we agreed Thanksgiving 2015 would be a good time for this.

The excitement grew over the next couple of months as Thanksgiving approached . . . What a perfect holiday for this occasion! Jill and I spent a lot of time talking one-on-one, but it was also nice to get to know both her son and her husband. We discussed small but important details. How would we address each other, how would we introduce each other, what would her son call me? I now introduce Jill to people simply as my daughter, and her son calls me the name my other grandchildren use. We also talked about important things regarding our individual life stories but also, and very important to both of us, our beliefs and philosophies on life. It was a wonderful five days!

I know I had, and continue to have, a strong commitment to creating the best possible relationship with Jill, and I believe she has the same commitment too. I am thankful for each positive thought and event we experience together, no matter how minor it may seem, and Jill has expressed her similar feelings to me as well. I see Jill when we are visiting other family close to her home. She and her husband have hosted us at their home, and with her family. Jill and her "boys" made another visit for the high school graduation of my youngest daughter and my sixtieth birthday. This visit also included all my children and their families, my brothers and sister, and my mother. I mention this because everyone seems comfortable with our new relationship and with their individual relationship with Jill and her family. I like that very much.

Throughout my entire life, I have been tremendously blessed by God with family, friends, and what I call "lifelong teammates," people I can trust and who have loved me and helped me in my successes. They have supported and loved me when I have failed, too. The past few years of getting to know Jill, expressing my love for her and feeling her love for me, have truly been an additional tremendous family blessing to me—another blessing in an already blessed and fortunate life. I hope and pray she feels blessed as well. Jill, if I have failed you greatly or in the slightest way by my actions, or inactions, I hope and pray you can forgive me and you can still love me.

I have learned many lessons through this experience. I believe a father's love enhances the life of a child, and when a child reaches adulthood, the love of a father can continue to enrich his children's lives. In the case of the four children I raised, my love was open, articulated, and demonstrated from the moment I witnessed their birth and throughout their lives . . . and will continue to be. In the case of Jill and I, this love came later in our lives, but that does not at all diminish the goodness and enduring power of that love.

It's never too late to begin or mend a relationship with your child, regardless of adoptive status. I did not reach out to Jill, and I often wonder if this was a mistake. Under the circumstances of her adoption and the relationships of everyone involved, I will never know. But I would, however, encourage natural parents to seize the opportunity, should it present itself, to develop the best possible relationship with their natural son or daughter.

I am sure I made mistakes. After all, I had twenty years of additional life experiences than Jill, but I don't know how things would have changed, or been better, had I been more active in establishing a relationship sooner. I can say that our situation may have been more complicated than most, but perhaps at the very least, I could have shown her warmth and affection when we did occasionally see each other. I could have openly expressed an interest in her life and family. But I honestly did not know what to do. I still feel some occasional guilt as I wonder what may have been, but I also realize that I let go of parental control incrementally with the four children I raised, letting them live their lives according to their desires as they grew and matured. Perhaps I let Jill decide how and when we would have a relationship, and I'm forever thankful she chose to do so.

I take comfort that any guilt, anxiety, or ill feelings I have about what I did or didn't do has been extinguished by the beautiful love I feel now with Jill. That is a good feeling.

Now for the platitudes: be loving, be honest (with yourself and your child), be open and available, be forgiving of yourself, and with others if needed.

CHAPTER ELEVEN

A CALENDAR YEAR

Tiffany Barson

Tiffany is forty-two and works as an aquatic supervisor in the Chicagoland area. She has been happily married to Peter, a bicycle mechanic, for twenty-three years. She is the proud mother of two boys, ages twenty and nineteen.

I turned seventeen on October 28, 1991. In November, ironically right after Thanksgiving, I was confronted with the plus sign on the pee stick. Before the stick was dry, I had made an appointment for an abortion. I didn't want time to think. The appointment was two weeks away . . . so turns out I had lots of time to think. The Friday before the scheduled appointment, "he" and I had another fight. It made me realize that decisions were not going to be made for me, and something needed to be done.

I told my mom that night. I sat calmly with my mom, "him," and a lovely lady I had met only minutes before and told them all that I was going to have this baby and give the baby up for adoption. After all, one of my brothers and two of my cousins had been adopted. This was my choice, and it was the best choice, and that was my plan. We sat in the living room with the only light coming from the Christmas tree, and I was shocked to the core when my mom said that I could either get an abortion or pack my bags.

Friday and Saturday night, I stayed at "his" house. Sunday, I stayed with a friend, and by Monday, I was in a shelter for delinquent girls. Christmas Day I was told I needed to find other arrangements because my mother refused to attend the required counseling sessions. New Year's Eve I moved in with a stranger. I didn't see my mother again until long after the baby was born.

Near the end of January, my Catholic high school politely asked me to find a different path to graduation. I was enrolled in night school before February. In night school, I learned that I wasn't "giving" my baby up for adoption—I was "placing" my baby for adoption. The change in language made a tremendous difference to me. It was explained to me that you give *things* away: old clothes, furniture, and things you simply don't want anymore. When you place your child in a loving home with parents who want more than anything to complete their family, you are weighing that decision with your heart and mind. It's not an action that you go into lightly but one that requires months of sleepless nights.

On February 25, I learned I was having a boy.

In March, I met the wonderful people from The Cradle and the lovely couple with whom I would place my son to complete their family. In April, I was put on bed rest for the remainder of my pregnancy. I was due in July.

In May I was treated to stories of my friends and their adventures during prom and post-prom, and I heard all about their graduation ceremonies.

On June 8, I had yet another trip to the hospital, where it was determined that this time they may not be able to stop the labor but they would desperately try. In order to prepare for everything that was in store, I underwent what was, for me, a very painful amniocentesis. On June 9, labor stopped, and I was sent home. The good news was that the amniocentesis showed that the baby boy was, in fact, ready for the world. On June 12, 1992, during my doctor visit, my contractions were strong enough and I was dilated enough to send me, once again, to the hospital.

Kenny was born at 3:36 p.m. He was 7 lbs., 10 oz., 20.5 inches long, and *wonderful*. His parents came to visit us in the hospital, and on Sunday, I brought him home with me. On Monday, I signed the papers and placed my little guy in his mother's arms.

I saw him twice, just before his first Christmas and shortly after he learned to walk. I also received letters and pictures. It was way too hard to keep this kind of contact. Each time I saw him, it felt like I had to say goodbye to him all over again. The pictures and letters ripped new holes in my heart. I asked to stop contact in October of 1993. In the time between the day he was born and the day I stopped contact, I was handed my diploma in the night school office. I moved into my very own apartment, I enrolled in community college, and I met the boy who would become my husband.

When I moved, I called The Cradle and changed my address, and when I married, I called The Cradle and changed my name. When Kenny was seven years old, I got an unauthorized update that had me beside myself for well over a year.

When Kenny was seventeen years old, I got a letter from The Cradle. He wanted to know me. We exchanged letters for what felt like forever. We talked on the phone. We texted and became Facebook friends. We finally met.

We have been in contact for eight years now. Last week I took him and my two sons, his brothers, bowling.

Thank you for letting me share. That is my story.

Here are my thoughts about adoption and being a birthmom.

My connection with adoption is actually twofold: my oldest brother and two of my cousins were adopted, which helped me make the decision to place my son for adoption when I discovered I was pregnant at seventeen.

The meaning of being a birthmother has changed for me many times over the years. I am now very proud to be a birthmother, but for the first few years after my son was born, I often felt very guilty. In those early years, I felt that I took the easy way out. It took reconnecting with my son to change that feeling forever. It is now easy to look back with no regrets. Choosing adoption was such a difficult thing to do—for me, I wanted no reminders because of my guilt. But now I know I made the right choice for both of us. I would tell birthmothers to trust your gut, and trust that in the end, things will work out. It isn't an easy thing to do when you are dealing with all the emotions tied to such a decision, but later, when you look at it in hindsight, things are much clearer.

My primary piece of advice is to *keep an open mind and an open heart*. There will always be things you wish were different or that you will worry about, but that doesn't mean your choice was wrong. I wished that my mother would have been more supportive, and I worried that it wasn't possible to really love someone else's child. When I reconnected with my son and began to talk to his mother, I realized that it was more than possible, and that I had spent too many years worrying for nothing. She is his mother, and she has a mother's love for her son.

I am happy that our triad is complete. There are times that the relationships I share with my son, his mother, and my grandson are very satisfying, and times when they are not. Navigating these relationships is difficult, and I always wonder if I am doing enough or perhaps too much. But again, I try to keep an open mind and an open heart.

The other suggestion I would give a birthmother is to talk to everyone you can about adoption. Birthparents, adopted children, counselors, teachers, doctors, Planned Parenthood. Read everything you can get your hands on to educate yourself about *all* of your options. *Talk to everyone!* Listen to all the advice that comes your way. You will find that there are kind souls out there who have wonderful words of wisdom to share with you, and you will find that there are others who will try to bring you down. Always consider the source and ask yourself what they have to gain. Know that even when you are receiving bad advice, there are important lessons to be learned from that as well. In the end, it is your life and your choice to make, and it is a decision you will live with the rest of your life.

Lorri, thank you again for sharing your story with the world. Thank you for the opportunity to be a part of this book, even if it's just about sharing my story with you. Maybe one person will have an easier time after reading this. My son's mother and I always joke about the fact that there was no "how-to" guide for us; it is wonderful to imagine that there will be now. For us and for others.

PART THREE

Adoptive Parents

CHAPTER TWELVE

WHEN YOU LEAST EXPECT IT

Laura Stout, EdD

Laura is an executive director of school leadership services in Corpus Christi, Texas. She and her husband, Brian, an aircraft avionics technician, live in Fort Worth, Texas, with their four adopted children.

When my husband and I had been married ten months, we decided that we would look into having a child. I was forty, and he was thirty-seven, and I knew from previous years that I couldn't get pregnant on my own. We decided to go see a doctor about in vitro fertilization. We were at the final stages of preparation when I received a phone call from my great-nephew's friend.

Perhaps a little background is in order. I am from south Texas, but I've lived in Dallas since 2000. I used to go visit my mother once or twice a year when she was still living down in south Texas. During my visits, I would go places with my family. The young lady who called me that day was friends with my great-nieces and -nephews and would sometimes tag along with my family on these visits. On a couple of occasions, she went with us to the beach on South Padre Island. I saw her, but we never really spoke. On one of my visits, I noticed that she was pregnant—I would guess about seven months.

Fast forward several years later to 2009, and I got this phone call from her. She knew from hearing me talk with my family that I wanted to adopt. These were conversations that I'd had with family prior to getting married. She knew that I wanted children. So, when she made the decision to place her child, I was the person she thought of, and that was the reason for the call. I told her to think about it and call back when she was sure. We hung up, and within a week I received a call from her. She said she was positive that she wanted me to have the baby. It was a boy, and he was five weeks old. She asked that we come get the baby right away.

She was five hundred and fifty miles away. I told her that we'd be there in the next week or two, and she said that we needed to go down there right away because she didn't have bottles or nipples or any way to feed the child. That was a Tuesday night. On Friday morning, we were headed to pick the baby up. We couldn't believe it. We arrived at the child's grandmother's house, and we were met by Child Protection Services. Long story short, it turns out that CPS was involved, and they wanted to remove the child from this young lady's care. Everyone signed consents, and we brought the baby home.

Just like that, we were a family of three. In September of the same year, we received a phone call from the birthmother again, and she informed us that she was pregnant again. She was asking us for money for an abortion, but we told her that we could not give her money for that. We did say that we would be glad to take the child in to give our first baby a brother or sister. She agreed, and that is when we brought her to live with us in our home in Fort Worth.

During the time from November to February, when our second baby was born, she and I spoke about a lot of things, and I learned a lot about postpartum depression from her. It was a tough time because she had homicidal thoughts. It turns out that the reason we got the original phone call about the first baby was because she had tried to suffocate him with a comforter. She asked us not to leave her alone with our first baby because she didn't want to hurt him and she was experiencing those thoughts again. We removed the baby from the nursery into our room, and she slept in a separate room. She was unpredictable and constantly crying. We took her to the doctor, and she was diagnosed with major depression and postpartum depression.

She and I talked about tubal ligation so that she wouldn't have any more children, and we both thought that was a good idea. We went to talk to the doctor, who said that this young lady was too young to have her tubes tied because she was still capable of having more children. That was the second time that I realized that not every adult makes the best decision for kids. The first time was when the judge who presided at the request to remove the first baby from the birthmother's custody refused to terminate her parental rights despite her having homicidal thoughts and even trying to murder the child.

We saw her through this pregnancy, and saw our child be born in February. We were now a family of four.

Fast forward two months, when we got another call from CPS. This time the caseworker told us that the same young lady had two children in foster care, born before she even contacted us the first time, and they were getting ready to be adopted out into the system. She asked for us to consider taking the older children in: a girl, age five, and a boy, age two. We prayed about it and decided to keep all four siblings together. By June 2010, we suddenly had four children. We were our forever family of six.

So . . . our story is that we took one child in, then took his brother in, and they were adopted privately. We also took permanent custody of their two older siblings from foster care. Although they have some learning disabilities, we believe that our children are perfect. They try their hardest, and whenever they have any bit of achievement in school, we celebrate. Two of them are in special-education classes, and two of them are high achievers. All of them do their very best.

I sometimes think that there is a reason there are women out there that can't biologically have any children. It is because there are children out there that need mothers, and these mothers might not adopt if they were able to have children of their own. I believe that this is God's way of solving the problem of children not having parents when their birthparents are unable to care for them. I do commend the birthmother for choosing to give the two younger children a better life with us, and I love her for making me a mom. She was not happy that the older two children were placed with us because she loves them. She had no emotional connection to the younger children, but I think that is understandable because she chose someone to love them when she could not.

That is where my husband and I come in. Our children have been to the symphony and on vacation every summer; they play with the latest technology, they play outside and get dirty, and they have everything they need when school starts. We teach them how to bake, how to tinker in the garage, how to play fair, and how to take good care of themselves. We are trying to raise them to be smart young adults and to take care of themselves and make good choices and be productive citizens, and I think we are well underway.

I would like prospective for parents with no children to consider adopting children from foster care because they are waiting for good people to take care of them. They are in foster care through no fault of their own and deserve a family. I love the drawings, the paintings, the crooked ceramic pieces that I receive on Mother's Day, the misspelled poems, and the mispronounced words, and everything else that I have received from these beautiful children. Again, our children are perfect, and we wouldn't change a thing. Thank you for the opportunity to share my story. I know I'm not the best or the most perfect mother, but I do try my best, and that's OK.

CHAPTER THIRTEEN

GOD IS IN CONTROL

Kathryn Jackson

Kathryn is a fifty-two-year-old mom from Dallas, Texas. She and her husband, Rick, have been married for twenty-seven years and have three adopted children.

Adoption entered our world twenty-two years ago when our plans to start a family did not work out the way we had originally envisioned. After years of infertility, we grew so weary of all the medical demands. Through all the continual heartbreaks, we finally came to this realization . . . that our strong desire to be parents far outweighed our desire to be pregnant. What had previously seemed like "Plan B" became our "Plan A," and we set out to pursue adoption and never looked back! I've said many times that if God were to come to me and give me the choice of birthing my kids or adopting them, I would now say "Adopt!" hands down every time because of all I have learned along the way. I count being an adoptive mom as one of my life's greatest privileges!

We have three children, all through domestic adoptions, with the first two being twins (surprise!). Our twins are now finishing college, and our youngest is a senior in high school.

For us, this whole process is directly connected to our belief that there is a God who is in control, that He causes all things to work together for good for those who love Him, and that He longs to adopt each one of us as His child. This belief not only is central to who we are but became central to our passion for earthly adoption and how we have approached it with our children since day one. We have always shared with them Psalm 139, especially verse 16: "All the days ordained for me were written in your book before even one of them came to be." We believe that in His foreknowledge, He chose these children for us long ago, and us for them. And just as He longs to redeem, restore, and renew each one of us, earthly adoption is an amazing picture of Him doing just that, for all parties involved: birth-parents, adoptive parents, and adoptees! I love how adoption redeems all parties at the same time: a birthmom in crisis, a couple desperately longing for a child, and a child able to grow up in an environment that wasn't possible otherwise. *Regardless of your spiritual beliefs*, the idea that your kids are not "unplanned" but rather part of a grand plan is a very powerful and grounding encouragement for them throughout their lives.

Early on, their adoption was a part of regular conversation in our home. We never wanted to have a big, sit-down "talk" about it. Instead, we wove it into our everyday life. When they were young and noticed a pregnant woman, we would remind them that they had a "tummy mommy"; it just wasn't me.

"When will I meet my tummy mommy?" they would ask.

"Maybe when you grow up someday. If you want to then, Daddy and I will help you."

We often talked about every detail of the amazing day we got the call that we had been chosen to be their parents. We told them how excited our friends and family were, how everyone came with us to the adoption agency to pick them up (literally everyone . . . I'm not sure they had seen such a crowd at placement before), how special friends and family were in court with us on the day their adoption finalized. We showed them pictures of those days. We reminded them how we so desperately wanted them, how long we prayed, how amazed we were when God chose us for them.

We also had the privilege of meeting both of their birthmothers, so we told them every detail we remembered about their birthmothers and our time with both of them. Our goal was to make them as comfortable as possible with any questions they might be having. I think as a result, their adoption was really just always a part of them, a part they embraced.

One of our favorite family traditions is "Gotcha Day," the day we brought them home. In addition to their birthdays, we celebrated their Gotcha Days with special gifts and dinners, every single year. From the get-go, adoption was celebrated in our home. An added unexpected benefit of this was that at least once a year, they had a natural opportunity to positively tell their friends and teachers. I loved how teachers would tell us about the children standing up in class and proudly announcing, "Today is my Gotcha Day!" I love how special they have made that day, even now as young adults. I love how it gave us an opportunity once more to talk about their birthmoms or tell them about that special day. (And the extra present was a bonus. Ha!)

Our youngest especially loves to tell the story how we drove from the adoption agency after her placement straight to our favorite restaurant to celebrate, ten-day-old baby in tow! (Not sure what I was thinking taking a new baby into a public restaurant like that!) But it has made for a great tradition on her Gotcha Day: every year, same restaurant!

A great piece of advice was given to us regarding when and what to tell them about their adoption and birthparents: when they ask you for a hamburger, don't give them a steak! Meaning, when kids are kids, they just ask simple questions, expecting simple answers. So, when they ask, "What color is my birthmom's hair?" don't overwhelm them with a serious detailed conversation about how the whole adoption process works. As an adoptive parent, you tend to think, "Oh, this is my chance to have this deep conversation," when all they really want to know is "Is she blond or brunette?" Typically, my kids would ask questions in spurts and totally out of the blue, with no rhyme or reason why. So, I learned just to take those opportunities as they came, even if shouted from the back seat, on the way to school, with a carload of kids!

This continues to be true even as they grow into adulthood. Recently, after seeing the movie *Lion* on spring break (such a fabulous film!), our college-age daughter FaceTimed us at midnight one night to tell us she really wanted to read the letters and see pictures that we had saved from her birthmom and possibly pursue finding her. Wow, that will wake you up at midnight!

We had held on to pictures and letters from the twins' birthmom until they were older and asked for them, and here was our moment. Funny thing is, I had always envisioned going through that box with her in some special, poignant ceremonial moment when we gathered the family and, drumroll please, opened the "special box!" Thankfully, my husband had much better insight than me, and said, "Sure, honey!" So, in millennial fashion, we retrieved everything from the special box and sat up in our bed at midnight, over FaceTime, with our daughter (and all her friends, mind you) as we all laughed and cried, showing her letters and photos she had never seen before. Forget Mom's sappy Hallmark-moment plan. This was apparently exactly when and how she needed it to be.

Since this experience, her siblings wanted to do the same, so they each have had their own openings of the box, without drumroll or drama. In hindsight, however, my waiting to share the box is one of my regrets. I regret saving the letters and photos for a time when they asked for them.

Instead, maybe it would have been more appropriate for me to ask them periodically if they would like to see them. Each of them have noted how cool the letters were to read and how, for now, they have sufficiently answered their questions about their birthparents, questions they always wanted to ask but were afraid to.

Another factor I really wasn't aware of is how adolescence may change the security they feel about adoption. While they may have readily asked questions when they were young, when they moved into adolescence, questions occurred less frequently. I would just encourage parents to be aware that no news may not necessarily be good news, and we must always be on the lookout for creative ways to keep the conversation going.

Currently, none of our kids are interested in pursuing a meeting with birthparents. I suspect, however, that someday one of them will. As long as they have fully thought out all the ramifications, we are great with that and will help them on the search.

I am certain there are additional things we should have done differently. As good of a job as I think we have done with embracing adoption, it would be foolish to say there weren't difficult things to navigate and won't be more in the future. What I have learned, however, is that my goal in navigating adoption as a parent has changed. My goal used to be to do and say everything perfectly so that our adopted children would never have questions about their adoption and its relationship to their identity. Could it be that a more appropriate goal would be to instill in my children the life skills and self-awareness necessary to deal with the questions that most certainly will come? A sign given to me by my daughter is hanging in the room where I am writing at this moment: "It is not what you do for your children, but what you have taught them to do for themselves."

As I mentioned earlier, in our particular worldview, that means spiritually leading our children to the God of the universe and His perfect provision of worth in Jesus Christ. We are convinced that the unconditional love we *all* are looking for is found there in perfect form. Whatever your worldview is, however, my prayer for you is that your goal in navigating your child's adoption will be the same.

CHAPTER FOURTEEN

IT TAKES A GLOBAL VILLAGE

Jill Larson

Jill Larson is an actress in New York City, best known for her role as the beloved Opal Cortlandt on the ABC soap All My Children. *She is a single mother who adopted her daughter from China.*

I was never someone who felt she had to have children to be fulfilled as a woman. As an actress, I was very focused on my career. Growing up the oldest of four daughters, I felt I had childcare responsibilities thrust upon me early on, and perhaps those experiences dampened my interest in motherhood. I also came of age during the seventies and the Women's Movement, with all its awakening consciousness about women finally realizing their own potential. A popular T-shirt image from that time had the face of a woman weeping with the caption, "Oh my God! I forgot to have children!!" Pretty much said it all.

In my early forties, having ended a challenging relationship with a man who was neither husband nor father material, I was cast as Opal Gardner Purdy Cortlandt on *All My Children.* Suddenly any vacuum in my personal life was filled with working very long days, memorizing pages of dialogue, and doing promotional and celebrity events on weekends. There was little time to notice that empty space next to me.

I've heard many adoptive parents refer to their adoption experience as a kind of destiny, which is exactly what I felt, and still do feel. It seemed like I awoke one morning with the thought that I would be adopting a baby. I truly don't know where this thought came from, and initially I found it somewhat amusing, but I quickly set to work researching for my future. My younger sister had already adopted two children from Korea, so after a few false starts, I looked to international adoption. Korea was not available to me—the requirements were that the parents be married for at least five years and be under forty—but China accepted single parents, and the age cut-off was sixty, so I began my application process.

In navigating the arduous process of adoption, I'm sure I'm not the only person who felt the invasion of privacy through FBI background checks and fingerprinting; deeply personal, probing interviews; bank statements, tax returns, references, family photos, and essays about intended parenting style, and so on. This is in comparison to the ease of the DIY, in-a-fit-of-passion method that creates biological families, no outsiders necessary. I, of course, understood the need for this depth of vetting, but I also felt the injustice of it, the requirement to prove myself worthy of being a parent.

But as I said, I felt throughout that I was on a preordained path and consequently none of these obstacles, and many others unmentioned, really disturbed me. They all just felt like pauses while *my* baby was getting ready to meet me. And then, on June 6, 1996, in a tiny room at the Shanghai Children's Welfare Institute, my daughter was placed in my arms. It is, of course, a moment I will never forget—both of us rather stunned, thrilled, frightened, everything all at once. Adoption is a very dramatic experience. In the taxi ride back to the hotel, I wondered to myself how it had taken me so long to get to this moment, and at the giddy relief I felt at realizing I now had someone other than myself to whom I could give my attention.

As an adoptive parent, I have encountered people, primarily men, who said they wouldn't adopt because "you don't know what you're getting," meaning medical background and so on, somehow suggesting that these adopted children are damaged goods. Of course, I never agreed with them, even though I could feel their own fear in their comments. And as my daughter has grown and our community of adoptive parents has widened, I can say that there are as many variations for adopted children, their successes or challenges in life, as there are for biological children. I see no substance in these fears.

You ask about lessons learned, things to offer other adopting parents. I'd say the thing I learned is that every single adoption is individual, and special in its own way. It has its own course, its own destiny. I don't know of any specific piece of advice to offer those beginning the process other than to say stay strong, and have faith, even in the midst of the most challenging bureaucratic misery; keep focused on being united with your child and remember that all this BS will soon be behind you, and you'll be dealing with the *real* challenges, those of being a parent!

As far as my daughter's birthmother, of course Chinese adoptees have very little hope of ever meeting their birthmothers. Due to the former One Child Policy in China, these girls had been abandoned, usually in public places. On rare occasions, there was a note pinned to them with a date of birth or other non-identifying information. It is a poignant situation. The adoptive daughter of a close friend was abandoned at nearly a year, which made a visible impact. The child, when she was perhaps five, saw a missing person poster on a street lamp and spent the next couple of weeks making flyers to post around Chinatown in hopes of finding her birthmother. My daughter claims she doesn't care about her birthmother, but I see signs of her heart's longing for connection or understanding, even if they're unconscious. This is the tragic side of these adoptions: these questions about abandonment, loss, and what is interpreted as rejection will never be resolved. I count on the strength of their souls to navigate these difficult waters as they grow into women.

Continuing with the notion of destiny, I've always seen this wave of Chinese adoptions from another, perhaps global, perspective. Here we were in our country, we women from the seventies, who had "missed out" on childrearing because we were working to overcome the limitations of a patriarchal society that undervalued women. We became aware of our own desires to be mothers but were often too old to become pregnant. And there, on the other side of the world, was this supply of baby girls, available and in need of mothering, abandoned in the face of a punishing patriarchal government that undervalued women. They became our daughters. That feels like destiny to me.

There will never be a dream of meeting birthparents for my daughter or most of the girls abandoned in China, and I watch them grapple with the pain of this huge hole in their story, often with anger and sometimes self-destructive behavior. Abandonment, an action that was forced on Chinese women by their government, is different from relinquishment. In New York, we have a large organization, Families with Children from China, and have invested heavily in Chinese cultural events, summer camps, homeland visits to China, therapy groups, and specialists, in an attempt to somehow fill this gap for our girls. I think the large majority of the girls have grown into happy, healthy, successful young women, thankfully including my daughter. There is, however, in my experience with my tiny family of two, an ever-present elephant in the room, a question we both know will never be answered. I must wait and hope that she will at some point be ready to confront and reconcile that primal loss, for the sake of her own well-being.

Early on in my motherhood, a friend gave me a book: *The Primal Wound* by Nancy Verrier, which explores the theory that a child separated from her birthmother carries a pain, an inner emptiness and longing for the birthmother throughout her life. An awareness of this possibility has helped me to understand and see my daughter more deeply. She is now twenty-one, in her last year of college and doing well. As with raising any child, we have had our ups and downs. Once she asked me if I wished I'd gotten a different baby from China. The question shocked me and broke my heart. "Oh, my Lord, *no!*" I answered. "*You* are my daughter, and you are the best thing that ever happened to me."

I hope she always remembers that.

CHAPTER FIFTEEN

MY CHILD HAS TWO MOTHERS

Tami Adcock

Tami, fifty-one, is a former Navy wife and nanny and current PTA mom. She and her husband, Michael, are proud parents to their adopted son, ten-year-old Noah, and live in Camas, Washington.

Most families celebrate their children's birthdays, but we have three days a year that we celebrate with our son: his birthday, our "Gotcha Day," and the day his adoption was finalized by the courts. The first day is all about him, but the other two are about us becoming a family. In our family, adoption wasn't a second choice but an amazing gift at the end of a very long road to parenthood.

After years of trying to start a family and lots of medical intervention, I was told I had almost no chance of getting pregnant. That was painful to hear, but it just sent us in a new direction, and we started researching adoption. The first big decision was international versus domestic adoption. Domestic adoption felt right to us, though I came to appreciate what a personal choice this is for any family. We explored adopting through the foster care system, but being a military family meant we might have to move, and that created extra obstacles on that path.

We signed up with a religious adoption program and took all their classes. At the end, they told us they were not accepting new families for six weeks, and then at the end of the six weeks they decided to close the program indefinitely. That was frustrating and felt like several months were wasted. We had to start over, but we did learn a lot in the classes, so all was not lost.

I found a private agency that sounded wonderful, but the very day we were to go to their informational meeting, my husband received orders to England.

The agency, however, was able to give me the name of a company that did home studies and post-placement reports for Americans living abroad. I knew we had to put everything on hold for six months until we settled in England and established a new home, but I was able to contact them and work on the paperwork so we could hit the ground running. I also contacted an adoption facilitator in our home state who was willing to work with us when the home study was completed. It seemed overwhelming to adopt in the United States while living overseas, but I was very determined and decided I wasn't going to let a little thing like the Atlantic Ocean stop us.

Once we were settled, we were able to start the home study. That part was actually fairly easy, compared to all the work we had already done. The only part that held us up was that we had to send our fingerprints back to our last address, and they were repeatedly returned as "not readable." My husband had his approved on the third try, but it took five tries for mine. I am convinced that it was the impassioned letter I included with the last set of fingerprints that finally convinced them to take pity on me. Jill, our facilitator, sent us information on possible adoption situations. A couple situations sounded promising, but the birthmothers picked other families. A few we decided to pass on for one reason or another, like the fees were out of our budget or there were requests we couldn't meet.

Finally, one day I came home to find an email about a baby boy who was to be delivered by C-section the next day in Las Vegas. It happened to be the day after my own birthday, and I had been feeling very sad to have yet another birthday without being a mother. The next weekend would be Mother's Day, a day I had come to dread. We said we were interested, and I held my breath. A part of me assumed this one wouldn't work out, like the other ones, so I didn't let myself get excited. The baby was actually born six hours after I received that email.

Two days later, they told us at 6 p.m. our time that he would be our son. By 7 a.m. the next day, I was on the train to Heathrow Airport after frantically spending the previous evening making arrangements and providing the agency with all they needed from us. My husband could not arrange leave that fast, so I went by myself, but my best friend flew in from Georgia to support me. I was excited but more than a little scared that something would go wrong. I decided I had to be OK with whatever happened. If she changed her mind, that would just mean we weren't at the end of the journey yet.

When I walked into the room to sign papers to take custody of our son, it was one of the most emotional times of my life. All I had to do was sign some papers and then I would get to finally meet our baby, the child for which my husband and I had hoped and prayed and worked and sacrificed for over the course of many years. I was nervous, hoping that everything would go smoothly, and a touch sad that my husband couldn't be with me. I was excited that it was all coming together and my dream was coming true. Mixed in with all those emotions was one I wasn't expecting—concern for a woman I didn't know. At this point I knew almost nothing about her, not even her name, but I knew she had just been through a huge medical procedure, having a C-section, and an even bigger emotional decision to make an adoption plan for her baby. I could only imagine what she might be feeling, and I was filled with compassion for her. She requested a closed adoption, and I might never know her or anything about her, but in that moment, I knew we would always have a connection, and I would always care about her.

Then it was time. After all the years and dead ends and tears and reams of paperwork, I was finally going to meet my baby. I stepped into the nursery and saw the most perfect little boy with tons of dark hair and sleepy eyes. He was four days old—tiny, just five pounds—but he was healthy and beautiful, and he was mine. I picked him up and whispered to him, "Where have you been? I have been waiting for you for so long!" and he snuggled in to me. It felt perfect. I knew at that moment that all the frustration and pain and waiting had been worth it.

The early months of our lives with Noah were blissful. We were so happy to be his parents and were convinced he was the most perfect baby ever born. Dealing with all the legal, financial, medical, and military paperwork was a bit overwhelming at times, but it didn't take away from how much fun we were having. Noah was a total joy. One day when he was about six months old and had just begun crawling, I was sitting on the floor with him, and he looked up at me with his huge brown eyes as he crawled to me. Looking into his eyes, I felt like I could see his other mother, and there was no denying that they were a package deal. I remember thinking that she must be a good person because she created this amazing boy, and he was a part of her.

I didn't feel any competition with her because I knew he needed both of us, and I was 100 percent his mother, but it felt like we were two parts that fit together to make the complete picture. I wanted to respect her privacy, but I also felt a deep desire to tell her thank you and to let her know he was doing well. I wrote her a letter and included pictures and sent it to the adoption agency with a request to give it to her only if she was open to it. A few weeks later, I received the sweetest and most gracious email from her.

Just like that, a door was opened. I wasn't sure what kind of a relationship she would want to have with us, and I wanted to be very respectful of her comfort zone and let her set the pace, but I was happy that my son would have a place to start looking for answers when he had the inevitable questions about his birth family. As a parent, it would be nice to think I could give my son everything he needs in life, but as an adoptive parent, I know he has a need for information and connection that I just can't provide. My husband and I can, however, be the ones who make sure he is able to get what he needs. We had to choose if we would stand in the way or pave the way, and paving the way seemed like the obvious choice for us.

My son is now almost ten, and it has been a gift to have a connection with Amalie, his birthmother. We text and email occasionally, and she and her family have watched him grow up on Facebook, and they send presents for special occasions. A couple of years ago, it became important to Noah to meet them, so I asked Amalie if she was ready for this big step. He was in second grade, and he said his wish for the new year was to meet Amalie and her family, so we made a trip that summer to meet them all.

To be honest, it was scary for all of us, but no one more than Amalie. I was worried that she might feel pressured into meeting us, but it all ended well and was amazing. It gave him answers that he needed, and I was grateful that he doesn't have to wait until adulthood to get them. It is not intimidating to me at all because she and her family are so loving and have never challenged my role as his mother in the least. His other mom has told me more than once that she is grateful he is with us because we can provide him with the medical, dental, and educational care he needs that she would not have been able to provide.

Most people in my life think I am crazy for encouraging this relationship, but it seems simple to me. This is good for my child, so it is my job to walk this journey with him. I give her the credit for it working so well because she is non-threatening. When something good happens, I can't wait to tell her because she is the one person who will feel as excited and invested as my husband and me. I am looking forward to having her in our lives in the years to come.

There are few times as a parent when you know for sure you did the right thing, and this was one time I knew we made the right decision for him. It wasn't easy, but it was about what my son needed, and as his mom, it was my job to walk through the experience with him. It helped that Amalie and her family are genuinely kind and loving people who I would enjoy knowing even if Noah wasn't in the picture. I don't know what the future holds, but I like knowing they will be there cheering him on and supporting him as he grows up.

I am very aware that not everyone is able to have this kind of a relationship, and I give all the credit for it working so well to Amalie and her family. They have always respected our place in Noah's life and never made us feel threatened or uncomfortable. I was able to get to know them slowly over the years, and I know they are safe and good people to have in my son's life.

I have a few words of advice for anyone thinking about adoption. The first is if you really want it, you *can* make it happen. It is not always easy, and as you can tell from our story there can be a lot of dead ends and false starts. That is frustrating while you are going through it, but looking back, it was all part of the path to our son. I learned something from each situation, and each led us a step closer. If you are persistent, almost anyone can make it happen.

Well-intentioned people will tell you that there are no newborns available in the United States, or that birthmothers always change their minds, or that you have to be a millionaire to afford it. These things simply aren't true. There are many available children, including newborns, and the fees differ depending on the situation. If an enlisted sailor and a nanny can do it without going into debt or borrowing from our family, most families can. It took some sacrifice, but it was worth it. Some adoptions, like those through the foster care system, can have almost no fees. Some people exclude themselves before they even start because they believe they are too old or not part of a traditional marriage or not rich enough, but people just like them are adopting every day.

Second, trust your instincts. Being an adoptive parent can feel at times like finding your way through a forest blindfolded. There are not a lot of signs to guide you or clear paths to follow. When you have questions about fevers or temper tantrums, there are plenty of other parents who have experienced the same thing and can offer advice, or the pediatrician can help. When the issue is directly related to adoption, there are not as many people around who can relate. There are always plenty of people who are willing to offer strong opinions, even doctors, but they often have no real experience with adoption.

I decided I had to trust my instincts about what was best for my child, even if it went against what well-meaning people in my life encouraged me to do. There were many who thought we were crazy for being open to a relationship with Amalie, much less let Noah meet her. It felt dangerous to them, and they thought Noah would choose her over us. We know our bond with Noah is unbreakable, so we didn't worry this would threaten our relationship. There were others who thought we should keep Noah's adoption a secret, even from him, as if it was something of which to be ashamed. That felt wrong on so many levels. Adoption is not the focus of our lives, but it is a fact of our lives and we try to deal with it honestly, as I hope we do most things. Trust yourself to make the right choices, even if you might not get a lot of guidance along the way.

Finally, get comfortable with the idea that people say ignorant things. Once you have gone through the process, you are more of an expert on adoption that the majority of people around you. People will say the craziest things, and it is usually not because they are being unkind but just because they don't understand how it works or the power of language.

For example, I had more than one person ask if I was sad I didn't have "a child of my own" or a "real son." I decided to be forgiving and maybe educate with humor instead of taking offense each time. Another time I took Noah to a new pediatrician for a check-up and she said, "Well, I really hope he gets to meet his real mom someday." I answered, "Oh, don't worry. We have met." I gave Noah a big hug and smiled at her. Then I added, "You know, when he throws up, I am the only one who runs toward him and catches vomit in my bare hands. Pretty sure that makes me a real mom." She laughed, but I think I made my point. A little humor can go a long way.

It feels a little strange to remember all these details to write this because adoption is not something we think about every day. I can't compare it to having a child born to me because I have not had that experience, but I cannot imagine loving or enjoying any child more than we do Noah. I am grateful every single day that we get the gift of being this boy's parents because he makes life so much fun. We have ups and downs like any family does, and we get frustrated when he leaves his socks on the floor or won't do his homework, but we never take just getting to be a normal family for granted. There are days when our house is full of little boys playing Minecraft, talking loudly, eating my cookies, and telling me their big thoughts, and I realize that this is everything I hoped my life would be. And more.

CHAPTER SIXTEEN

DESTINY'S CHILD

Elizabeth Kate

Elizabeth is an actress living in Los Angeles. She is the single mother of two daughters, one adopted and one biological.

I am very proud to be an adoptive mother. I got obscenely lucky and wound up with both an adopted daughter *and* a biological daughter. My "bio-baby" was a surprise, but then honestly, my adopted daughter was a surprise too. After waiting almost four years, I was amazed when our social worker alerted my former husband and me that a birthmother had chosen us.

We'd tried fertility treatment for years, unsuccessfully. I never got pregnant and eventually lost hope that pregnancy was even a possibility for me. I dove headlong into the world of adoption. I didn't care where the baby came from, I just knew that somehow, I was meant to be a mother. It was up to me to pave the road for that child, wherever she might be.

As it turned out, our baby was in South Africa, where we had lived and started the adoption process. We continued going through all the steps, even after moving back to the United States, and we spent a great deal of time and money traveling around the world to make that adoption a reality. But of course, I would do it again in a heartbeat. I knew from the moment I heard of this birthmother that this child was meant to be mine. Indeed, she is my little soul mate. Friends always comment and laugh at how ridiculously similar we are. I just smile. Yes, it was meant to be.

The one difference between me and other moms who didn't go through fertility treatment and adoption is that I am constantly grateful to have these little souls in my life. I wanted to be a mother for so long that even on my most trying of days with my children, I am still overjoyed that this experience of motherhood is mine. The good and the bad. All mine. I'm very blessed.

Being an adoptive mother means I am a mother by choice. I wanted to be here. I feel I owe it to my child and to God and to my child's birthmother, who so bravely entrusted her baby with me, to make this little girl's life the very best life it can be. I'm not rich and certainly can't give my daughter a life of luxury, but I will always love her dearly, take care of her, and fight for her to succeed. I am overjoyed she has a beloved sister with whom to share this childhood experience. Since I became "against all odds" pregnant just as our adoption was coming through, I would say their sisterhood is destiny, too. I would do anything for these little girls. Although my marriage didn't survive, I still can't get over my luck at becoming a mommy twice over when it once seemed like a pipe dream.

One time, I remember running into a neighbor near my house. Jokingly, she asked what kind of drugs I was taking. I had no idea what she was talking about. She explained with a laugh that I always looked so serene and happy while pushing my double baby carriage down the street; she wanted some of what I was enjoying. I explained that having these little ones was a dream come true. Even with no sleep and the normal struggles of raising two babies at the same time, I really was happy as can be.

Because I have both an adopted and a biological child, people sometimes ask me in hushed tones if I feel any different about the children because of the origin of each. It's kind of a strange and insulting question, but then again, I understand where it's coming from. Adoption is still regarded with a bit of mystery and fear. Many people are too scared to take the plunge because they "don't know what they're getting." But truly, even with biological children, we never know what we are getting. Life is funny that way.

There is absolutely no difference in my eyes between my two children. I never think about where they came from or why. They're just my kids. They are fun and funny and loving and silly and difficult and frustrating and everything I ever wanted my children to be. They're mine and I love them unconditionally.

I was fortunate enough to be present at the birth of my adopted daughter. It was thrilling. The doctor handed my newborn daughter to me, all wrapped up in a blanket. She was only five pounds and felt so light in my arms. Her eyes were wide open as she looked around with wonder. It was as though I recognized her. I knew that pretty little face right from the start. All I could say through the tears was, "Welcome, dear one. You're finally here!" Everything happened the way it was meant to be.

My daughter is still young, but she asks questions about her birthmother and siblings from time to time. I always answer her honestly. Her birthmother didn't want to keep in touch. She wanted us to "get on with our lives." We kept in touch with the birth-grandmother for a few years, but on my daughter's third birthday, I sent her an email with a selection of photos, and the email bounced back to me. The grandmother had changed her email address, and I couldn't find her again. Just like that, our communication ended.

I have promised my daughter that when she's eighteen, we can go back to South Africa and try to locate her birth family. I look forward to sharing that experience with her and my biological daughter too. It will be a special moment for us all. Everything in its own good time.

As words of advice to prospective adoptive parents, I would say don't ever lose hope. Yes, adoption is expensive. Yes, it's a long and difficult road. But don't give up. Believe the right child will come to you at just the right time. We had adoptions fall through along the road. They were heartbreaking and seemed inexplicable, but we carried on believing, and eventually just the right child arrived. And then another!

Adoption is the most wonderful blessing that has ever touched my life. I fully believe that somehow my biological daughter refused to enter this world until she knew the adoption of her sister was secured. Maybe that sounds crazy, but there you go. My dreams came true when I welcomed these two beautiful children into my life.

Believe in miracles. I do.

CHAPTER SEVENTEEN

FOSTERING ANGEL
TO ADOPTION

Sandy Horna

*Sandy is forty-six and is a pediatric physical therapist from Ventura, California.
She is the single mother of eighteen-month-old Julia, whom she fostered and has
since adopted.*

My name is Sandy, and I am a pediatric physical therapist. My journey
toward adoption began four years ago when I lost my baby at six months of
pregnancy. My physician explained to me that I would no longer be able to
carry and birth a child. After many months of healing, thanks to my wonderful family, church, and friends, I told myself that I needed to become a
mother in this lifetime.

If I could not have my own child, I would give a child who began life
with extremely meager beginnings a phenomenal life. My husband at the
time fought me on this decision. After many, many discussions, this area
of contention led to divorce. My desire to become a mother was never
stronger! If I had to be a single mother, so be it! I contacted my county
foster care program and then became a foster mother after attending all the
required classes.

One of my specialties in my career is newborn drug rehab. I see many
infants whose mothers have taken drugs throughout their pregnancies.
This specialty is called sensory integration. It involves specialized massage
techniques to integrate the nervous system after the drugs have severely
damaged it. Once I became a foster mother, I told the county my occupation
and specialty and requested a baby who was affected by drugs.

A month later, I got my baby girl, Julia, at eleven days old, straight from
the NICU. Her birthmother began her heroin addiction at twelve years old
and was on heroin and meth throughout her pregnancy. Julia was actually

the fourth baby of this mother, and unfortunately all three siblings prior were miscarried secondary to drug exposure. Julia had to take methadone for the first three months of her life to wean her off the heroin and meth. Julia's infancy progressed beautifully. Mercifully, there were no complications, and she thrived!

As far as Julia's health throughout her life, I have no concerns. The sensory integration I provided Julia during infancy healed her nervous system, and there were no lasting effects. She demonstrates age-appropriate behavior. I would strongly urge adoptive parents who know their child was exposed to drugs in utero to seek a pediatric physical therapist trained in sensory integration. Many children who have been affected by drugs require physical therapy, occupational therapy, and speech therapy to ensure they obtain age-appropriate levels of cognition, as well as finger articulations and mobility skills. Of course, I can't predict the future, but I know that so far, I have given Julia the best chance to be healthy.

On the other hand, my baby's birthmother and father fought for custody. While Julia was in the foster care program, her birthparents had the right to have supervised visitation once a week . . . Tuesdays. I *hated* Tuesdays! A social worker would pick her up from her daycare and take her to a county facility for an hour, then bring her back. This went on for about five months. The birthmother and father were required to attend a drug treatment program; however, they refused. After the social worker and court realized there was no hope of sobriety, the judge closed their case, and the adoption process began.

Being a foster parent is full of mixed feelings. On one hand, you are doing an incredible service to the child: providing love, comfort, and a stable home in which they may thrive. On the other hand, your role as a foster parent is a *role*. You have no say, and the social workers and the courts make all the decisions. If the birthparents do the bare minimum, the case could last for months to years.

I don't, however, have any fears associated with the risk of becoming a foster parent and having the child reunified with the birthparents. That is part of the game. I have learned that I need to look at all sides in this situation. You cannot be egocentric going into it. The birthparents might have their addiction to drugs, but many times they are good people and want to change their lives. The county offers a lot of help to these people, and if I could be a part in making their lives stronger and better for their child, then that is a win for me as well. It is an amazing and gratifying feeling to help somebody in such a profound way. And I must say, I came across many wonderful social workers throughout this process. They were very eager to offer support every step of the way. I never felt alone.

In fact, this scenario of reunification did happen to me. Julia was the second baby I fostered. My first little one I received at one-day old, and she was meth-exposed. From the start, the county told me that her aunt wanted to adopt her. So, I told myself that it was my absolute pleasure to do everything I could for this beautiful little creature to have a fantastic life. I had her for a month and provided all the sensory integration for her. Her aunt adopted her, and she is now thriving! For me, that feels like a million dollars! There is no better feeling than to know you have profoundly helped an infant and family! So, am I ready to do it again, and risk the same outcome of the baby being reunited with their parents? Absolutely! Even if a child is not my forever child, I know I will nurture and love that child and give him or her a beautiful start in life.

Many of my friends and family have asked me, "What are you going to tell Julia when she is older about the adoption and why her birthmother did not keep her?" When Julia is young, I will tell her that her birthmother was sick. Every child can relate to that. When she is in high school, and if she asks more details about her birthmother, I will explain to her that she was a drug user of heroin and meth. I will then educate her on what drugs do to the body, have her watch videos, and if she needs to, she can talk to a drug counselor to have any other questions answered. I believe education and honest, upfront communication is the key.

Many people have asked me if I am worried that Julia will be drawn to drugs because they were in her system in utero. My answer is absolutely not. I believe that being drawn to drugs is often an environmental issue. People can be pulled to drugs because they offer solace to poor upbringing, dysfunctional lives, and trauma. I believe raising a child takes tons of love, of course, but also rules, guidelines, and limitations. As a result, she will mature through life with a healthy foundation of family, love, and support, and drugs will never have to be an issue. I realize that even with a healthy foundation, and even when adoption is not an issue, the risk of drug experimenting can happen in any family. But that is the risk of being a parent, and being a parent is worth it to me.

And I truly have no negative feelings. I only wish the process could have been shorter, as my little girl is now a year and a half. Next year, I plan to adopt a second drug-exposed infant and find Julia a sister. The decision to become a foster parent was one of the best and most profound in my life. I am extremely grateful for all the amazing support I have received. I am so very proud to be a foster parent, and as far as being an adoptive parent, I couldn't be prouder! It fills my heart with joy every time I see my beautiful baby girl walk, speak new words, and run into my arms for a hug! This has truly been the best and most gratifying adventure I have ever had!

CHAPTER EIGHTEEN

BUILDING FAMILIES

Mandie Carroll

Mandie, thirty-two, and Shane, thirty-three, have been married for nine years but have been together for sixteen. She is a recruiting coordinator, and he is a drafter. They live in Denham Springs, Louisiana, and are the parents of an adopted toddler.

Shane and I met when we were in high school. I was sixteen, and Shane was seventeen. We had geometry class together, and I sat next to Shane. We became friends, and throughout the semester my feelings started to change. I could tell he was feeling the same way, so finally on the last day of school I got the nerve to ask him out. We have been inseparable ever since. Shane asked me to marry him on Christmas Day 2006, and we married on May 17, 2008.

We always knew we wanted a family. Before we were married, we would talk about how many children we wanted, baby names, activities they would be in, and so on. After two years of marriage, we started trying to become pregnant. We tried for two years, and during that time we found out we were not able to have children of our own. We didn't think twice about adoption. We knew this was in God's plan for us, and we began doing research on adoption and local adoption agencies.

We found three local agencies and decided to visit them. When we left one in particular, we just knew in our hearts this was the place for us. This was where we would begin our journey. Once we completed the process (classes, training, information binder, and our profile book), we began the waiting game. Our total wait time was twenty-six months until we received the call that would forever change our lives. That call came on November 4, 2014, around 2:30 p.m. Our social worker called me at work and asked if I was sitting down and could talk. She began telling me that they believed a perfect match had been found and asked if we could come to her office to talk about the birthparents' situation. Shane and I met with our social worker the next day, which happened to be Shane's birthday! When I left there, I had the feeling that this one was meant to be.

One week later, our social worker called us stating the family had picked Shane and me and wanted to meet as soon as possible. We had an appointment to meet the birthparents and their families at the agency one week later. The appointment was scheduled for one hour, and after two hours we finally said our goodbyes. We all left there feeling like we had known each other our whole lives. We began meeting quite often and became very close to the family. The first of the year, they invited us over for dinner and revealed that the baby was a girl!

On January 31, 2015, at 6:03 a.m., we received a phone call that the birthmother had gone into labor! Shane and I quickly got dressed and rushed to the hospital. The hospital was so wonderful and supportive. They made sure our needs were met, and they provided a private room next to the delivery room where our social workers, new combined families, and extended families could share this special moment together. At 11:31 a.m., Mia Grace was born! Mia's adoption was finalized on September 11, 2015.

Mia is now two-and-a-half years old, and I couldn't think of a greater gift than being picked to be her parents. As far as her birthparents, we could not have asked for a better extended family. We do not live that far from each other, so we see them often. Every other Friday, Mia goes to the birth-grandmother's house for the day. We celebrate all birthdays and holidays together and have even gone on vacation with them to the beach.

The most special memory I have with the birth family happened on August 16, 2016, three days after our house was badly damaged by the August 2016 flood in Louisiana. The whole family showed up to our home without asking and helped us gut our home. Over the next nine months of rebuilding our house, they were by our side, tearing out sheetrock, helping test moisture levels, setting up crews from other states to come help us, bringing us items we needed, cleaning the house at various times before the next stage began, watching Mia countless hours so we could work on our home, and most importantly, praying over us every step of the way.

Being an adoptive parent is the greatest gift we both have received; knowing that a family chose us to raise their daughter means the world to me, and not one day goes by that I don't say a quick thank you for their decision. If it were not for them, our family would not be complete. I am forever grateful for them and their selfless decision.

If I had to give any piece of advice to families, I would tell them not to settle in their haste to have a child. Go with your heart and pray about it, because the right child will come along in due time. I know in the moment the only thing you are thinking about is completing your family, but truly think about the big picture and consider carefully. If the adoption is open, you are sharing your lives and your child's life with this family forever. The dynamics between the families need to work in order to make their child's adoption story successful.

Shane and I received two calls before Mia; the first one was for twin girls, and the second one was for a boy. Shane and I put our hearts out there in hopes for the twin girls but were not picked. Looking back, in my heart I knew it was not a good fit. I just had a feeling, but I tried to shake that feeling because I wanted a baby so badly! The call regarding the baby boy was a very hard call to take, because it was two months after we lost out on the twins. Shane and I turned down the option of our profile book getting shown to this family. As hard as it was, I had learned from the last situation that it was not meant to be, and we had to learn patience and wait. As I stated earlier, when I received the call about Mia, I knew in my heart it was right.

This whole process truly made us look deep inside ourselves, our marriage, and our relationship with God, our family, and friends. This process made us become stronger, more mature, and ready to raise our child. It made us realize we can set goals in our lives, but that doesn't necessarily mean the goals we believe are best for ourselves are necessarily the outcome we will receive. The outcome will be even better.

CHAPTER NINETEEN

INCONCEIVABLE

Brad Hurtado

Brad is fifty-six and lives in Brooklyn with his husband, Sean, and adopted daughter, Grace, who is sixteen. Brad and Sean have been together for twenty-three years and got married in Hawaii. Brad is a television producer, and his current project is co-executive producing the Bravo TV reality series Xscape: Still Kickin' It.

When I was a young boy, I always felt that I'd be a father one day. I loved little kids and thought that being a father was something I was destined to be. Then in my teenage years as I realized I was gay, I felt a profound sadness that getting married and having children was no longer ahead of me, and for years I lived with that understanding.

When I was in my late twenties, I was working as a producer on *The Phil Donahue Show* and began to read articles about gay men and women who were becoming parents despite the challenges. I decided to produce an episode titled "How Gays Become Parents." I was able to bring together stories of traditional adoption, surrogacy, foster parenting, and parenting your gay partner's children from a previous, heterosexual marriage. It was a very well received episode, and I was able to tell these amazing stories to millions of viewers. Because of my research into that show topic, I quickly realized that being a father *was* a possibility for me.

Later that same year, I met a handsome Australian actor, and we began to date. Very early on I told him of my desire to adopt one day, and while he wasn't initially of the same mind, over the next few years he began to come around. When we'd been together seven years, we took the step of going to a NYC adoption agency that we knew worked with gay couples and had an introductory meeting with them to discover what might be ahead of us if we took this step. We didn't fill out any paperwork or sign up with them—it was just about gathering information.

We learned that it was indeed possible for us, that it might cost approximately $40,000, give or take, that it would likely take about two years, that we'd have to have all sorts of normal background checks and social worker evaluations. When they asked us what kind of child we'd like, we told them simply white or Hispanic, healthy, and an infant. We left their office with a lot to think about and did nothing further.

Six weeks later, the adoption agency called us asking if we were still interested; they had a Hispanic woman in Texas who was four months pregnant with a healthy baby and who'd specified that she would be OK if her baby was adopted by a gay couple. As you can imagine, we were shocked by how suddenly this was happening and didn't have an answer for them. They said we could have three days to think about it and make a decision.

So, for the next seventy-two hours we ran through every possible scenario. Were we ready? Should we wait? Was this the right time for us? Were we *really* serious about this? When they called back three days later, we still hadn't decided and asked them for another fifteen minutes, which they gave us. Then we took a few deep breaths, talked some more, and told them *yes*, we wanted to become the parents.

Over the five months between our first contact with the birthmother, Belinda, and Grace's birth in San Antonio, we set up a weekly call where we'd check in with each other and just chat for twenty or thirty minutes. She'd tell us how her body was changing, what she was eating, what was going on at home for her, and we'd tell her about how we were preparing on our end, and we'd swap family stories with each other. On one of those calls, Belinda asked us if we ever worried about her changing her mind and keeping the baby. I paused and thought about our good friends, Jeffery and Josh, a gay couple whose birthmother had backed out in the days after the baby was born and devastated them. After a moment of quiet I said, "No, Belinda. I don't worry about that because in all the time we've been talking, you've never given us any reason to doubt you."

"Good," she said. "Because this baby is yours. I have my own five children at home, and I'm not adding a sixth, so get ready!"

She then asked us if we were hoping to come down for the birth, and we told her we definitely wanted to do that. She asked us if we wanted to be in the delivery room, because she'd be OK with that.

"Yes! We'd love to," we told her.

Then she said, "If you ask the doctor in advance, he'll let you cut the baby's umbilical cord, which you definitely should do."

We took her advice. When the baby was due, we came down to San Antonio and had dinner with Belinda. The next day, we were in the delivery room when we learned we were the fathers of a baby girl, and I then cut Grace's umbilical cord with one hand and videotaped it with my other hand! (I am a television producer, mind you!)

Later that evening, when we were looking through the big window into the nursery, watching Grace sleep, the hospital chaplain came into the waiting room and introduced himself to us. Belinda had warned us that people in Texas may not be as liberal as up in New York City, and she encouraged us to keep a low profile in the hospital. The chaplain spoke with us for a few minutes, and we carefully answered his questions about us, all the time wondering how this would end. He then asked how the hospital workers had been treating us, and we answered, "Very nicely. Everyone has been lovely." He got a big smile on his face and said, "Times are changing, and people are evolving on their positions on our community."

Our community?

Sean and I were totally taken aback as the chaplain told us that he had been married at one time and had a grown daughter, but that he'd come out about being gay ten years ago. He told us that things might still be different out there in Texas, but here in the hospital he was confident we'd be treated very well. And it was true. The doctor and nurses who cared for Grace were so very kind to us and made sure we had plenty of time with our new daughter. We were invited in to give Grace her first bottle, and we were there for her weighing and even her footprints on the birth certificate.

Twenty-four hours after her birth, when it was time to discharge both Belinda and Grace from the hospital, a nurse was pushing the wheelchair with Belinda sitting in it and holding Grace in her arms. Sean and I walked alongside Ernesto, Belinda's husband, each one of us silently experiencing this life-changing moment from our very different perspectives. Outside, Belinda took a last look at Grace and put her into my arms. Then Ernesto helped Belinda into his pickup truck as we put our daughter into her car seat for the first time in our rental car and slowly drove out of the hospital parking lot: two new dads and a six-pound baby girl named Grace. It's been sixteen years now, and our family is strong and happy and proud, and we love telling our story of how we all came to be the Hingston-Hurtado trio.

My advice to *any* LGBTQ man or woman out there considering whether to become a parent: You are *no different* than any straight person who wants to have a baby, and the love you want to give your child is just as all-embracing as any straight person's. In fact, I always say that anyone who adopts must really want to be a parent because there are so many financial and emotional hurdles that you've got to overcome in order to change that first diaper.

When my husband and I first began considering adopting around 1998, there were very few gay and lesbian moms and dads in our circle of friends, and it wasn't as widely accepted as it is now, twenty years later. While we definitely weren't pioneers in gay adoption at the time, I can tell you that here in New York City it was a rare sight to see two dads pushing a stroller anywhere, but not once, in all of our time as dads, did we ever receive any sort of public negative reaction to us being parents. Quite the opposite, in fact: the number of smiles and encouraging words that were offered to my husband and me was rather overwhelming.

It was actually in my own family, from my two sisters in Ohio, where we felt the negativity. I knew they didn't approve of my homosexuality, but after twenty years, it finally wasn't a topic of conversation. When I told them that Sean and I were going to adopt a baby, however, they each let me know just how wrong they thought this was. I firmly told them that I wasn't asking them for their opinion or approval. I was informing them of our intention, and they could either embrace my growing family or unfortunately miss out on the wonderful opportunity of welcoming a new child into their lives, and having a relationship with him or her. Thankfully, after Grace was born, they came around and fell in love with her.

This issue of family acceptance is a hard one for many of us, especially when our families disagree with our lifestyle. I follow the advice of columnist Dan Savage when it comes to family acceptance: if someone in your family is giving you a hard time about being gay, or becoming a gay parent, explain to them that when they can accept your family just as you are, then you will be happy to be a part of their lives. Making family inclusion a bargaining tool is one of the few ways we have to influence negativity in moments like this, and it's rather powerful.

When Grace's birthmother told the adoption agency what kind of home she'd like for her unborn child, she made sure they knew that she would like to have her baby placed with a gay couple. It wasn't a random decision. Years earlier, when Belinda had become pregnant for the first time, she was in her late teens, and she made the decision to go with adoption. During her pregnancy, she became familiar with the workers in the adoption agency she was using, and after her delivery she returned to that agency and began working as a birthmother coordinator. She would check on her birthmothers to see if they were making their doctor visits, taking their medications, and generally taking care of themselves during their pregnancy.

She did this work for a few years, and during that time she noticed that when the agency began working with a new birthmother and were trying to match her up with adoptive parents, there was a pattern of behavior that would take place. If the baby was going to be born with potential Fetal Alcohol Syndrome, or the birthmother had been using drugs, the agency would reveal this information to their waiting adoptive parents. Over and over again, the straight couples on the list would pass. They'd decide to wait for the next baby to come along without the potential health issues. Eventually, the agency would work its way through all of their straight couples and finally offer the baby to any gay couples on the waiting list.

Belinda told us that she saw these gay couples agree to become the parents of these babies, and then a year or so later, the gay couples would return to the agency with their babies and share with them how happy they were and how the babies were flourishing, despite their troubled beginnings. Belinda took note of this, and when she became pregnant with Grace, she made sure her agency knew that she was going to have a healthy Hispanic baby, and that she wanted to place it with a gay couple if possible.

It just so happened that six weeks before this moment, my husband and I had met with our agency and told them we were a gay couple looking for a healthy Hispanic or white infant. My mom likes to call this "a God moment," and I totally agree. Our two families became connected because Belinda, a low-income Hispanic woman from San Antonio, Texas, had come in contact with a few gay couples whose stories touched her heart, and in return she gave Sean and me the amazing gift of being dads.

CHAPTER TWENTY

SOMETIMES NO PLAN IS THE BEST PLAN

Azadeh Stoelken

Azadeh is a forty-eight-year-old "melting pot." She is of Middle Eastern descent, and both she and her husband of nine years are German immigrants and long-time naturalized and proud Americans. She lives in Santa Monica, California, with her husband, their adopted son, and her stepson. She works as a holistic health coach and is currently also working on her diploma as a classical homeopath.

We were trying to get pregnant for a while, but doctors told me at age thirty-seven that I was peri-menopausal and that it would be difficult to conceive. Two half-baked attempts of IVF (they overmedicated me) and one miscarriage later, we decided to adopt. At least we knew that there would be a baby at some point. We were referred by a friend of mine to an adoption agency in Los Angeles that specialized in open adoption, and after some research, we went with this recommendation.

The paperwork and the various rounds of approvals by different social workers took about four months to complete. Once everything was sent in, I finally was able to relax! I was looking forward to months and probably even years of not thinking about follicles, ovaries, bloodwork, and timed intercourse. At least that's what I thought.

However, three months later—on my birthday—we received a phone call from our adoption agency. They found a birthmom in Brooklyn, New York, who had received our profile and who had expressed interest in meeting us for the potential adoption of her unborn child. I almost fainted. I was not prepared for this to happen so soon! I had my yoga retreat booked and a knee surgery scheduled. But I also saw it as a sign that she was from Brooklyn. We had just moved from Brooklyn a year earlier. I love Brooklyn and consider it my second home.

So, we scheduled a call with her—me in Los Angeles, the potential birthmother in Brooklyn, and my husband somewhere out of town. The young lady sounded lovely, even though we both admitted that we were super nervous. To get a better idea of who she was, I decided to book a flight to New York the next day. To refresh your memory, the phone call from the agency came in on Monday, July 18; we spoke to the birthmother on Tuesday; I flew to New York on Wednesday and met our very pregnant birthmom that evening in New Jersey in her hotel room, which our agency organized for her. We decided we would both go to the hospital at 8 a.m. the next day to get her very first sonogram!

So that's what we did. The doctor confirmed that the baby was a healthy boy and that . . . she was already dilated! *What?* Yes, sonogram at 8 a.m., booked into her room at the hospital at 10 a.m., she was induced at 3 p.m., and the baby came at 6:21 p.m.!

In the time between 10 a.m. and 5 p.m., I frantically placed one phone call after the next: to my husband to tell him to get to New York as fast as he could; to the adoption attorney in New York, who seemed unfazed and decided to skip traffic and stay in his office until after the birth; and to my own mother in Europe to brainstorm baby names.

And in between all this craziness in the hallway of the hospital in New Jersey, I had the most beautiful bonding time with our birthmom. We were both so happy and so grateful that we found each other! We chatted and laughed and cried together. I immediately had warm, sisterly feelings for her. When the contractions started, I held her hand; I wiped her sweat off her face. She pushed, and I held her hair and cheered her on to push harder. It was truly the most beautiful experience of my life.

It sounds awkward to bring a baby into this world with a woman that I had only met the night before. But something else takes over—it's hard to describe. It's the glorious wonder of birth. The only thing that mattered was the health of that little boy who was about to see the world. Pure love and gratefulness. And, to be honest, also a bit of relief that it was not me who had to push and push—and then be sewed back together again!

I felt a very close bond to the birthmother, and I know she felt the same for me. We stayed in touch after the birth for a few months, and then she slowly withdrew from me. Although I have her email address and phone number, I need to respect that decision of hers, even though I still would like her to be in our lives, especially for our son.

We have never met the birthfather. He went missing as soon as he heard that our birthmother was pregnant. We have no idea who he is; we just have the subjective description she gave us about him.

There are many ways to become a family, and adoption is one of them. Our little boy is now five-and-a-half years old, and he rules our world. Literally. He is the boss! We try to tell him that usually parents are the boss, but he doesn't believe us. Honestly, if it wasn't for this beautiful story that we can, and do, enjoy sharing, and the wisdom that came with it, I would forget that I did not push him out of my own body. The adoption part is only the story of how we came together to become this family, but it does not define us or our everyday lives.

The advice I would give to other potential adoptive parents is *relax!* We get so worked up about not getting pregnant—the *why's* and *when's*, the frustration, depression, self-doubt, anger—that we forget to trust our destiny. In the end, it will all work out fine. Our life goes exactly the way it is supposed to go if we keep the energy channels open and receptive. Trust your life's path, breathe, and find your peace. If you can't get pregnant, adopt! The right baby will find you.

If I could change any part of our story, I would wish I had more time with the birthmother. I had to ask her all of the questions I had in a day or two at the hospital, before we went our separate ways. I wish we had more time together. Usually you get matched at the beginning of the third trimester, not a day before the birth! I would never have believed that it was possible to become a parent within a day. It can happen. Nobody told us this, but I'm telling you now!

Some people worry about the question of bonding in an adoptive situation. I was not sure about the bonding part. When you don't have a baby inside of you growing, I wasn't sure how long it might take to really bond with the baby that is "given to you." Well, in our case, we were new parents within a day! I was still somewhat in a state of shock when this little boy came to us. But you have to keep it together and focus and learn (How do I prepare the bottle again? How do I change him?), so bonding came naturally. And since we adoptive parents are so desperate to become parents, bonding is not one of our problems. I learned that. The love for your baby is instant and 100 percent, and it does not matter whether the baby grew inside of you or inside someone else.

In thinking about lessons learned, what can I say? I flew to New York to meet with a pregnant young woman, and twenty-four hours later I was a mom! What did I learn from this experience? Life has some funny plans for you sometimes, and you better be flexible and adapt to whatever is thrown your way.

Be prepared to answer the following question: "Mommy, what was it like when you had me in your tummy?"

This question hit me in the car while driving home from preschool. I stuttered something but did not want to lie to him. So, I told him a tale of the brave, good woman who gave her beautiful baby to Mommy as a birthday present because he was such a special boy and Mommy could not carry a baby in her tummy herself. He was quite happy about the story, smiled, and asked me a couple of follow-up questions before we moved on to discussing whether to buy ice cream or not. He was only four. I'm not sure if my story really stuck or if I will need to repeat it, in a more refined version, when he's older.

I was always a pro-choice kind of woman. I believe in the right to decide what's good for your body and your life and ultimately the life you create. However, our adoption has changed that, or better, added some nuance to this difficult subject. If more people would be open to adoption, then women wouldn't have to abort their fetuses! They can carry their baby to term and then place it for adoption, as it happened in our case. Our birthmom went in and out of abortion clinics several times. Thankfully, she never followed through. The choice of adoption was presented to her at the clinic, and our agency reached out to various abortion clinics to find birthmoms for their clients. I see this as a win-win situation and a great way out of the state of despair in which so many pregnant women must feel stuck.

Adoption gives you the feeling of doing something meaningful. If you believe in God, the Universe, or just your fateful path of life, you can trust it will all happen the way it is supposed to. You need to surrender to the higher forces that sometimes take over your life. Try not to panic, don't lose control, but keep it together, focus, and go with it. Surrender and believe that this is your path and a higher force is looking out for you. It was a life lesson I learned on that July day in 2011.

CHAPTER TWENTY-ONE

ALL GOD'S CHILDREN

Teresa Fillmon

Teresa, fifty-six, splits her time between Tallahassee, Florida, and Ukraine. She and her husband have five children, two of whom were adopted from Ukraine. Teresa is the founder and director of His Kids Too!, a Ukraine orphan ministry, and she is an orphan advocate.

I have a unique perspective as both an orphan advocate and a mother of two adopted children from Ukraine. I've experienced firsthand what happens when you remove an orphaned child from their culture and environment, and I can tell you that sometimes, things don't go as you planned. While I believe adoption can be wonderful, and sometimes the only viable option for a child, I don't believe it is always the best for all children.

My husband, Rich, and I started a ministry in 1986 to help impoverished local people, and we expanded that to work with five other international missionaries in Albania, Cuba, Mexico, and Italy; supplying clothing, shoes, and medical supplies to those in need. Our local pastor traveled to Ukraine after it gained its independence from the Soviet Union, and he brought a group of doctors back to the United States for training, introducing them to us. We met the translator and learned more about the poverty in that country, and it was an easy decision to add Ukraine to our service countries. Never did we expect the turn of events that would result from that decision.

Speaking with the translator, we arranged to ship aid to her for distribution. We did this for four years, and the recipients often asked that this "Mother Teresa" (who I definitely am *not*) would come for a visit. In 1998, I finally made my first trip to visit the people of Ukraine.

The trip was amazing, long, and inspiring. The need was quite visible; poverty was widespread. Children would kick around a flat soccer ball or pick through trash. Teens were bored and stood idly on street corners smoking and drinking alcohol. Adults were kind and very appreciative of the years of support. They treated me like royalty, which is something that makes me feel very uncomfortable. People would spend money, which I knew they didn't have, on gifts of appreciation. I tried hard to discourage this but without much success.

During the trip we visited several hospitals, orphanages, and facilities for disabled children. Conditions were deplorable. Sanitation was questionable at best. My heart ached for these children, and I *knew* that I had to do something to help them. I prayed and prayed that God would make it clear as to exactly what I was to do. I didn't have a lot of financial resources, but we serve a *big* God, and no task is too big for Him. With a visit to an orphanage, my heart told me that I must advocate for orphans. Children wore rags, ate food that I would not feed to my animals, and disabled children were left to lay in their waste. I *had* to let the American public know of these conditions; I had to help these innocent children. This was the official start of His Kids Too!, my Ukraine orphan ministry.

During the month-long visit, I spoke to my family only two times. I wept when I shared with my husband about the conditions in which the children lived. He told me, "Find a child, and let's save at least one." I visited the local orphanage several more times to get to know the children, all the while researching the adoption process. After my visit, I returned to the United States with a new vigor to not only help those I visited but also collect all the documents and return to adopt a certain boy with whom I had bonded. In March 1999, Rich and I left for Ukraine with our three biological children and the same translator who I met through our pastor.

Upon arriving, we made it to our first official adoption appointment, where the director firmly and heart-crushingly told us that we would not be adopting this boy. We sat in her office stunned, shocked that someone would deny our desire to adopt a child that no one else wanted. This was a child who I had just seen five months prior, who was alone and needed a family. I tried to contain my tears but could not, and then I looked at her and asked her if she could make an exception and allow us to adopt this boy. She then screamed at me, "What part of *no* don't you understand?"

I will never forget that . . . the disdain in her voice, the willful anger. Why prevent a little boy from having a family? It was so odd to us all, and still is to this day. But she was not going to budge on her decision, so we had no other choice but to look at other available boys. We were shown six boys from three different facilities, and we chose to go to Mariupol, Ukraine, which is in the far, far southeastern corner of the country, a twenty-seven-hour slow train ride away.

We arrived at the Mariupol orphanage late the next day, and we met three four-year-old boys. One stood out to us: Artur, a gypsy boy who had no siblings and no obvious illnesses. Gypsies are not kindly looked upon in eastern European countries due to their habits of stealing, lying, sneaky behavior, begging, and general living conditions. Gypsies clearly have a different lifestyle, living in colonies in specific areas of town; they even have their own cryptic language.

Prior to the trip, I had done some research on international adoption, but really, we didn't prepare enough. One thing I had decided, however, was that with any child we would consider, we would go to their main room, watch them interact with the other children, and have a staff member discreetly point out which children were available for adoption. We had seen how children "put on a show" for prospective adoptive parents, and we didn't want that. So, we watched the three children from a distance. Each of the boys had their good qualities, but as we stood watching, Artur was given his food last. He went and sat at the table to eat, then looked over, noticing us. He walked over to me and said, "You look hungry. Do you want my food?"

I almost started to cry. This boy, who had nothing but a small bowl of soup and a piece of dry bread, was offering it to me. I looked at my husband and said, "Him." He agreed.

The staff was mortified and discouraged us from adopting Artur. They told us that he was deaf, that he wasn't a "true Ukrainian" (not blond and blue-eyed), and that he was nothing but trash because he was a gypsy. It didn't matter to us, and we pushed through all the negativity and began the great adoption "paper chase."

Rich and the three children left after the court hearing, but I remained for four more weeks doing paperwork and visiting Artur daily. His auditory hearing was absolutely fine—selective maybe, but completely functional. The first sign of trouble was when I moved back to Kiev to complete the paperwork at the embassy, and I stayed in a hotel with him. Artur was a very inquisitive boy, to say the least, but one evening, I set him in front of cartoons and went in the bathroom to wash my hair. I suddenly felt a presence, and I peered out and saw Artur standing in the doorway with a very wide-eyed look on his face. I jumped from the shower, grabbed a towel, and went into the room, where the bedside table was fully engulfed in flames. Artur had plugged in my travel immersion water boiler and laid it on the table. Running to the table, I was able to put the fire out. That was the first of many fires that Artur would later set.

We arrived home to the United States to a big welcome fanfare; Artur was oblivious to it all, and we settled into life. Little did we know the roller-coaster ride that was ahead for us. It seems that the Post Trauma Stress Disorder (PTSD) and Reactive Attachment Disorder (RAD) were quite severe. Artur had been left in a local open market at fourteen months, so he was fairly bonded to a mother, and then she just abandoned him. This greatly troubled him, and bonding to our family was virtually impossible. He continues to be haunted by the "why did she just leave me?" question, even though he has visited Ukraine several times and seen the poverty and hopeless conditions firsthand. He was, and still is, a very angry person, but his anger is misdirected at the people around him instead of at his birthparents. This has led to a life of chaos, confusion, poor choices, and, later, jail time. Sadly, he has not been able to understand and grasp the "golden ring" that adoption afforded him, though we have diligently tried. He has suffered with addictions and has struggled with submission to all authority figures throughout his life. At present, he is in a residential treatment facility, where we prayerfully hope they are able to help him.

In 2000, while visiting orphanages in Ukraine, I came across a little girl born without feet or fingers. She was eighteen months old, having been left at birth in a local maternity hospital. We questioned the orphanage director about her future in Ukraine, and she responded that any child with an invalid diagnosis would be transferred at age four to the invalid facility in their region for their lifetime. I specifically asked the location of the one that this particular little girl would be sent to, and the director, knowing why I was asking, replied, "Teresa, you don't want to go there . . . It is horrible. The last time I went there, I had nightmares for a week."

Of course, that only served to make me more determined to go. I contacted the facility and was given permission to visit. After just one trip, I was determined to find homes for any invalid children in the area in order to prevent them from ever ending up there. It was a horrid place, where children were left to lie in filth, fed terrible food laced with sawdust as filler, and were not able to ever leave. After years of trying to work with the staff and directors without success, I was on a mission to either change the staff or shut that place down. (I was later contacted by the *London Times*, and I took them to the facility to expose the mistreatment of invalid children.) And as for that sweet little girl with no feet or fingers, I was on a mission to find her a family.

Unfortunately, I was having no success with that search, and as the girl, Alla, approached her fourth birthday, the director tearfully told me she would be forced to move her to this institution. Our other four children knew her, and as a family we prayed over this little girl's future. But this time, God pressed upon our hearts to adopt her ourselves, and we made the family decision to move forward with the adoption. We gave the orphanage director the news, and she was elated; we quickly put our dossier together in three weeks. We arrived on Christmas Eve to visit Alla, and we asked her if she wanted a "mom and dad . . . and a big family?" Though she knew us, because we provided aid to her orphanage, she hesitated; she finally agreed, and said, "I'm ready to go," thinking that we were leaving right then. We explained that we could not go yet, as there was paperwork. She had heard that before; six previous families came to meet her but never returned for her. Her face was sullen as she walked off with the caregiver, deflated.

The next day was Christmas (2002), and we arrived at the facility mid-morning. We anxiously waited in the visitation room, and as our daughter rounded the corner, her face broke out in the biggest smile, and she fell into our arms screaming, "My mama is here, my papa is here!" She then proceeded to tell everyone in the room, over and over, that we were her family, and we came for *her*. There wasn't a dry eye in the room, and it was the best Christmas gift!

Though the adoption trip seemed successful, the past fourteen years have not come without much heartache. Alla seemed to bond with our family, but at puberty, she started to withdraw. She started counseling to deal with issues in middle school. Kids can be so mean, and she was frequently the brunt of jokes and ridiculed about her appearance. Instead of communicating with us, she turned to her friends, and she started cutting. She didn't want to kill herself, as she tells us now; she just wanted to redirect the pain of the verbal jeers and jabs from classmates. Our hearts hurt for her, but unfortunately, she also acted out toward other children with physical challenges, which took her down a road of more rejection. Watching her spiral out of control, we were desperate to help our child, so we sought the help of counselors. She was very resistant to anyone "prying into her life," saying, "No one will ever understand my horrible life," and "Why did God make me look like this?" She could not grasp that we didn't have anything to do with the way she looked and that we could not change it, but we could and would love her, encourage her, support her, and help her with adaptable equipment.

Alla was, and is, an angry person; she continues to displace her anger on all the people, teachers, pastors, family, and friends that try to help her. She has Oppositional Defiant Disorder (ODD), in addition to RAD. She just graduated from high school and attends a local community college. She wants to be a coroner, and her reasoning is "Dead people don't talk; I don't have to communicate with them."

This is not to say I have never seen a good transition for an orphan from Ukraine. I know of a few cases, and the families are doing well. Most, but not all, successful instances were single-child situations. There may be some connection with that: children having their parents' undivided attention. Unfortunately, I am usually contacted by people who are having problems because I am one of the pioneers in Ukraine adoptions, and people know the difficulties we've experienced.

Both my adopted children have RAD, and anyone familiar with that understands the struggles of this disorder. If you are inclined to consider this type of adoption, you must understand what our goal was. It was to give two children a loving, Christian home. It wasn't to "save" them, or "rescue" them. We didn't expect anything from them, although we would have been thrilled had the bonding gone better. Both would have had very difficult lives in Ukraine. Gypsies are treated very badly, and the disabled are forgotten, or worse. Alla would have been begging on the streets, crawling on the ground (she would never have gotten prosthetics), she would have received no education, and she would have had a high probability of physical, sexual, and most definitely emotional abuse. We had to adopt her, and we felt called by God to do so.

Many people adopt to have a family or complete a family. We had three children. This was about seeing a need and following my calling to help. I have actually talked with my other children and husband, and after everything we have been through, we aren't so sure we would have adopted. Both my adopted children are so full of anger. Artur threatened our family many times and set fires in his bedroom, saying he was "going to burn the house down with us in it" because we asked him to do his homework or take a shower. When he was in fifth grade, he went after his teacher with a pair of scissors because he made him stay in from recess for not doing his homework. Alla's rejection of us and hostility toward us continues, and takes a toll on the rest of us.

However, we went into the adoptions as a strong family of five, and we wouldn't allow Artur's and Alla's behavior to tear us apart. We know they have ODD, RAD, and other disorders as a result of their early years. We went into these adoptions fully aware that children coming from these beginnings would have developmental delays and emotional issues. Even so, we were not prepared for what we experienced, but we love them, and we tried our best to give them the help and the reassurance they needed. There does come a time when you have to let them go. We are thrilled Artur is in treatment and hopeful that in time, and with more life experience, they both will mature and eventually receive the love, support, and help that the family has tried to give them. We never give up hope on either child, but we are careful to not be too vulnerable because we've been so hurt in the past.

When we adopted, international adoption was relatively new to the adoption arena, and information was scarce. Now I share with anyone considering adoption from a country in chaos or without a strong orphan structure in place the caution that your child may never bond with your family, and they may reject you, your values, and your help. There definitely is a place for adoption for some of these children. Our moral compass tells us that we saved our two from impending death, or at best, a life of horrors, had they remained in Ukraine. However, I think for many of these orphans, a better way to help is to advocate for policy change in these countries. There are now some very good programs in Ukraine that provide orphans with good, clean basics in a home-type environment, and many thrive in these programs. Decisions about adoption should be made on a case-by-case basis.

The key to a successful adoption is education and flexibility; the key to a successful transition is prayer and to know there are no guarantees. There is, however, always hope. God extends His hand to everyone, until we take our last breath; we also extend our heart and hands to our children. It is up to them to grasp it.

For more information on adopting in Ukraine, and general international adopting suggestions and tips, please visit Teresa's website www.HisKidsToo.org. It contains a wealth of information to prepare you for foreign adoption.

CHAPTER TWENTY-TWO

FIREWORKS

Aubrey Bergman

Aubrey is a relatively new mom with a one-year-old adopted daughter. She lives in the Pacific Northwest, and has been married for four years.

When I went through the adoption process, I posted about the events and all the emotions we were experiencing. This is a sampling of some of the posts I wrote later, looking back; together they do a good job of telling our story.[1]

MATCHED

It was a regular day. We had just moved into our new house three days before, and we were starting to get settled. Furniture was placed, boxes were being unpacked, and we were waiting on cable and internet. A few days earlier our adoption consultant had informed us about an agency they had been working with a little bit and told me I should send an application to them ASAP. In the craziness of moving, I somehow got the paperwork sent. The agency emailed me about a baby due in San Antonio in July. They didn't have very much information but thought we would be a perfect match. They spoke with Mama One and showed her our profile book. On May 10, 2016, at 9:54 a.m., our lives were changed forever. *Matched!*

Our hearts were bursting at the seams but we were also so cautious. We wanted to shout from the rooftops that we were paper pregnant, but we were also so scared to let our hearts be so open. We decided we would tell people but also make sure that everyone knew it may not work out. Looking back now, I'm so glad we celebrated and let ourselves prepare for a baby but also respected the fact that this baby was not ours just yet. It was, however, love at first sight.

---

[1] Posts have been edited and headings have been provided by the publisher.

LITTLE WHITE ONESIES

I can't believe I will have a year-old baby soon! This time last year, we were washing baby clothes and packing a hospital bag just to make sure we were ready to hop on a plane to Texas. I remember packing the bag. I cried washing those tiny white onesies. I couldn't bear the thoughts of our match failing, but, oh, that reality was so real. When I think of all the emotions we were going through, I can't help but think about what her Mama One was going through, too. Two women who didn't even know each other, but so connected by this one little soul.

DUE DATE

Amelia's due date was July 11. We knew if we got a call that Mama One was in labor, we would have to jump on a plane and travel to San Antonio, which would likely cause us to miss the birth. So, we decided on this day last year (a week before the due date) to head down to Texas and just wait it out and have a little fun while we were there. Best decision we ever made, because Amelia was born two days later.

LABOR

We got to the hospital and found the correct room. We immediately went to Mama One and hugged her. She was in the middle of a contraction. I held her hand, and we chatted in between and got to know each other face-to-face. What a way to meet your daughter's birthmom for the first time! Labor progressed quickly, and shortly after that, our little Amelia was born. There is nothing more miraculous than watching a baby enter the world. This tiny little human, who had no idea how much joy she would bring to so many people, entered the world at 8:13 p.m. in San Antonio on July 2, 2016. Our lives were changed forever.

TWO MAMAS

After very little sleep and so much anxiety, we headed back to the hospital early in the morning to spend the day with Mama One and Amelia. I couldn't eat a thing. My stomach was an absolute wreck at the thought of leaving Texas without Amelia. It was very much a possibility; that is the reality for so many families in the adoption process. And if Mama One had decided not to sign those papers, I know she would have been an amazing mama to Amelia. All day, we got to know her more, helped care for Amelia, and just waited. Amelia had to be forty-eight hours old before termination of parental rights could be signed and she could be released from the hospital. So, this tiny little human spent her first forty-eight hours being cared for by her two mamas. I will always tell her how special that was. We shared feeding her, changing her, and comforting her when she cried. Sam was a rock star at keeping me focused and calm, and reminding me to just enjoy these moments, whatever the following days may bring. And so we loved on this baby girl as much as we could until we knew what the outcome would be.

FAMILY

Mama One had some family visit the day after Amelia was born, and they wanted to meet us. We were already feeling the nerves big time, but meeting family and hoping they liked us was huge! Talk about being a nervous wreck! Mama One warned us her mom would be very emotional. They walked in, and I handed Amelia to Mama One's mom. She cried and spoke to her in Spanish. I know she was telling her how beautiful and perfect she was. I could feel it. Some other family also came, including two children. They immediately took to Sam and wanted him to play with them and hold them. Mama One and her family were shocked and said they never do that with strangers. We somehow felt it was their way of approving of us and telling us everything was good. It was a very special moment. After the visitors left, Mama One got a text from her mom saying she loved us and knew we would treat Amelia like a princess. Cue all the tears.

WAITING

After another night of hardly any sleep, we woke knowing today was the day: the day we would have a daughter or the day our hearts would be shattered into a million pieces. We headed back to the hospital to spend the day with Mama One and Amelia again and find out when they could be discharged. We knew it would be a long day, since they couldn't be released until Amelia was forty-eight hours old. So, it would be later that night. We paced the halls, signed a massive amount of paperwork, looked for every ounce of reassurance from our adoption agency rep, and continued to love on baby girl and get to know Mama One as much as we could. Oh, and I *still* hadn't eaten a thing! My stomach has never been such a wreck as it was during those waiting days.

NOW A MOM

Before Amelia was born, we didn't know the gender, so of course we just had all gender-neutral stuff with us. The day of discharge, we decided to take a quick trip to Target to buy some girl clothes. It was also July 4th (Independence Day!), so we wanted something patriotic to put her in to leave the hospital. The only thing left was a Minnie Mouse onesie, so Minnie it was! However, we didn't want to put it on her until we knew we were indeed taking her home with us.

In a few more hours, we would learn the fate of this tiny, amazing baby: whether we would be her parents or would be saying goodbye forever. It was excruciating. We tried to focus our attention on Mama One. We wanted to know everything about her in case we became her baby's mommy and daddy.

Discharge papers were beginning to come into the hospital room, and movements were being made. The plan was that we would take Amelia with us upon discharge and would be informed when or if papers were signed.

We dressed her and walked with her and Mama One and our agency rep out of the hospital. We hugged and said our goodbyes, and I cried a lot. Mama One was so confident and calm—which is one of the traits I loved about her, among many more! She gave Amelia a kiss on the forehead and helped strap her into her car seat. As we drove away from the hospital, we released. Every single emotion came out of us like a flood. I honestly don't know how Sam was able to drive through the sobbing. We still didn't know if Amelia would be staying with us, but we were one step closer—the closest we had ever been to calling this girl ours! So we waited again.

We listened to fireworks the whole way home from the hospital and silently believed they were celebrating us. We got back to my friend Linda's house with Amelia, and I ate the biggest meal ever and drank the biggest glass of wine ever. We spent the rest of the time just staring at her. Then it came: the text from our agency rep that would change our lives forever.

"Do you feel any different? Because you are now a mom."

And just like that, we had the most amazing, sweet, perfect daughter we could ever dream of.

Lorri's Note: Aubrey is only one year into a new journey and doesn't feel that she has a lot of sage advice at this point, but her story points to the careful balance between hope and caution. You must be patient and remain hopeful, even when the wait for a child takes time. The hope is important to stay positive and upbeat, but you also must be realistic and know that it's not final until it's final. You must keep the faith while not leaving yourself too vulnerable. It's walking a tightrope, but I'm sure Aubrey and all adoptive parents think it's worth it in the end!

CHAPTER TWENTY-THREE

WORDS OF LOVE, NOT RESCUE

Patrick Gray

Patrick Gray lives in Idaho with his wife and three children. One daughter, Olivia, was adopted from China. He is the author of The Push, *a children's story of friendship, and co-author of* I'll Push You, *the story of his lifelong friendship with Justin Skeesuck, which led to Patrick pushing Justin's wheelchair on the epic Camino de Santiago pilgrimage in Spain. Patrick and Justin have appeared on* The Today Show, *and their story has been made into an award-winning documentary released in 2017.*

With a variety of careers come a variety of experiences and a variety of dark conversations. I've worked construction crews and thus spent hot days swinging a hammer while my coworkers tried their best to bring me into the most vulgar conversations. Road construction meant long hours, hot days, and some of the most disgusting exchanges you can imagine about what happened the night before. Teaching high school was rewarding and frustrating at the same time, and the hallway discussions among teenagers never failed to amaze me. Bedside nursing lent itself to dark humor, heavy conversations with families facing the loss of loved ones, and awkward family dynamics. As a hospital administrator, I had many conversations with angry physicians or families, and the majority of my social interactions defied all social norms. And as dark as these conversations were, never have I heard anything quite so cruel as the words spoken by a mother as she denied her daughter affection; I overheard this as I worked in inpatient child psychiatry. The words *damaging* and *cruel* are all that come to mind.

The girl was nine, adopted only three years prior by her mother. She'd come into her "forever home" from a foreign country, and adjustment to the United States had not been easy. The trauma she'd experienced in her first six years of life had led to mistrust and behaviors that were challenging, and her adoptive mother had reached a tipping point. I watched as this woman refused to hold her little girl, who was reaching out for comfort. The mother was angry because of a previous outburst and was embarrassed by the girl's behavior. In that moment, she leaned in close so she was eye to eye, nose to nose with her daughter. Piercing stare, clenched teeth, and finger in the tiny face, the woman scolded, "I saved you from your life! You should be grateful for the love I give you!" She then leaned back, crossed her arms, and looked away while the little girl cried. A social worker who was facilitating the meeting intervened, but the damage had been done.

I couldn't believe what I was hearing! Regardless of the chain of events that brought this mother to this point, her words were vile, and they broke my heart . . . I can't imagine what they did to that little girl's. Her understanding of love was being painted with ugly colors and wickedly jagged brush strokes.

It was a defining moment for me. I'd always believed in the power of our words and actions: the power to build up and the power to destroy exist in so much of what we say and do. But as I watched a part of that little girl torn apart by sixteen words uttered by someone who claimed to love her and refused to hold her, I witnessed a remarkable and terrible force—the force of manipulative, guilt-filled love.

The girl was discharged from the hospital, and I never saw her again. But what I witnessed had a profound effect on me as a father. If one person's words and actions could cause so much pain, surely the opposite is true, too.

Those damaging words I heard so many years ago have motivated me to make sure my words are filled with love and are ones that build up, ones that empower. Don't get me wrong; there are many things I have said to my children I wish I could take back, and I am definitely a work in progress. But the beauty I see in my children, their potential to love others, the future change-makers I see in them, tells me whatever I do with them . . . for them . . . and to them must have one single motivation. If I am going to look at myself in the mirror each day and have a shred of pride in who I am as a father, that single motivation is love. Love in my words and love in my actions. Nothing less.

My wife and I have three amazing children. Our eldest daughter, Cambria, and son, Joshua, joined our family biologically; and our youngest daughter, Olivia, blessed us through adoption from China. The five of us are complete when it's the five of us. We are family. We are blood.

Every child needs the same things to survive: food, water, warmth, and rest. Even more, they need a safe place where they experience love, affection, intimacy, and support through their successes and failures.

That little girl from so many years ago had what she needed to survive. But thrive? I hope something changed, because when I saw her she wasn't experiencing a safe place filled with love, affection, and intimacy. Her world was emotionally unsafe and lacked any sense of what a little girl needs to go beyond just making it through each day. In fact, she needed more than my two oldest children because her world had been turned upside down, much the way my little Olivia's was turned upside down for the first seven months of her life.

I imagine that little girl asked many of the same questions my Olivia has asked: Why did my mom give me up? Why don't I have a birth story like my brother and sister? Why do I look different than the rest of my family? The first few of many difficult questions we will undoubtedly face. And while the answers to these questions are so very important, my response to her uncertainty, her questions of self-worth, and her wrestling with abandonment are just as important.

Just like every child, Olivia needs to know she is loved, even when she wrestles with difficult questions. She needs to know that my arms are a safe place to rest, a safe place to laugh, and a safe place to cry. She needs to know the power of loving touch, and that I say what I mean, mean what I say, and that my words align with my actions. She needs to know I love her when I say it, and when I show it by stroking her hair, in the moments I cup her face in both my hands and tell her how lucky I am she is mine, when she crawls in my lap and just rests because it is safe there. She needs to know how beautiful she is—not because of how she looks, but because of who she is. Olivia, like my other children, needs to know there is nothing she can do to earn or lose my love. She will always have it just because she is my daughter, not because of how she behaves, who she is, or who she becomes. But so much of who she is, and who she will one day be, depends on how I behave, who I am, and who I become.

As fathers, we have a remarkable amount of power over and in our children's growth. How I treat my wife is how my daughters will expect to be treated, and how my son will treat the women in his life. The words I choose and how I say them, my inflections, my tone, my facial expressions, and my posture . . . all of these have power and shape the expectations of my children. How I show affection to my wife is what will shape my daughters' expectations from their future relationships.

Olivia is wonderful, beautiful, funny, silly, rambunctious, strong-willed, intelligent, sweet, and kind. But these aren't the reasons I love her. I love Olivia because she is my daughter. This kind of love isn't earned and it isn't taken away. It just is and always will be because she is my daughter and I am her father.

My daughter Olivia was never someone to be rescued; she has always been a beautiful creation that I should embrace, love, and thank every day for making my life better and making my family whole.

To every father and to every mother: your words and actions have remarkable power. Regardless of how your children enter your lives, to be a parent is a privilege and a blessing. Every day we have the power, as parents, to bring heaven or hell into the lives of our children. Let your words and actions show love; love without condition, love without manipulation, love without motive—just love.

Spend time with your children, play with them, wrestle with them, hold them, and read to them. Whisper, "I love you so much" into their ears as they sleep in your arms. The future of our world depends on each new generation. Our children's capacity for love, their understanding of love, is dependent upon how we love them. The fate of so many in this world is dependent on how our children will love others.

CHAPTER TWENTY-FOUR

BREAKING BARRIERS

Helen Trauntvein

Helen is a single mother and former hospital administrator from Salt Lake City, Utah. Helen adopted her daughter, Nanci, out of foster care in 1969, when Nanci was six years old. She was awarded the first single-parent guardianship given by the state of Florida. Nanci's story is featured in Chapter Thirty, and Nanci's birthmother's story is in Chapter Eight.

The hallmark statement, and what it truly means for my daughter and me, is, "Where there is understanding, no explanation is needed. Where there is no understanding, no explanation will suffice."

I have the wonderful blessing of being an adoptive mom to a very *special angel*, Nanci. The beauty of our intertwining, which led to a journey of love, was based on a deeper understanding of each of us and our desire to have a positive outcome of our sojourn together. At times, that seemed impossible.

Another quote often guiding our journey, which made all the difference then and still does now, is the following from Edwin Markham's poem "Outwitted":

> *He drew a circle that shut me out*
> *Heretic, rebel, a thing to flout.*
> *But Love and I had a wit to win:*
> *We drew a circle that took him in!*

The opportunity to be a legal guardian and then an adoptive parent came to me out of the blue. At the time, I was a thirty-eight-year-old single woman with a career in nursing administration at All Children's Hospital in St. Petersburg, Florida. I was making plans to leave Florida in October 1969 to return to Salt Lake City, Utah, and start in nursing administration at Primary Children's Hospital.

Since we were the only children's hospital in the St. Petersburg/Clearwater/Tampa area, all the children who were in foster placement care were brought to our clinics for their medical needs. One of my friends was a caseworker with the State Children's Services; she would bring the children for their appointments, and on occasion, would seek me out and introduce the children to me. This is how I met Nanci. The social worker informed me that Nanci, at almost six years old, had serious, chronic medical issues and because of this, had not been medically released for adoption, so she had been in foster care since birth.

In September of that year, the caseworker came into my office to let me know Nanci was in the clinic and the doctors had determined a release for her to be adopted could be issued. She also said her department was concerned about finding a placement for Nanci due to her age and the medical needs she would always have. They knew a placement would be difficult, if it would happen at all. Without much thought, I said, "Maybe I could take her."

She said single-parent adoptions were not allowed in the state of Florida; however, she asked if it was OK for her to check with the appropriate authorities. Within several days, the caseworker called to inform me the appropriate person at the state had said thanks, but no thanks. The state of Florida was not willing to make an exception, even for single-parent guardianship.

I started my new position in Salt Lake City in mid-October. The week prior to Thanksgiving, the caseworker called me and asked whether I could come down to Florida the following week and get Nanci. I asked what had changed. She informed me the state of Florida had reviewed Nanci's case and felt they were not going to be able to place her for adoption due to her age and medical concerns, and it would continue to cost them an enormous amount of money to pay for her care. I was told that if the state of Utah would work with me for home visits and conduct the adoption through the state of Utah, Florida would give me legal guardianship.

I flew to Florida, and by Nanci's request, she and the caseworker met me at a designated park, which had a pond and some ducks, for our official introduction. It was decided right then that she would come with me. It was interesting to me that nothing would be sent with her: none of her belongings, whatsoever.

We stayed overnight with some of my friends. The next morning, we went to the judge's chambers where legal guardianship was established.

We went straight from there to the airport. This was Nanci's first plane ride, and we were not aware of, nor prepared for, the trauma this would cause her. We arrived late that evening on a dark, cold, and snow-covered tarmac. Nanci had only lived in Florida in the warmth and sunshine, and had never seen or been in winter's cold. This occurred in the first week of December. This whole experience came to fruition within about nine weeks of my first visit with the caseworker.

As one considers what occurred so rapidly and so abruptly, it is mind-boggling. The whole world for a not-quite-six-year-old child was shaken. She was taken from the mother, father, and siblings she had known for three years, from the foster home in which she had lived, loved, laughed, and developed. She left behind toys, a tricycle, and other familiar security items to go to cold, snowy weather, with one person—me—whom she had only just met, to start living in a home with no other children, no father figure, no stay-at-home mom. She immediately started going to a daycare with other children and teachers she didn't know and started living a completely different way of life. Little wonder there were such challenging years ahead for her and for me. I marvel she survived, but survive she has! She has become a most beautiful, gracious, outgoing, creative woman.

What being an adoptive parent meant to me then, and now forty-eight years later, is worlds apart in learning and understanding. We had to work through so many situations regarding my daughter's pain, confusion, and desires, as well as my own feelings, hopes, and wishes.

A piece of advice for adoptive parents: Obtain as much information on your child as possible, including information about the child's social background, any foster/temporary care, medical care, and anything else anyone can give you. Have an adequate amount of time together with the child and family members before a transition occurs, especially when the child is not a baby. Had I had more information about my daughter and understood more about what this all meant to both of us, my responses to various situations would have been much different.

While she was growing up, she and I often talked about not getting too caught up in the current situation so that we wouldn't lose track of what we wanted for each other and how we wanted to relate to each other in years down the road. We kept our long-range goals in the forefront. As my Nanci and I have often shared, in this we feel well rewarded.

You don't raise an adopted child differently. Whether you have a child biologically or through adoption, there is much to do to build your relationship and continue to develop the love, understanding, respect, and bond you both would like to have throughout the years. There is no manual, no matter how your child comes to you, and time, patience, and maturity are great teachers.

I feel our story is one of learning. It is one of being willing to listen, to share, and to maintain a safe environment for each to respectfully be heard and make decisions. One example of this: Nanci and I spoke from the very beginning about my willingness to help her in any way possible to search for and locate her biological family, especially her mom, when she was ready. Over the years, I would repeat this offer, but never had success with the search.

Later, Nanci decided to pursue the search, and she kept me updated on the progress. I received a phone call one day from Nanci informing me she had just received her original birth certificate. She was so excited, but before opening it, she called me and said, "Mom, this is what I have, unopened, in my hand, but first, I want to know how you feel about it because I don't want to hurt you."

Nanci has always been so thoughtful, from writing notes around the house to drawing me pictures, many of which I still have and treasure. Of course, I was very happy for Nanci since she had wanted this so badly since the day I met her. We were, and continue to be, so happy she could get her answers and meet her biological family.

I wouldn't change anything I have learned and experienced. I have only to say that, had I had the kind of understanding I do now, I know I could have taken that wonderful, frightened little girl, my special angel, in my arms and helped her to better understand what was happening to her. I feel I may have been better able to help her with her fear and pain so she could better enjoy her precious life. A tip I would give to new adoptive parents, especially those coming from difficult beginnings, would be to look at all situations through their child's eyes. While the relationship may be new for everyone, the child will need to feel unconditional love and support in order to sort out challenges.

Nanci's biological mom, Judy, along with Nanci and myself, met in a park during the summer here in Salt Lake City and had a lovely picnic together and just enjoyed sharing stories. It was a wonderful experience to meet her, and she expressed so much gratitude to me for taking care of her baby, which is something she readily admits she just wasn't able to do at the time. Nanci's biological family, who all live out of state, often inquire about me and are very considerate. Judy and I exchange cards and express gratitude for each other and for our being . . .

1. Mom number one: Judy
2. Mom number two: Alice (Nanci's beloved foster mom, who remained close)
3. Mom number three: me

What an amazing, stretching, and growing experience, and one I would not have wanted to miss.

CHAPTER TWENTY-FIVE

MY VERY REAL DAUGHTER

Rachel Tucker

Rachel lives in Phoenix, Arizona, with her husband, Collin, and they have been married for twenty years. They have three children: two biological daughters, aged eighteen and sixteen, and an adopted daughter from Ethiopia, who is age nine.

For as long as I can remember, I wanted to adopt. I grew up having friends who had been adopted as infants, and I always thought it was a beautiful thing. I've never believed that families must be connected biologically.

I chose to adopt a child born in Ethiopia because I'd read that, as a result of the AIDS epidemic, there were somewhere around four million orphaned children, and the futures of those children seemed especially bleak. In America, there is a system in place for children who need support. Children in the United States usually go into foster homes and hopefully end up being adopted; they are also educated and have their basic needs met. I'd read that in Ethiopia, once children "age out" of the orphanage, they are pretty much on their own in the world.

We started the adoption process, and after about fifteen months of paperwork and waiting, we were emailed a photo of our baby. It was estimated that she was about a month and a half old. Several months later, I was on a flight to Addis Ababa to meet our daughter. I was able to bring her home after being there for five days. A few days after Violet was home, my husband confided in me that friends had been asking him if he thought the baby would feel like "his." Looking down at her, sleeping in his arms, he said, "I love her so much. She just couldn't be any more 'mine.'"

Being adoptive parents hasn't been so different to us than simply being parents. Before a person becomes a parent, they may not fully appreciate how each baby comes with his or her own personality, quirks, and preferences. Having a biological child doesn't always mean the child will look and act just like you. Because our adoption was transracial, it is very obvious to most people that Violet was adopted. Kids at school sometimes ask why Violet doesn't look like her parents. They sometimes even ask about her "real" parents. We've also dealt with some racial discrimination. Some friends and even some family members had to be cut out of our lives. Once you become a parent, you realize that your child and her well-being have to come first. There is no room in her life for people who will only bring her down.

I remember that the adoption process was overwhelming. The massive amount of paperwork and home studies seemed never-ending. There were times when I was just obsessed, frantically looking through photos posted by our adoption agency of the orphanage, wondering which baby was ours. Even after we finally had pictures of her, there were times when I felt like she'd never come home. I constantly had to convince myself that the nurses in the orphanage were giving her all the love and attention she needed. Once she was finally home, all of that stress just melted away. The process had been an emotional roller-coaster ride. Having Violet home was the best feeling in the world.

My husband and I are often told what "amazing people" we are because we adopted. We find that attitude awkward and embarrassing. The truth is, we loved being parents and wanted another child. We didn't do it for Violet; we did it for us. She never chose this life. In an ideal world, her biological parents would have been able to care for her. We're just a consolation prize after suffering such a tragic start in life. Please don't tell my little girl she's lucky to have been adopted. It diminishes all that she went through before she had us. If you must call her something, call her resilient. Call her a survivor.

During our adoption process, we had to cut off contact with my husband's parents. I guess we never fully realized how much of a struggle our adopting would be for his mother. For whatever reason, she just couldn't get behind it. I also assumed that when the baby came, my mother-in-law would come around. She didn't. We knew that she would always treat Violet as less than her sisters. It didn't take long to come to the conclusion that this baby and our little family were more important than that relationship. That was painful and it continues to be. That being said, I wouldn't do anything differently. We've been extremely successful in surrounding ourselves with wonderful friends and family members who love and support our family.

It is very unlikely that we will ever be able to track down Violet's biological parents. The officials involved in her case claim that a woman (perhaps her mother) brought her to a hospital and said she was unable to care for her. That's it. That's the only information we were given. I like to tell Violet that I can only imagine that her biological mother must be incredibly beautiful, funny, and kind, just like her. I often wish we could contact her, if only to let her know that Violet is happy, healthy, thriving, and so completely and totally *loved*.

For me, adoptive and biological parenthood are very much the same. Parenting is such a day-to-day thing. I'm no expert on parenting or parenting a child of adoption. My tip for the waiting period: when you are trying to adopt, try as hard as you can to be patient. Once that child is yours, she is yours forever, and I promise, just like a biological child, she'll be driving you crazy in no time! Just know that your family will come together, and it will be wonderful. The wait is absolutely worth it.

Another tip for adoptive parents is to consider keeping your child's personal history private to just her immediate family. A child's story is hers to tell, and she might not want all the neighbors and all of her classmates knowing all the very personal and likely painful details. Respect your child!

Each of my daughters has managed to take hold of my heart in a way I never imagined possible.

CHAPTER TWENTY-SIX

MALENKY ZAICHIK AND ME

Andrea Robinson

Andrea is a studio singer and live performer from Burbank, California. She is the single mother of Alex, a recent high school graduate, who she adopted from Ukraine shortly before his second birthday. Andrea's film singing credits include singing for Sister Mary Robert, the shy nun-turned-diva in Sister Act, *and for Queen Athena in* The Little Mermaid: Ariel's Beginning.

I am a single adoptive parent. I never thought my life would end up like this, because after all, I was raised in Burbank with two loving parents and a fantastic brother. We were the perfect 1950s, "Mayberry" family of Southern California. Our household was filled with professional musicians, intelligence, photography, art, love, respect, kindness, and a lot of laughter. I thought my life would automatically have the same reality. Good grief, I could not have been more off target.

I divorced at thirty-five after ten years of marriage. Four years later, I came to realize my baby window—physically and ethically—was coming to an end. Someone asked me, "When you reach fifty years of age, what would be on the top of your regrets list?" Without hesitation, my answer was not raising children. I knew my parents would be the quintessential grandparents, and although they never pressured me, they deserved grandchildren. Our family name was coming to an end. In 1978, they had lived through the tragedy of losing my brother. Greg, a *San Francisco Examiner* photographer, was ambushed alongside Congressman Ryan covering the Jonestown Massacre. The press coverage was relentless, and the devastating effect of his loss on our parents was compounded because he had no children. I wanted a child both for myself, and for my parents.

My career was abundant, and my home had a giant grapefruit tree in the backyard waiting and ready for a swing. Most of all, an orphaned child would be coming into loving arms of family and friends. My parents raised us with so much love, I was positive that I could do the same for a child. These were enough valid reasons for me to adopt on my own, so I met with a few single mothers who had adopted internationally and started researching.

Sadly, the current data states that there are twenty million orphans in the world waiting to be adopted. In the Eastern Europe Bloc, children are aged out at sixteen years of age. Ten to twenty percent commit suicide in the first year; survival is extremely harsh. These kids have no life skills, and they are gullible. Some go into the reserves; some will get a menial job and may share apartments with other orphans, but they are targeted by many. They often get swindled out of apartments given to them by the state. The boys are targeted and are used by the Mafia to run drugs. If the girls are not placed into jobs, they end up prostituting. There is absolutely nothing positive about being an orphan in those countries.

Since I couldn't bear the statistics, I decided to adopt from Ukraine; their adoption system was unique, and I am of Ukrainian descent. Upon arriving in Kiev, we went directly to the adoption center. After looking through books of poorly produced photos of available children, we went to meet a boy in a region known to be difficult. After meeting two boys, the director demanded a $1,000 cash donation for their water boiler. No donation meant no child. My facilitator immediately said, "We're leaving," and we returned to Kiev. The adoption center then recommended a boy with a 5/5 health star rating and high APGAR score. My facilitator and I traveled for eight hours to the now war-torn area of Donetsk, and we immediately met with the orphanage director.

Within five minutes, my beautiful Alex was brought into the room. He had the typical dull, thin orphan hair and beautiful hazel eyes. He was attached to his caregiver, which was both a sad yet ultimately good sign. Additionally, at two years of age Alex was not talking and was the size of an eighteen-month-old, but these were typical delays. I knew he was my son, and I wanted to immediately proceed with the paperwork. I was warned to spend a few days evaluating and connecting with him. We visited and played for two more days, and I confirmed my initial instinct. Everyone says there is a deeper connection that happens, and you "just know." The judge hit the gavel on the table and said, "Congratulations—you are now a mother!" I was forty-five years old.

As we prepared to leave, Tanya, his caregiver, was quiet as she took him out of his orphanage clothes and into overalls that my mother had bought. They allowed me to keep his red shoes, which he continued to carry and sleep with for several weeks. His shoes were his anchor of familiarity. As Tanya handed Alex to me in the car, Alex tried to crawl over me reaching for her. He was crying, as was I. I felt horrible that my innocent Alex had to experience this. If I have one regret, I wish I had spent a few weeks seeing him every day. I was still a stranger to him. On the way back to Kiev, he finally had a diaper to wear, so he could sleep through the night; no more marching in the middle of the night to sit on chamber pots. As we returned back to Kiev, Alex slept soundly for eight hours.

I've learned so much about adoption on this journey of mine, both generally and concerning foreign adoption. These are my words of wisdom, starting with how my life has been enhanced by my son's adoption. I have joined the parenting side of life, and I love it! While I know that someone's greatest loss became my greatest gift, I have no words to express my gratitude. I have made friends that I would have never met, and my life experience is far richer because I am a mother.

I did not force my son to call me Mama. I let the connection unfold. Four months after Alex came home, he woke up, walked into the living room, and called out, "MAMA!" I will never forget that moment and the impact it had on my life. He climbed into my lap with his bunny, I kissed and rocked him as we had been doing, and said, "*Malenky Zaichik*," his Ukrainian pet name meaning "Little Rabbit." I may not have seen his first smile, or shared in his first laughter or first steps, but since the first day he was officially mine, we have had thousands of firsts, and we continue to have them every day.

My beautiful mother passed in 2003, and within three years, my father passed. My family was gone, and I was devastated. One time when I was deeply grieving, four-year-old Alex wrapped his little arms around me and said, "I'm here for you, Mama, and I will catch all your tears in a cup." His compassion was, and is, so amazing.

Now at eighteen, Alex always asks me, "You OK?" Then he adds with a huge grin on his face, "You know who I love the most in this world? I have two favorites: you and Crystal [our cat], but Crystal is *first*."

It's amazing how much his happiness and success affects my life. As a parent, I get great joy as I see his tremendous art talent emerge. One piece of his art hangs in perpetuity in the hall cases at his high school. Happily, he is no longer small for his age. He presses 200 pounds and has been approached by modeling scouts. I am elated to say that things have worked out. He has been more joy for our family and myself than I could have imagined. I am one proud mother.

That's not to say there have been no difficulties. I wish I adopted my son ten years earlier so we would have more time on the planet together. Additionally, I regret he does not have a father or sibling. My dear father helped me raise my son for five years until his passing, but that was the main male influence Alex has had.

No one could have told my single friends or myself how difficult this would be. And if they had tried, they would not have swayed our intentions. I wish I could have lived the life of a full-time single parent for a few months before I'd adopted. This is a two-person job, and I agree wholeheartedly that it does take a village to raise children. For single adopters, as scary as it may seem, go forward; it all works out. Google "Single Mothers by Choice," (SMC) a national support organization, which is basically for women who have "run out of time." I have made lifetime friends from those meetings.

I've learned a few specific lessons that apply to foreign adoptions. Unless you are purposefully seeking to adopt a high-risk child, I would suggest to those who are adopting internationally to google the facial characteristics of FAS or FAE (Fetal Alcohol Syndrome or Effect). The fewer surprises, the better. I actually taught the FAS facial features to my adoption facilitator in Ukraine. I know of a family adopting in Central America who had the child tested academically before agreeing to placement. It's best to at least try to find out the history of the family.

Also, if adopting internationally, learn baby or child vocabulary in their native language so you can help the child with "tender transition." Phrases such as "Can I have a hug?" "Hold my hand," "Are you hungry?" "All done," "Time for bed," and "I love you" are essentials. Find out if the mamas in the orphanage gave your child a nickname like my son's "Little Rabbit," and learn the pronunciation. My son's was pronounced in Russian as "Mahleenky Zycheek." Although children will learn English within four months, have a possible friend or translator available to avoid meltdowns. You will also avoid meltdowns with toddlers if you read the book *Baby Signs* (data based—it does not truncate speech). Start by using their native language and teach simple signing, then slowly add English. Another great book for new parents is *How to Talk So Kids Will Listen and Listen So Kids Will Talk* by Adele Faber and Elaine Mazlish. It is useful for all ages, and trust me, you will need it when they are teenagers. This is fantastic for any parent, but the adoption arena has particular challenges.

In addressing the birthparent search, I will be by his side if he really has an interest, but so far, he and his friends who are adopted don't talk about their adoptions or searching. I have found it is a very personal subject to most of them. Of the books I have read, all have stated that, as the birthparent topic comes up—and it will—they will ask the number of questions for the answers they are ready to hear. I follow that advice to this day. Also, the major difficulty in international searches includes complex language barriers, but parents do hire people through the internet for this purpose.

I also have some advice for anyone embarking on any adoption path. Keeping adoption a secret is old-fashioned and damaging. My cousins were adopted here in the US in the 1950s. After their parents passed, my cousins were both over fifty when they discovered they had been adopted. We thought they knew, and it was deeply devastating to them. Your kids won't love you any less if you don't share DNA. I brought up the word *adoption* early on to Alex and talked about all his friends who were also adopted in the neighborhood. Our adoption support group play-dates were filled with children who knew they were adopted. It was an open and normal part of life.

Additionally, if you find out the age of your child ahead of time, do the upfront work regarding schools and daycare. You won't have time for this once your child comes home. Go to greatschools.org, find public schools that are highly rated, and move to that district unless you plan to have them attend private schools. Be sure to have a support system of family, or strong finances for daycare, nannies, and babysitters. Just remember: you won't be going out all the time as you did before. It is expensive every time you walk out the door.

Most of all, during the adoption process, keep your eye on the prize. The dossier takes months to complete; they will fingerprint you and request tax returns, physicals, and more. The paperwork seems endless. Just chip away at it daily. In the meantime, get your house ready, research schools, and find a good pediatrician and any adoption support groups in your area.

When your darling first comes home, don't overload him or her with too many toys, and, if possible, be ready to stay home for several months. Kids from foreign or older-age adoptions are in shock. They can acclimate pretty quickly, but they do need serious bonding time. Most of all, give lots of hugs, kisses, tickle time, serious nutrition, play dates, and, as my father said, "Keep them laughing."

Having or adopting children is a leap of faith, but know that the child who is meant to be in your family is waiting.

CHAPTER TWENTY-SEVEN

REMEMBER THE BIRTHMOTHERS

Ellen Porter

Ellen is a stay-at-home mother and the founder of BraveLove, an organization that honors the heroism and bravery of birthmothers. She lives in Dallas with her husband and four children, two of whom are adopted.

For my husband and I, adoption was never a plan B. Early in our marriage, Reid and I attended a Steven Curtis Chapman concert. During the concert, Chapman did a wonderful presentation on international adoption, sharing his story of adopting from China. Before we even got home from that concert, Reid and I both knew that we would adopt one day. There was no angst or heartache about it. Maybe the snap decision seems immature or foolish, but we just knew it was something we both wanted to do.

Fast-forward about five years, and we were finally ready to begin growing a family. I was not getting pregnant easily. I had one miscarriage, and after two-and-a-half years of trying month after month, I was done! I was tired of receiving infertility treatments, and receiving birth announcements, and receiving baby shower invitations, and *not* receiving that coveted little plus sign on a plastic stick. My heart was ready to be a mommy, but clearly my body was not having any part of it. Reid and I decided that since we had always wanted to adopt, why not start the process? I just wanted to be a mommy—no matter how that happened.

We attended an international adoption information session with the Gladney Center for Adoption. We learned about the ins and outs of international adoption from the varying countries from which they placed children. We learned that there are certain boxes you have to fit in for each country, and we learned into which boxes we did and did not fit.

Initially, when entering into this process we thought we would be adopting a little girl from China. After all, that was Steven Curtis Chapman's story, and we had learned about adoption through him. That is what we had always envisioned for ourselves. But as it was, China was not the box into which we fit. Both of us had to be thirty-years-old to adopt from China, so we were too young! After careful thought and consideration and prayer, we decided to enter into the process through Guatemala.

At that time, children in Guatemala adoptable through Gladney were being cared for in a foster-care environment rather than in orphanages. Guatemala had a relatively short process in which you could be placed with a very young child, and since we were going to be new parents, we longed to have "the baby experience."

After being accepted into the program, I became pregnant. Now, dear reader, I will tell you that nothing is more frustrating than when somebody says to you, "Of course you got pregnant after you started the adoption process! That *always* happens. You just needed to relax." As if the adoption process is remotely relaxing! Clearly, these people have never been through a home study! I have many friends that I have met through our adoption process who have never experienced pregnancy. So, no, despite what someone in the grocery store line might say, entering into the adoption process is not a guarantee to become pregnant.

After finding out that I was pregnant, Reid and I were ecstatic and desperately wanted both children. Thankfully, we were able to continue in the adoption process even though I was pregnant. Finally, we got "The Call." Our caseworker told us that a precious little Guatemalan boy was available to adopt. He was our firstborn son, Caleb!

When Caleb was only eight weeks old and I was about four-months pregnant, Reid and I traveled down to Guatemala to meet our child. We stayed in a hotel in Guatemala City for four days, delighting in our first opportunity to finally be Mommy and Daddy.

For four straight days, we stayed in the hotel and spent every waking hour marveling at the love we already felt for this child we just met. Caleb became so very precious to us in that short time. By day two, I was already an emotional mess thinking about handing him back over to his foster mother and returning to the US without my baby. When it came time to actually say goodbye until his paperwork was completed, I thought I would never stop crying. This might sound gross, but when we got back to Dallas, we didn't wash everything in our suitcase so we could still revel in the smell of our son.

It was about five more months for our paperwork to pass through all of the government procedures in Guatemala. In November of that year,

Caleb was officially made a Porter. Our caseworker called and let us know that we could expect to travel the first week of December. This was a bit of a problem since my due date was December 5. The Lord took care of the details, since I went into labor the day after she called. We welcomed Caleb's younger brother, Bennett, a month before Caleb came home from Guatemala.

The first week of December, Reid packed up and headed to Guatemala to pick up our Caleb while I stayed at home caring for Bennett. Bennett was one month old when Reid got off the plane with a seven-month-old Caleb. I had gotten so used to holding a five-and-a-half-pound baby that when Reid put Caleb in my arms, he felt enormous to me! This was definitely not the eight-week-old we left in Guatemala. This kid had teeth!

To say that the first week we were all home together is a blur is a huge understatement! Rather, I would say the first two years of the boys' lives are a blur. I know I was there, because there are pictures and videos to prove it. I look happy, but I honestly don't remember much. If I had remembered, we probably would not have entered into the same scenario a second time. But as gluttons for punishment, we did it again.

When the boys were both two, I found out I was pregnant with our third son, Silas. We were a happy, full family with a three-year-old, a two-and-a-half-year-old, and an infant. Once again, I have very little memory of this time in life.

I agreed to speak at an adoption conference at our church, and while I was preparing for my talk, I was reading a book called *Adopted for Life* by Russell Moore. I felt that familiar tug on my heart that our family was not yet complete. Reid and I discussed and prayed, and when Silas was just eight months old, we entered into the adoption process again. This time, we got to adopt a child from China. There are benefits to aging! China deemed us "old enough."

When the boys were four, four, and one, we were matched with a precious little girl, Micah. And believe it or not, she was only six months younger than her big brother Silas. Functionally, we entered into the world of two sets of twins aged five and under. My memory is just now seeming to resurface.

Being a mother does a lot to change a person. When we entered into the adoption process in our late twenties, Reid and I were not particularly introspective or thoughtful about the process. We felt we were ready to be parents, but we had no idea what that really meant. I suppose we are still learning. But we never really thought specifically about what it meant to become parents through "adoption." Now we know two times over.

Having two babies just seven months apart raises a lot of eyebrows in the grocery store. Having four kids five and under is as startling to people as if I had a unicorn horn growing out of my head. I don't like when people use hyperbole in excess. However, I think I am being truthful when I say that I have never, ever stepped out in public with my four children and somebody hasn't said something ranging from, "My my! You have your hands full!" to "Do you mind me asking, is your husband Asian or something?" to "Tell me about *this*!" (said while pointing a finger to all my children with a frowning, confused, and semi-disgusted face). For the most part, I really don't mind. I know we look pretty interesting, and I would probably want to ask, too, if the tables were turned. I delight in sharing our story as long as one of the kids isn't pitching a fit in some checkout line. That is never a good time for any mom to talk.

Mostly what I want people to know is this: it's really not that big of a deal! Yes, we look unique, and having that many kids close together is not the easiest thing in the world. When it comes down to it, though, I'm just a normal mom that really loves her kids—all of them. They are all different in personality and character, as well as looks. No, I don't love them all the same, but I have a mama bear–sized love for each and every one of them. For me, it feels like I love our kids so much and think they are so cute that I kind of want to eat them, or murder anyone who wants to harm them. I feel that way about each of them from time to time.

I don't get carried away with thoughts that would tempt me to think I love one more than another because that one is biological and the other one is adopted. An adoptive parent's mind has a tendency to go that direction if you have biological children as well. The truth is, even when your house is full of biological children, you are going to do a better job loving some of your kids than others. That's normal human nature. Some kids you just "click" with more easily than others. That doesn't mean you don't love the ones that are not as easy to parent or that you wouldn't take a bullet for one. It is the same for my heart when I parent biological and adopted children. They *all* have their moments when I would prefer to be with one over the other. I feel sure they feel the same way about my husband and me!

Adoption always begins from a place of brokenness. It comes from parents who are not able to care for their child for a myriad of reasons. It comes through the relinquishment of a baby into the arms of strangers, through authorities taking away a child from a parent who is not fit to be a parent, or the literal abandoning of the child. This broken beginning produces great loss at the start of any adoption.

Reid and I really didn't think about this beginning and brokenness until we were looking into the eyes of the babies that became part of our family through adoption. Two of our children grew in the wombs of other women. Two of our children have completely different biology running in their bloodstreams than Reid and me. There are women out there in the world who had babies that they never got to know. And two of those babies live with me. They are my babies now. I am just now learning to grieve that loss for those women and that loss for my children.

It makes me sad that I will never get to introduce my children to the ones who birthed them. I will never be able to say thank you for what they did in the life of the child who is now mine. They could have made a different choice, and we would never know all that we had missed. But we know now. We honor those women, we respect them, we thank them for their courage, and we grieve for the loss that is our gain.

I founded an organization called BraveLove out of a desire to honor, respect, and encourage any woman who has placed her child for adoption. Bravelove.org has become a hub of adoption information and resources not only for women who are considering placing but also for women who have already placed and need to hear that they are not alone. I have never viewed the biological mothers of my children as weak or unloving. The real tragedy is that most of us never think of these women at all! I don't know the circumstances of Caleb's and Micah's birthparents at the time they decided they could not parent the baby in their arms, and I probably never will. But one thing I do know: those two women were brave enough and loving enough to carry my babies to term. Every time I get to look in the eyes of my Micah and my Caleb, I feel so very thankful they did.

PART FOUR

Adoptees

CHAPTER TWENTY-EIGHT

ONIONS, DANDELIONS, AND GUARDIAN ANGELS

Mary Beth McAdaragh

Mary Beth is a fifty-three-year-old television marketing executive from Los Angeles. Her experience has taught her that our cells never forget and things always work out for the best.

I was born a leap year baby, adopted at seven months in Sioux Falls, South Dakota, through Catholic Social Services. My birthparents couldn't decide whether to keep me or place me for adoption. Their situation was complicated, and many decisions had to be made, so while they tried to figure it out, I was passed from one foster home to another.

My birthparents were having an affair. Charlotte was married and had three small daughters. It was an abusive marriage, and she was trying to get out of it. They were living in the Grand Forks/Fargo area of North Dakota, and she had fallen for Paul, who was married with two kids of his own. I was the product of that affair. I am already crying as I write this, and I don't know why. It's funny . . . I, of course, don't remember any of this, but I do believe our cells never forget.

I found out a lot of this information when I was searching for my birthparents later in life. Growing up, I never knew anything, and I didn't care to know more. Betty and John McAdaragh were destined to be my parents, and that's all I needed to know.

My mom had my older brother twelve years before me and then got endometriosis and couldn't have more children. They had an opportunity to adopt another baby before I came along, but it was through a doctor rather than a lawyer. They worried that there was a greater chance that someone might change their mind, or show up later, so they didn't adopt that baby. They had applied to become adoptive parents with Catholic Social Services, and they got the call that there was a baby girl and they could come get her that same day. For some reason, they were not told to go to Social Services but rather to my third foster home, where I was living. They went to pick me up in a trailer park. The mother wasn't there—some kid was watching me. It was in September of 1964 when they took me home and became my parents. A very short time afterwards, a woman came knocking at our door when my mom wasn't home. My brother answered and discovered it was a member of that foster family, who said they wanted me back. That obviously didn't happen.

In the beginning, I didn't eat much, and it took a while for me to come around. Those seven months in foster care probably weren't optimal. It's probably best I don't know my living conditions. I had a wonderful childhood growing up in the Midwest and not knowing anything about my start in life. I always knew I was adopted. I can't say when I was told . . . it was just who I was. What I do remember, and it's strange, is that we were dusting the wood floors in my mom's bedroom when she told me. I don't remember the exact words, but I remember the floors and that that's when she told me.

My parents made me feel very secure and very loved. As a teenager, I remember some angst and telling them, "I'm going to find my real parents!"

They would just say, "Go ahead." They said they would help me find them if I wanted that, but we never did. I wasn't really ready. Since I was twelve years old, however, there was one thing I did know. I wanted to work in television broadcasting. I loved the news. It made no sense . . . In South Dakota, we had no access to Hollywood or any of the networks. My dad was a virologist at South Dakota State University, and my mom was a homemaker and a receptionist. Why would I have this desire to be in broadcasting when we were literally and figuratively so far away from that world?

There comes a time in an adopted child's life, whether it's as a teen or a young adult, when he or she looks in the mirror and says, "Who am I? I'm not like these people." I wanted to get out of South Dakota and explore, and see the world, and my family was content to never leave our hometown. It's like peeling back an onion—you don't know it until you become older and more self-aware, and you start discovering who you are, and what you like. For so many years, it was great, and I didn't feel different from my loved ones, and then I got older and said, "Wait a minute—there is a big world out there to explore."

When I was fifteen, Dad had a business trip in Lincoln, Nebraska. By this time, a dear family friend named Deb was working at a TV station in Lincoln. Deb was ten years older than me; she and her husband were friends with my older brother in high school, and she was the only person I knew who worked in television. I asked my dad if I could go with him and hang out with Deb that day at the TV station since I wanted to be a newscaster. He took me with him, and Deb gave me a tour and showed me the ropes, solidifying my determination and our friendship.

I went to South Dakota State and majored in broadcast journalism. By then Deb had moved to Kansas City, so when I was a sophomore and needed to do an internship, guess who I called? That summer I worked in the programming and news departments at KMBC-TV in Kansas City.

It was the summer of 1984, and something else had happened just eight months before. My dad had died suddenly of a heart attack. It was shocking. He went on a business trip to Chicago and died in his hotel room. We didn't see that coming, and it was devastating. I went back to college and graduated in 1986. Needing a job, and wanting to finally get out of state, I once again reached out to Deb, my guardian angel, who was now a station manager in Nashville. She told me to come down and be her assistant. She said, "You'll get out of South Dakota and at least be working in the business." I spent six months there and then went to New York and spent six months there. I was on my way—exploring the country and working in broadcasting. In 1987, I moved to California and got a job at Columbia Tri-Star Television doing research and marketing for some of the most popular shows on television.

Now I was living the life that felt right to me. I met my husband, and we got married in 1992. This was when I began to feel the need to peel back the onion. This was when it hit me that these questions of who I was and where I came from had to be addressed. At first, I told no one of my plans, not my mother and not my husband. I reached out to Catholic Social Services to get some non-identifying information. I was only looking for health information at that point; I wasn't ready for more than that. They told me there was nothing health-related in the file, and they couldn't help. It was a dead end.

Four years later, my marriage was falling apart, and the need to find out where I came from returned full force. I called the agency and asked, "How difficult is this? Do I have to hire a lawyer, or what will it take to get my file?" To my surprise, this time they said, "Send one hundred dollars and a self-addressed, stamped envelope, and we'll send you your file." I was stunned, and sprang into action.

In July of 1997, that envelope landed on my desk. I sat and stared at it. This was it. Until this point, I had spent my life not knowing anything about the story of how I'd come to exist and what transpired in those first seven precious months of my life. Now, once I opened that envelope, there it would be. This was so personal; it went so deep that I didn't even tell my husband. I told no one, afraid of what I might find. I finally opened the envelope.

On the cover sheet, there it was. The names of my birthmother and my birthfather. That explained my Irish eyes and fair complexion! It showed she already had three daughters. I wondered if they knew about me. There was paperwork from her first divorce, as well as handwritten letters from the priests at CSS saying there was money needed for clothes and medicine for me as I spent those seven months in foster care. These letters also urged them to make a decision about me since I was going to get attached to these foster families, and they needed to get me placed permanently. I found a response from my birthparents that said, "Don't worry, you'll get paid, and if you have any questions, please contact Paul at KTHI-TV in Fargo."

I stared at the letter. That blew me away. KTHI-TV? My birthfather worked in television? This was life-changing. Flashes of old thoughts of nature versus nurture . . . it just hit me. For thirty-three years, I'd been on autopilot, assuming this is who I was, this was my name, and now, in a heartbeat, things slowly started to make sense.

I was again peeling back that onion as I went through the file; I went from knowing nothing to knowing all this. Seeing her handwriting, knowing that she was going through a divorce when I was conceived. The handwritten letters back and forth between her, Paul, and CSS in those seven months also explained the delay in placing me in a permanent home. North Dakota law stipulated that "a baby born during wedlock is presumed to be the legal child of the married couple [her and her ex]—and relinquishing of parental rights would then be the responsibility of the presumed parents." In a letter from Paul, he stated it was imperative that Charlotte's former husband not become aware of their problem. This man was not emotionally equipped to handle the news. The welfare of the baby was foremost, but preventing a disaster was also essential.

Notes in my file also indicate that to avoid her ex-husband knowing about this situation, just prior to my birth, she inquired with CSS to have me placed in various foreign countries: France, Sweden, Mexico, British Isles, or Canada.

Paul was in television, and there were names of the various foster parents. I went from zero to a hundred in five minutes. And then, I saw the name Paul and Charlotte had given me . . . Beth Lynn. My heart stood still. My adoptive parents named me Mary Elizabeth, but to this day, my family calls me Beth.

This was monumental for me. I needed to take a breath. There was so much information, and I needed to process. I told no one and did nothing. It was time for a divine intervention from my guardian angel. Deb had a brother who was going to adopt, and she came to Los Angeles for a business trip. We got together, and were talking about her brother's situation with the adoption. I had told no one about the file, but out of the blue, she asked, "Have you ever thought about getting your file?"

I paused, then replied, "I just did."

"*What?*" she yelled.

"Deb, you of all people, will not believe this—my biological father worked at KTHI-TV in Fargo!" I told her about my one attempt to call the station he had worked at to find out if, somehow, after thirty years, he still worked there or if anyone knew him. No one recognized his name.

Deb said, "I think I know the people who used to own the station! I will call and find out if they know him."

A little later, she called me and said, "Are you sitting down?"

I held my breath. She had not only had a huge influence on my career, but now she was helping me find my birthparents. And apparently, we were starting with my birthfather!

Deb had gotten more information than she ever thought she would. He had been a news director and on-air talent at that station in Fargo! This stopped me in my tracks. He had been doing exactly what I had grown up wanting to do—a broadcaster and news reporter. This was life affirming. At twelve years old, I wanted to be in television, and I find out my birthfather was doing just that.

But that wasn't all. Deb had found out he had moved to Georgia and had gotten a job at another TV station. She had called the station to see if he was still there. They told her, "No, he doesn't work here anymore, but he has a restaurant in town, and here's the number!"

Now we were really peeling back the onion. I knew nothing, then I knew the names, then I knew the locations, then I found out about his job, and now I had the number where he worked. I dialed the number and heard his voice for the first time on the restaurant's answering machine.

Deb was about as excited as I was. She told me that, coincidentally, she had a former nanny who lived in that town. When she inquired, the nanny indicated that Paul was like the mayor—everybody knew Paul. Deb and I decided we would make a trip to Georgia. She would reach out to Paul and inquire about having a party for her former nanny at his restaurant.

The next thing I knew, I was on a plane to Nashville to begin the adventure of my life. At this point, I told my husband everything, but he wasn't interested in coming with me for this pivotal moment. I met Deb, and we drove eight hours to Georgia to meet him for lunch and check out the restaurant. As we were driving, she asked me what I wanted to know about him.

I thought for a minute and said, "What are his hobbies, how's his health, things like that," not knowing how she was going to work it into the conversation. I was driving and as nervous as could be; I even missed our exit.

We pulled up next to a green Cadillac with the name of the restaurant on the license plate. I was parked next to my birthfather's car! I can't remember the moment I saw him—it's a blank. Deb introduced me as her friend, Mary, from LA, and we sat down in the restaurant and proceeded to have lunch and talk about the party and the TV business. In the process of planning this trip, he and Deb had talked a lot about broadcasting. For the first time in my life, I was sitting across from somebody who shared the same flesh and blood.

When Deb got up to use the restroom, he asked me again what my name was and where I worked in Los Angeles. I hesitated, wondering if he had known who adopted me. We weren't trying to deceive him; we only thought if we had told him prior to the trip, this might not have happened. I only used my first name and told him I had this fantastic job at CBS. He offered to give us a tour of the restaurant's facilities. He was lovely, and at one point during the tour, we both laughed at something he said. I was immediately aware that we laughed exactly the same. He then offered, "I'd love to give you a tour around town."

I remember I sat in the back seat, and all I could look at was the back of his neck, and boy did his hands look like mine as they maneuvered around the steering wheel as we drove around town. This was so poignant to me. There I was . . . inspecting every detail of this utter stranger. I'm crying again now as I remember that feeling. He had brown eyes. I always wanted brown eyes.

As we continued on our tour around town, Deb would proceed to nonchalantly get answers to the questions I had: "How's your health?" and "What do you like to do in your spare time?" All the things I wanted to know. We were all getting along famously, and out of the blue, he took us to his home and introduced us to his wife. I didn't know what to think at first. Could this be my biological mother? We quickly surmised that it wasn't, and we walked around and visited, never expecting to spend all that time with him. He was really such a nice man.

And then we were back in the car, driving back to Nashville. I was crying, sobbing like the rain that was pouring down. It was raining so hard you could barely see the road. They were tears not of sadness but of relief. After thirty-three years, this had been a life-changing day. It was such a relief to know he was a good guy.

Then Deb asked a question I never expected. She said, "I have to ask you . . . How do you feel about abortion now?" I was shocked; it was a question out of the blue. I have always believed that a woman has the right to choose. "Deb, I would never judge what someone chooses to do with her body, but I thank God my birthmother didn't choose that."

I was in shock for a while. I was now not the same person I had been for the first thirty-three years of my life. For the first time in my life, I had a better idea of who I really was. Back in LA, I needed to process, and I was distracted by the unraveling of my marriage. But I couldn't let go of the fact that Paul didn't know I was his biological daughter. We had a really nice day with him, and he deserved to know. Deb and I discussed it, and soon afterward, Deb set up another meeting with him and flew down, bringing papers from my file that were proof that he was my father. They had lunch, and then she said, "Paul, I need to tell you something. That girl that was with me . . . I have every reason to believe she is your biological daughter."

He looked at her and said, "If her birthmom was Charlotte, then yes, that was me." Then he went on to tell her, "I can't do anything about it now. My current wife doesn't know about Mary Beth. It was a very stressful, difficult time back then. After we gave Beth up for adoption, Charlotte and I got married, and I moved her and her daughters to Georgia when I got the job, and then she left me for somebody else. I ended up taking care of her girls. But nobody knew about Beth. I cannot open that can of worms with my family, and I can't have a relationship with Mary Beth."

He then gave Deb one more bit of information. He said, "I wanted Charlotte to have an abortion, but she wouldn't do it. She was Catholic."

That was sobering.

Four years later, I had to finish what I started. I had more of the onion to peel away, and once again, my guardian angel made it happen. Finding my birthmother would prove to be more difficult. Deb knew a private detective, and finally we decided to try that route. We provided him with all of the information in my file, and to my surprise, it wasn't long before he provided us with her current married name and address. I didn't set my expectations too high, but I wrote a letter to her saying that, as an adoptive child, I was naturally curious about where I came from and just wanted to know about medical history and basic information. She never wrote back.

One day, I just picked up the phone and called her. I figured I might as well give it one more try. I asked, "Is Charlotte there?" and she replied, "This is Charlotte."

I caught my breath and said, "This is Mary Beth. Is this a good time?"

And she said, "There will never be a good time."

Ouch.

She went on to tell me she had received my letter and that she could have nothing to do with me. That the man she was married to didn't know about me. That she had a defibrillator, and her heart couldn't take the stress. She was cold and distant but began to warm up a bit as I asked her questions.

"Are you petite like me?"

"Yes."

"Do you have blue eyes?"

"Yes, and that's the first thing people notice about me."

"Me too."

I told her I had a great life, a great career, and amazing people who had always taken care of me. She asked if I'd met Paul, and I told her I did, and that I'd gone into the same field of work as him.

Finally, I asked her if she would send a picture of herself to me.

"I hate getting my picture taken."

"Me too."

She said she would send a picture if I sent her one of me, but followed that by saying she wanted no more communication after that. To my surprise, I received a letter from her indicating that she was having three pictures made, and they would be sent to me in a few weeks. It also stated that she would write on occasion to tell me about her life. She said, "If it makes you feel any better, I want you to know I did think about you often, but I'm sure you had a better life than what you would have had."

I gathered up a baptismal picture (there are no pictures of me prior to seven months), a picture of a six-year-old me in a ballet tutu, and a third, of the present day. I wrote a note, thanking her so much for the picture exchange. I added that I wouldn't contact her anymore and that I had a great life.

Lo and behold, a few weeks later, I did get the pictures from her and a letter. Not a friendly letter. The sentiment had changed. It basically said, *here's what you wanted, hope you're happy, don't contact me again.* But there was something important in the picture. The dress she was wearing in the picture matched the dress I wore to my senior prom. Same color, same style. We looked exactly alike. Same eyes, same cheekbones, same lips. And that was it. I'd heard her voice. I'd got the picture. End of story.

I have quite a few thoughts about adoption and its place in my life. I have never discussed this journey of finding my biological parents with my adoptive mother. It's so private. I never wanted to hurt her feelings, so I haven't really told her about Deb's and my search, or our findings. I've alluded to things, but we've just never gone there. But having examined all of my history for this book, I think that will change. Each year that she gets older, and frailer, I worry that I haven't told her how much I appreciate everything she and my dad did for me. I never got a chance to tell my dad . . . I was young, and it took time to realize the sacrifices they made, the unconditional love they have given me. They chose me, and I would hate for her to never know that I realize this and what that means. As a result of this examination, I am going to take the file with me on my next trip back home, walk her through each page, and most of all, thank her.

I have come full circle. I found my birthfather, and he seemed like a good guy, and I was thrilled to have learned of the career he had chosen. I found my birthmother. I am thankful that we shared pictures. I have my answers to many questions. My birthparents have given me more reasons to wonder about nature versus nurture and the gift of unlocking some of the mysteries in my life: the dress in her picture, his career path. And the most important thing they gave me, the thing that Deb so presciently suspected . . . they could have gotten rid of me, and he wanted to, but she chose to give me the gift of life.

To adoptees, I would say this: go find who you are. Do not take rejection from your birthparents personally. That's their life, their prerogative. Their rejection doesn't make us any less worthy of living a complete and deserving life. The rejection isn't about us; it's about them. In my case, the fact that she didn't want to see me isn't about me. That's about her. That was probably guilt, and having to unearth the terrible things she was going through at that time. Both of my birthparents said the exact same thing: I can have nothing to do with you because that was a very stressful, difficult time.

To adoptees and birthparents, I would say that we deserve to know who we are and where we came from. That is our birthright. We need an anchor. If we don't, we're like a dandelion that someone has blown into the air, with no tether.

And to adoptive parents: let your children go find themselves. Let them do the work to become whole. I understand the fear that you have. You have loved and nurtured them. Don't take it personally. It's not about you. It's about our natural curiosity. Where did these blue eyes come from? Was it just a coincidence that our dresses were alike? Why did I want a career in broadcasting? And there's one more thing adoptive parents need to hear: thank you.

I also want to thank my guardian angel. My story proves they really do exist.

CHAPTER TWENTY-NINE

EMBRACING ACCEPTANCE

Jennifer Outerbridge

Jennifer is a stay-at-home mom from Naples, Florida. She has three children, and she and her husband have been married for nine years.

Writing about this, and actually putting words to how I feel, is harder than I had expected.

My name is Jennifer, I'm twenty-nine, and I'm an adoptee. I always knew I was adopted. I couldn't pinpoint a specific time I found out; it was just a part of me. I clearly remember being in first grade telling my friends on the playground how I was adopted when I was ten days old. I always thought it was pretty cool and unique.

I grew up yearning for information on my birthparents. What did they look like? Did I have any siblings? Growing up as an only child and not looking much like my parents, those two questions were a big part of my childhood. I never resented their decision to give me up; I just felt curiosity. As I grew older, I learned my parents had met with my birthmom, Anne, on a few occasions before my birth. Ten days after I was born, I was left at a church by Anne and then picked up by my parents.

I love my parents very much, but we are very different from each other. I moved out when I was eighteen due to the conflict at home. I later told my mom I wanted to try to find my birthmom and see what she was like. She then handed me a piece of paper with her full name, address, and phone number written on it. I found out that years prior, my birthmom had reached out to my mom and gave her all the info I'd need if and when I wanted to reach out after I turned eighteen.

Anne's information sat on my nightstand for probably a month or two before I could even consider making that step. I remember having so many questions and fears that had crept in as I got older. I wanted to know why. I wanted to know what she looked like. Did we act similarly? I wanted to know if she missed me, if she thought about me. I was never angry. I just wanted to know and understand. I ended up chickening out and had my boyfriend (now husband) make the first phone call. I can remember pressing my ear so hard up to the phone hoping to hear her voice. A younger girl answered, who I now know was my half-sister Emily. Anne wasn't home, but my boyfriend was told she would call back. So, I waited. She called back later that day, and that's where my story really begins.

We absolutely, completely hit it off. We laughed the same, we ate the same weird food combinations. We were and are so incredibly similar, it is simply amazing. Something that stood out to me during our first conversation was she kept telling me over and over that I was conceived in love. I found that strange, because to me, an eighteen-year-old girl, I was just like, "Okay that's nice." I later found out that she was adopted as well, and her birthmom was too. I was the third generation of adoptees. And I later joined their ranks as the third generation of women pregnant at nineteen, baby at twenty. Anne had found her birthmom in her thirties and was told she had been conceived by rape. She was also told her birthmom had been stabbed and left for dead, and her attacker later died in prison. Now, ten-plus years later, the validity of what Anne was told is being questioned, but that was a lot for her to take in at the time.

I immediately flew to the state of Washington, where Anne lived. I finally was reconnected with the woman who gave birth to me and loved me enough to let me go. We had an amazing, overwhelmingly beautiful visit. Our first day together, we got matching tattoos. I also visited the hospital room in which I was born and met her nurse friend who helped deliver me.

On that trip, I also learned my birthfather was a gay man who had a tough childhood with the suicide of his father and his own inner demons.

My favorite big moment of my adoption story was seeing Anne for the first time in the eighteen years of my life. The small, amazing moments were reconnecting and learning about each other, and how eerily similar we are.

For me, being an adoptee has not always been easy. There have been issues between all parties involved. I have learned to keep my relationship with Anne very separate from my parents, especially my mom. I think my mom resents and is jealous of the relationship I have with Anne, even though it's more of a close friendship than anything else. It is by no means a mother–daughter connection as much as a deep understanding of one another. We just get each other in ways others don't.

My birthmom has dealt with a lot of the same struggles that I have in the past (anxiety, depression, alcoholism), and we are very similar in many ways, so I feel that maybe my mom feels threatened by all of that. For me, finding out my biological family has had a lot of the same struggles that I have had was, in a way, very healing for me. Growing up, I always felt something was off in my head and never understood why. I know now that genetics played a huge role in all of that for me, which was comforting to find out. My mom still doesn't accept that genetics play a role in my makeup.

My parents, and especially my mom, have made it clear that they don't want to know about my birthmom, including how she is doing and how our relationship is going. I never mention my birthmom's name in front of my mom because she gets very worked up about it if I do, and it's a shame. I feel it's a secret I have to keep and something I can't talk about with her.

I've learned a lot from my experience that I could pass on to others. To adoptive parents: accept where your child comes from and all the imperfections that come with his or her situation. That acceptance is something I truly wish I had in my life. My birthmom has been a part of my life for over ten years, but it is something I still can't talk about with my mom. As an adoptee, I don't know how it feels on the other side, but I do know that the way my mom has handled my meeting Anne, my relationship with her, and our similarities has been a secret struggle that eats at me. They both love me dearly, and I wish the roles they play in my life were embraced by everyone.

My parents did, however, do a lot of things right that I would suggest to others. When I was growing up, before I reconnected with my birthmom, the fact that I was adopted was never a secret; they never kept that knowledge from me. My parents told me stories at bedtime of how my birthmom loved me so much, she gave me to my parents. I never felt any anger toward my birthmom for giving me up. I also never felt unwanted, which I feel is such a delicate issue with an adoptee. I remember telling my friends stories in first grade about how I was born with a different name and could have a whole clan of sisters and brothers. I remember feeling proud of my story from a young age and thought it was pretty cool.

I think being as honest as appropriately possible with your adopted children is super important. Obviously keeping certain things from them until the time is right is also important. I couldn't imagine not knowing I was adopted as a young person and later finding out my parents kept that important information from me. Being adopted or adopting a child is beautiful, and although sometimes difficult, no one should feel ashamed or have anything but positive feelings about the adoption.

Although sometimes challenging, at the core it means I have a huge amount of people who truly love me. My kids have more grandparents than most, and in the end, I know where I came from.

CHAPTER THIRTY

FULL CIRCLE

Nanci Done-Nemeth

Nanci is a fifty-three-year-old entrepreneur currently residing in Park City, Utah, with her husband, Dave, a national television host. Nanci and Dave have been together twenty-two years and raised three children in a blended family household. Now empty-nesters, they enjoy the outdoor lifestyle with their dogs. Her birthmother is Judy Craig, whose story is featured in Chapter Eight, and her adoptive mother is Helen Trauntvein, whose story can be found in Chapter Twenty-Four.

If someone asked me, "What does being adopted mean to you?" my first answer would not be what one would expect, especially because I've experienced the most amazing love from my adoptive mom, and we have a wonderful relationship. I've also been lucky enough to have my birthmother come into my life, and we are all very close. But my adoption experience is complicated, and I would have to answer that being adopted also means a loss of what could have been, confusion over what is, and paralyzing uncertainty of where I fit in the world. It means incredible trepidation on how to navigate the future. Crippling fear of losing my "new" parent, since it happened before. Chronic agitation and despair about the probability of being abandoned again. Habitual conviction that I'm not "good enough" and being in a monophonic state of being "abandonable."

A riddle for you: I am one of thirteen children. I'm the oldest child, the youngest child, and the middle child, but I grew up an only child. Who am I? This is an answer for which I have been searching for much of my life.

I was born in May 1964 in St. Petersburg, Florida. It was determined I would be placed for adoption before my birth. My birthmother never held me, saw me, or knew anything about me other than I was a girl, and she was told I had a birthmark. From what I would learn, more than four decades later, she understood I would be immediately placed in a loving, adoptive home. After all, I fit a highly desirable placement request as I was a female Caucasian.

Immediately upon my birth it became clear to the doctors something was terribly wrong. I was diagnosed as having neurofibromatosis ("elephant man" syndrome). It was also determined I wasn't expected to live for long. I became a ward of the state and deemed "medically unadoptable." My birth records were sealed.

I would spend almost six years in several foster homes. Not all would be nurturing; in fact, some were quite neglectful. Due to this neglect, I wouldn't learn to speak until I was almost four years old, and I missed critical developmental milestones along the way. My last foster home would be a loving, nurturing environment. While with this family, at the age of five and a half, it was determined there had been a huge mistake in my diagnosis. I did not have neurofibromatosis. The doctors were not certain of what I did have, but they knew it wasn't that. My status was then changed to "medically adoptable." The time had come. I would need to leave the current foster home since they had just had another baby, and now they had too many children in the home. "Last one in is first one out." That was me. Due to my age, my condition, the uncertainty of the ongoing medical care I would need, and the amount of money I was costing the state, they were desperate to find a medically suitable placement for me, and the odds of finding a new home were not favorable.

A lady named Helen worked at All Children's Hospital in St. Petersburg, Florida, as their nursing administrator. Her friend Ida was my social worker and would often take me to the hospital for my care. Ida shared with Helen my plight, and Helen casually mentioned that maybe she could adopt me. Helen had not been looking to adopt a child; she was single, and the state of Florida did not allow single-parent adoptions or guardianships at the time, so she was denied.

Helen then moved to Utah to take a position with Primary Children's Hospital as their nursing administrator. Meanwhile, finding a placement of any sort for me was proving to be almost impossible. The state of Florida then determined if Helen could get Utah to conduct the adoption, they would award her guardianship of me. She did. Helen was awarded the first single-parent guardianship given by the state of Florida. Our adoption would be finalized in Utah, two years later. My name was changed, and I was issued an amended birth certificate, which had no identifying information. Due to a typewriter ink issue, it had always been unclear as to whether my birthday was in March or May. They decided to go with May. It was as if I was handed a completely new identity at the age of seven.

Helen is a kind, wonderful, nurturing, religious, loving woman who has a huge heart. This incredible human being has certainly earned her angel wings. She also was a single woman, never married, had no biological children of her own, and had a demanding position in the hospital with heavy responsibility. Out of necessity, Helen would end up being at work much of the time, and I became what was known at the time as a "latchkey kid." I would spend an incredible amount of time alone.

When Helen received me, she received only me and none of my belongings. I literally came to her with only the clothes on my back. There were no pictures of me before the age of five and a half. No information regarding me and my childhood, my past, or where I had originally come from. Nothing. The theory at the time was to sever all ties with any previous life, including any tangible items, and I was to have zero contact with those involved prior in my life. This was believed to promote forward attachment to my new life by extinguishing any memories of my earlier years.

As most can surmise, I was already through my critical developmental stages (birth to five years old), and this was not the most appropriate way to handle my transition. This, combined with so many previous developmental traumas, would set me on a personally destructive path in my pre-adolescent, adolescent, and early adulthood years. My earliest memories (good and bad) were etched in my mind forever, and I was already wired for who I was going to be. I had grown to know my last foster family as my family and had an extremely difficult time understanding why, in just one day, they were no longer my family and I was suddenly with a new mom, in a new state, with absolutely nothing to call my own.

We had yet to learn how incredibly pernicious this severing would be moving forward. I would end up having a very difficult time in school, and I struggled with self-esteem, relationships, anger, rage, depression, anxiety, substance abuse, and failed marriages. My health was always a concern, yet I was so fortunate to have multiple, perfectly timed surgeries and treatments that were critical to my physical development. My mother provided me with access to the best in medical care. In my twenties, I gave birth to, and raised, my own daughter. After her birth, I was unable to have any more children.

I was a very scared, insecure, and emotionally fragile child. I held on for dear life to my earliest memories, probably because, at the time, they were my only and closest connection to where I had originally come from and so desperately wanted to find again. It was an obsession from my earliest memories to find my "mommy." My social worker knew very little about the circumstances surrounding my birth. She had a possible name of my mom, but it was so common it sounded made up. It was believed that my birthmother already had a child when I was born and that she was not married and unable to care for me. It was also rumored she was from up north and had come to, or had been sent to, Florida to hide the pregnancy.

My new mother seemed to understand my sadness and obsession with finding my birth family, and on the day of our adoption, she promised me she would do everything in her power to help me find my family one day. Helen would fulfill this promise thirty-seven years later. From time to time in my adolescence and early adulthood, we would try to find them. Research methods being the limited way they were back then, we would quickly run into brick walls and abandon the search. A lot of my drive came from the fear that if the stories were true and I did have a sibling, that sibling might also be in the foster system. My mother also knew of the strong desire I had to find the last foster family with whom I had been placed, since I had such an attachment to them. Over the years, we would send many cards and letters to the Department of Welfare in Florida requesting them to be forwarded to my foster family. None of these were ever answered.

I was living in Rochester, New York, working for Eastman Kodak when I was twenty-nine years old. One very cold, dreary November day, I received a phone call from my mother. She asked me if I was sitting down. She proceeded to tell me she had just received a phone call from Alice, my last foster mother. Alice and her husband, Glenn, were up in their years and selling the family home, the home in which I had lived. Alice had come across the one and only letter that had been forwarded to her from the department of welfare that had been written by my mother, Helen. In that letter, Helen had told her I was doing well and was adjusting to my new life, and she had thanked her for everything she had done for me. Since my mother never married and still had the same name, Alice called information for her number.

As would be expected, this news was welcome but equally frustrating. The anger and resentment I had felt for so long, and suppressed, came back with a vengeance. Why now? Where have you been all these years? Why didn't you ever respond to my cards and letters? Why didn't you keep me?

The flood of emotions hit me like a freight train. It would be months before I summoned the courage to return her call. Little did we know at the time, this would begin a very painful, albeit necessary, cycle of healing.

I returned to Florida a short time later to meet them as an adult, and see and be in the home of which I had such etched memories. I met all my foster siblings again (six of them), and they shared stories about our time together. To this day, all of us foster siblings remain in contact. Alice shared so much with me about myself, how I was when we first met, how I came to be with her family, and what they did to try to help reverse much of the damage that had taken place from the previous years of neglect. She said when I had come to them at the age of three I couldn't or wouldn't talk or cry, and how sad it was that I didn't even know my own name when they got me. We would later learn the previous foster family was deaf and dumb, so they never spoke to me. I wasn't held, and no bonding had taken place.

Over the next couple of years, we talked, exchanged letters, and continued to bond. Alice and my mother would as well. Sadly, a few years later, Alice was diagnosed with cancer and, ultimately, lost her battle. Soon after, her husband, Glenn, fell ill and passed as well. One of the greatest gifts I was afforded was to be by both of their sides to care for them in their final days and be with each of them when they passed. It was a true blessing and serendipitous that I could be with them at the end of their lives when they were so instrumental in my early life. The full impact of this reunion on my life would not unveil all its treasures for another ten years.

My desire and emotional need to find my biological ties, and answers to my nagging questions, was increasing exponentially, as were concerns for my health, and it was becoming critically important to obtain familial medical history. I was now married again and in a healthy relationship in which there was much love and support. I finally felt safe enough, and emotionally mature enough, to take on the search to find my biological roots. With the help and support of my adoptive mother and a referral to a great attorney by my recently found foster brother, I hired a lawyer to help with the search. We tried several avenues with the courts, and we were denied each way we turned. We were informed the only way the court could even consider opening my sealed files was if I had reason to believe I was marrying a sibling, or if I had a medical issue that could result in death.

In July 2008, my husband and I were living in Tampa, Florida. I was forty-four years old. I was once again hospitalized for a severe case of cellulitis, a dangerous infection I often get because of my underlying condition.

I became so ill, in fact, that they ran additional tests to see what else could be wrong. I woke up one morning to an oncologist sitting on the side of my hospital bed telling me we needed to talk. He proceeded to tell me it had been determined I had multiple myeloma (a cancer of plasma cells) and that it had spread to the point that it was not treatable. His recommendation was I should get my affairs in order. I was informed I had, in the best case scenario, four to six months to live.

As you can imagine, this news was shocking. I had a hard time accepting this news. Most would call that denial; I call it instinct. I immediately called my attorney to give her the news and asked if we now had what we needed to petition the court to unseal my records.

This latest development with my health caused a rapid ascent in the court involvement, and within days, my petition was granted and my records were unsealed, on one condition: I allow my attorney to make first contact should we locate the biological parents. Within days, I received my original birth certificate as an attachment in an email.

You would think I would just rip into that information. After all, I had only waited my entire life for this day. It caused me great pause. I was taken aback by my hesitancy in opening this email. My answers were all in there, just a click away. Would this change everything? Change everything about me, who I believed I was? My biggest concern, and what caused so much heartache for me, was what this might do to my dear, sweet, amazing mom, Helen. Even though she has always stood by my side in support of this, would it break her heart? Would she be threatened? Most of all, would it change our relationship in any way? I ached with such empathy, and, at the same time, with such desire to finally have my answers.

I chose to call my mom first, to let her know I had it but hadn't opened it. We talked about what it meant for me and what it meant to our relationship, and she reassured me this would only bring us closer and affirmed how desperately she wanted this for me. After we hung up, I still didn't open it. I sat with my feelings for a while, and I chose to journal about these feelings. I did this because I knew I would never feel this way again. I would never live in the unknown again. It was all I knew, and as much as I wanted this, I had become afraid of what I would learn. A lifetime of desire was being trumped by a new fear: What if I can't find her? What if she has already passed? What if she doesn't want to meet or talk to me? What if I was a product of rape? The "what-ifs" were paralyzing.

What seemed like an eternity passed from the time I received the birth certificate until I opened it. The feeling of seeing that birth certificate for the first time is almost indescribable. For the first time in forty-four years, I felt legitimized. I felt normal. I felt like I counted. Baby Girl Williams was the name on the certificate. My birthday was indeed in May. My mother's name was on it. And, yes, it was the name that it had been rumored to be over the years.

My joy turned to despair. I had looked for this name for thirty-plus years. But there was one little detail that would turn out to be the key to finding her: a middle name. The search began.

Remember how I had mentioned earlier that I had a hard time accepting the news that I had multiple myeloma? I argued with the doctors that they had to have made a mistake. I was convinced they were confusing my symptoms and test results with my underlying health issues. Deep down, I was convinced this just couldn't be true. I received the diagnosis of multiple myeloma on a Friday. I received my original birth certificate the following Wednesday, and on the Friday of that same week, I received a phone call from my oncologist with an apology. They had misread the reports and misdiagnosed me with multiple myeloma. There was a lot of confusion because of the rarity of my underlying condition, and that I absolutely, unequivocally, did not have multiple myeloma. While extremely grateful with this recent development, it was hard to deny the coincidences in my life. My original medical misdiagnosis at birth had cost me a chance at a family, and now, forty-four years later, another medical misdiagnosis had given me the possible opportunity to find my own family.

Six weeks later, through a series of serendipitous events, I would find her. I had her phone number. I was sitting in a Target parking lot when I found this latest information. Again, paralyzed with the fear of the unknown. The what-ifs were screaming in my head. The fear of the ultimate rejection . . . being rejected by her twice . . . was almost more than I could handle.

I've always been impulsive and not one to have much patience. This would test my impulsivity more than any other thing in my life. Although I was the one to find the number, I followed protocol and allowed my attorney to make first contact.

What happened to me physically while this process took place was something I didn't expect. I couldn't walk, talk, or think a cohesive thought. I shook uncontrollably and made myself sick. I had multiple panic attacks and cried. How I cried! I hadn't been able to really *cry* since I was five years old.

Strangely enough, the awareness that I was now able to cry gave me the strength to compose myself and begin to face whatever would be the outcome of this phone call. My attorney finally reached my birthmom on the phone, and although she was quite shocked that I had found her, she readily admitted that she was the birthmother, and she welcomed contact. She then told her husband, for the first time, about me. I'm so grateful for his support to her. His response was fantastic: "Great! I can't wait to meet our new daughter."

A time was scheduled for us to talk on the phone. She lived in Ohio, and I was in Florida. My husband is a television host, so we were always documenting everything with video. Knowing how emotionally difficult this was for me, we agreed to set up a camera to capture everything so I could focus on the phone call and not on trying to remember what was being said. Nobody knew at the time if this would be the only phone call or contact we would have. I was fearful she would be angry with me and tell me to never contact her again. I had no idea what to expect. I was hoping for the best but was trying to be prepared for the worst. I had a list of questions for her, just in case this would be our only contact.

The camera was on. I placed the call at our scheduled time. The phone rang, and rang and rang. No answer. There was no answer! I went into complete physical and emotional shock. I wasn't prepared for her to not answer. My worst fears were realized. I was being rejected, again. A flood of my worst memories, anger, hurt, and abandonment issues hit me all at once, and I curled up in the fetal position hoping to die.

Approximately twenty minutes later, the phone rang. It was my birthmother, Judy. She was so apologetic. She had been at church involved in a volunteer project and lost track of time. While I was stunned and confused as to how you could lose track of time with such a significant life event, this soon gave way to a most incredible conversation. We shared, we cried, we laughed. She let me ask every question I ever wanted to ask. She shared the hows and whys, who my father was, and that I had an older brother and a younger brother. She apologized. I would go on to learn she had no idea about my health issues or that I had not been adopted as an infant, and she certainly didn't know about me going into the foster system and what transpired there. We set a date to meet in person. That day just could not come soon enough.

I flew to Ohio, where she lived. We had agreed I would stay for three days. Three days turned into more than a week. We looked at family pictures. We told stories. We laughed. We cried. I met my little brother (six years younger), who had not known anything about me until I found my mom. I talked with my older brother (eighteen months older than me), who of course hadn't known about me, and we set a time to meet and ultimately have become very close over the years. I met my grandma, aunts, uncles, and cousins. Judy's husband welcomed me into his heart and home and proudly calls me his daughter. It was unbelievably emotional and wonderful.

There's a great saying: "You don't know what you don't know until you know you didn't know it." What I didn't know up until that point in my life was what it felt like to look into the eyes of where you came from. I didn't know that by doing so there was a different type of depth, a feeling, a sense of belonging, an awareness of wholeness. This was an unexpected delight. It was almost as if I had entered another dimension of being. No one knows they have this if they haven't missed it their entire lives. Me, my biological mother, my stepfather, my brothers on this side, and her entire family continue to bond and grow our relationships. We are all close, and I'm so humbled and grateful for this in my life.

My birthmother was very forthcoming about her shortcomings and whom my father was and how I came to be in this world. The only people that were aware of her pregnancy were her, her mother and father, and the biological father. She was then sent to live with her grandparents in Florida to give birth and return to Michigan to never mention it again. My biological father had been involved in legal proceedings with her for financial assistance in regard to the pregnancy, so he was aware that I had been born and placed for adoption. My mother had saved these court documents all these years. She gave these documents to me, and so began my search for my father.

I would find him six weeks later, and, as with my mother, my attorney made first contact. He did admit he was the father and asked for a few days to process the information. It appeared he would be open to contact but just needed time. A week later, we would find out he would refuse contact. I was heartbroken. I had, of course, always wanted to find my mom, but I also had such a strong desire for my "daddy," particularly because I had never had one. This news was more devastating than I had expected it to be. He did give my attorney the medical history with which I was legally entitled. If you have never believed in serendipity before, you might now. The incorrect diagnosis I received that would set the wheels of discovery in motion, as you will recall, was that I had multiple myeloma and only had four to six months to live. We would learn from my birthfather that his mother had died a few years earlier from a rare cancer, multiple myeloma.

I would learn I was the oldest child on his side. He married shortly after my birth and went on to have four more children, all of us eighteen months apart, succinctly. A few months later, I would meet a brother and a sister on that side. When their mother learned of the meeting, they were forbidden to have further contact with me. You can imagine the feelings I would wrestle with again in regard to rejection and abandonment. It was so painful.

Despite his adamant refusal to meet me and the fact we lived more than two thousand miles apart, three years later I would arrange circumstances, in a covert way, so I could meet my father. We had a couple of drinks together, watched the last game of the World Series, talked, laughed, and joked for a couple of hours. He even introduced me to his beloved dog, Gus. It was magical. However, to this day, he doesn't know it was me he met. Meeting him, on my terms, was what I needed to allow myself to accept what is and move toward healing this part of me.

This brings us full circle. You would think having found my answers, and the missing pieces of me, would have been all I would need to move forward in life and let the past be in the past. In so many ways, you would be correct. It's critically important to understand, finding one mother did not replace the other mother. Quite the contrary. It only strengthened the love and bond I have with my mother, my adoptive mother, Helen. The strength, courage, and the ultimate show of love she had for me, her daughter, to do everything in her power to care for my every need—physically, spiritually, and emotionally—called upon her to make huge sacrifices and risk losing everything to help make this happen for me. She had no guarantee that my loyalty wouldn't shift, that I wouldn't leave her for what I had desired for so long: the connection with my biological roots. I know she must have lived in so much fear, and I can't imagine the pain and tears she went through in the process. She exhibited the love, strength, and courage of what it is to be a mother. She put my needs ahead of hers and fought a valiant fight to make my dreams come true. My depth of gratitude, respect, and undying love I have for her is immeasurable. Every child should know and experience this kind of love.

There is a moment I cherish more than any other in my life. This moment was when my two mothers met for the first time. To watch them embrace and cry, and to hear each of them thank the other for the part they played in my life, was surreal. The respect they showed each other was awe-inspiring. I can't imagine the courage it took for each of them to come together, for me. They remain close. They talk and exchange cards and letters. To this day, they each refer to the other as my mom, and I call them both mom, and everyone is perfectly okay with this. I love them both beyond measure. My loyalty is not divided. They are, both, my mothers, and they both have the perfect place in my heart, my soul, and my life. My only wish is that Alice, my last foster mother, had still been with us to be included in this special reunion.

I started life with no mother, father, sister, or brother. I had no one to love me, and ended up loved like no other.

CHAPTER THIRTY-ONE

MEANT TO BE

Heidi O'Neil

Heidi is a former college soccer player and lives in Charleston, South Carolina. She is a financial advisor, is married, and has two daughters.

My adoptive parents were not able to have children. Between problems both my mom and dad had, they couldn't conceive. They decided to adopt, and their first child, my older brother, was born to a twenty-year-old who was most likely drug addicted. They had previously arranged to adopt the girl's baby, but she went into premature labor ten weeks early. The baby was born deaf from complications of the drugs or too much oxygen. He also had to be on a feeding tube for a few months and had many other issues, including being learning disabled. The doctor asked my parents if they could take a completely deaf and disabled child.

Prior to any of this, my mom had a heart for the deaf and actually worked with deaf children. She felt it was meant to be for her to receive a deaf child, and they accepted my brother. I was born two years later, and this family became my family.

Enrique, my birthfather, was a college All-Star baseball player when he and his girlfriend, Beth, conceived me. Because Beth was a Christian, she carried me to term and opted for adoption. I grew up knowing I was adopted, and they couldn't hide that from me since I was five feet, two inches tall and had jet-black hair, and my adopted parents were over six feet tall, and I didn't look a thing like them.

Ours was a closed adoption. I grew up not terribly curious about where I came from. I wasn't that child who wanted to search out "my roots." I was satisfied with my status as an adopted child, and I loved my parents. As I grew up, I was a difficult and rebellious teenager. I was also very athletic, a high school soccer star, and I would sometimes dream about who my birthparents might be . . . Was my dad a professional athlete? Was my mom a model in New York? Funny, it turned out she did model, and he was a baseball player. But I wasn't that curious about searching, even though I was so different from the rest of my family.

Beth did a search to find me and waited until I was eighteen, of legal age. She then called my dad, who, at the time, was separated from my mom. My dad called me and told me to sit down, then proceeded to tell me that my birthmother wanted to meet me. He asked me if I wanted to meet and then told me that Beth and Enrique had gone on to marry and I had two full-blooded brothers.

This was unexpected, and exciting! I was a pretty typical self-absorbed teenager, and at first was like, "Wow, yeah, that's cool," but since I hadn't had the desire to search, this was all new, and I didn't have the anticipation or the maturity I would have had if I'd been the one who searched.

My dad flew Beth in for the weekend. We got to the airport early, and I watched her come through the baggage area. Even though I look more like my birthfather, she was twirling her hair the exact same way I do . . . I knew she was my birthmother.

It was exciting, and my dad thought it was really great. Mom was more cautious. She hadn't been involved in the decision to fly Beth in since the call came to my dad, and we acted so quickly. Mom thought it was too much too soon. She was very insecure about her place, intimidated by Beth, and thought we could be moving too fast. In retrospect, I think I didn't think that through. I didn't consider how this might affect my mom. I was a pretty typical self-focused young athlete, about to go to Penn State on a soccer scholarship, and didn't really think through how this would affect anyone but myself.

We had a great weekend and made a plan to meet my siblings in Wisconsin two weeks later. In retrospect, it was too much too soon, although I *loved* my time with my brothers. They were so much like me . . . We looked alike, we had the same chocolate-brown eyes, the same sense of humor. We had similar mannerisms. It was fun to be with people who were so like me.

I left Wisconsin feeling satisfied with the visit. I didn't anticipate how much this relationship would mean to Beth or my siblings. It was great to meet them, but I was good with how things had gone and was fine with leaving it at that for now. I now had to concentrate on college and soccer. Again, typical teenager.

Beth started to call a lot, more and more, and before too long I was feeling very smothered by her. Life wasn't easy for Beth at that time. She and Enrique had gone their separate ways, and she was having prescription drug issues. She would call and demand that we see more of each other, that she wanted me in her life, and rather than seeing it from her perspective, it scared me. Her calls became more frequent, almost blaming me for the failures in her life. It was very confusing and difficult for me. She began to ask me for money, and finally, my dad said no more. I didn't know this, but my parents contacted Beth and offered to put a down payment on a salon business she had told me she wanted to buy. There was one caveat: she could no longer contact me if she took their offer. They then told me not to reach out anymore, that if Beth wanted to contact me, she would. I loved her, but since I was struggling with everything anyway, I just accepted it. Beth never told my brothers what had happened, or how she suddenly was able to afford the salon. Contact stopped. They thought I didn't want a relationship, and I figured they felt the same. It would be ten years before we would reconnect.

I got married, and then at age thirty-one, when I was pregnant with my first daughter, I felt a longing to be back in touch. It was around that time when I found out the whole story, and I decided I wanted to get back in contact. I wanted to reach out to my brothers and explain what happened, and I yearned for forgiveness and love to replace the distance. Beth was upset, not understanding why I hadn't reached out to her, even though I explained that I thought the relationship had been cut off by her. My siblings were initially cautious but then happy to be back in touch, and we've enjoyed a close relationship ever since. We get together as often as we can living half a country apart. It hasn't been all roses with Beth—she still asks for financial help from time to time, and my husband doesn't want me to get sucked in again.

Because my brothers are full-blooded siblings, I also have a relationship with my birthfather, Enrique, and have ever since our reconnection. We are very similar and are on the same page about almost everything. I really enjoy noticing small ways in which we are alike, and it's the same with my brothers. One of my brothers is the godfather of my second daughter. We all get together for weddings and family activities, and as former athletes, my birthfather and I enjoy going to baseball games and watching soccer on television when we are together. We see each other about twice a year. My relationship with him is definitely a sweet side of my adoption story.

My dad is very supportive of all that's gone on and thinks it's all terrific. One thing looking back, I wish Dad had let Mom be a part of the decision-making process. She was left out of that, and I know it was all very hard on her. But I know God let it all happen the way it did for growth and learning. Now that I am an adult, and have children of my own, I am more understanding of both my mother's and Beth's reactions. My mother loves me and just wanted the best for me, and she wasn't sure the events that were occurring were in my best interest. I get that, and wish I'd been more understanding and sensitive to her position. And Beth . . . I can't imagine not having one of my daughters, and I'm sure in her desperation to have a relationship with me, and with all the issues she was dealing with, things just got out of control.

I think an important lesson from my story is to let the child dictate the pace of early contact, and let him or her proceed at his or her own comfort level. At the same time, if the child is the one searching and desiring a relationship, I would say he or she, too, must let the birthparent take the lead on when, where, and how much.

I feel like everything has unfolded the way it was supposed to happen . . . that it's all meant to be this way. The old cliché "God works in strange ways" is so true, especially in adoptive relationships. The funny thing is, even with the negative aspects and the break that took place, I wouldn't change my story. First, I've learned so much from all that went on. More importantly, if Beth had held back and waited for me to search them out, I can't say for sure that any of this would have happened. I might never have known my brothers. I was perfectly content with being adopted, and perfectly happy with my family, and I might never have done a search. And now I can't imagine my life without my birth family. Everything that happened with my adoption story happened in its own time, and for its own reason. I would recommend that anyone starting an adoption journey should remember that, and give time a chance. Things are meant to be, and sometimes it takes a while to see that.

CHAPTER THIRTY-TWO

THE TIES THAT BIND

Julie Braga

Julie is forty-five years old and lives in Redlands, California. She is married with two children.

I am an adoptee that was given up for adoption in 1972. My birthmother got pregnant with me in Minnesota. She decided she was going to place me for adoption, and she didn't want anyone to find out. She had an aunt who lived in California, so she told her parents that she was going to go visit that aunt and uncle. Once she was in California, she contacted the maternity home and made the arrangements to live there and prepare for the adoption. She told her aunt and uncle about the pregnancy, and they agreed to keep her secret. They would pick her up from the home from time to time for visits. There were conflicting stories about whether or not she revealed my birthfather's identity in the home's intake paperwork. I always assumed she told him about me, and I just found out he never knew.

Once she had me, she went back to Minnesota, got married, and had five beautiful children. She kept me a secret from her family for thirty-three years. When I first found her, she didn't want to meet because no one in her family knew about me. She did eventually tell my maternal grandmother and her husband. I have spent time with both of them, and I feel good about both relationships. My maternal grandmother kept the secret for many years and was happy to finally meet me.

My birthmother eventually filed for divorce from her husband after thirty years of marriage. Once she made that move, she was open to a relationship with me. She told my five brothers and sisters about me on my birthday, the fourth of July. I still have the email she sent me to tell me about her decision. She told her siblings, and it was quite a shock to them all that their sister was able to keep this secret for so many years. I think she is happier now that she let this out, and from what I hear from her sisters, she is a better person now.

I have always known that I was adopted, and my adoptive family has always made me feel special. The story I was told was that my birthmom was very young and could not take care of me, so she gave me to a family that could not have kids. My adoptive mother has always told me that I was an answer to her prayers and she was so lucky to have gotten me. My story is unique, and I have never felt shame about my situation. I was blessed to have a loving family who supported my search to find my birth family.

I found my birthmother through the internet and with the help of a woman who was also a birthmother at the same maternity home as my birthmother. I later assisted this birthmother friend in finding her birth son as well. We call each other our Earth Angels.

You probably need a little explanation about her and how my search transpired. I was actively looking for my birthmother on the internet, and I came across a registry that allowed you to register to look for a birthmother or child that was placed. I found someone born at the same home as me, and I printed the person's information out. I also found someone that gave birth around the same time, and I printed that woman's information out, too. I contacted the birthmother, and we started to email and exchange stories. She gave me her son's birthdate, and I was able to provide her with her son's adoptive name. They were reunited because of me! What a small world!

She then returned the favor by helping me write letters to find my birthmother. I visited the home where I was born in Los Angeles, and they gave me my non-identifying medical information. I received a tour from the nurse who actually helped deliver me. She gave me a copy of my records and neglected to cover up one area where my birthmother's last name was written. Mind you, that nurse was about to retire in the next few weeks, so I feel she was trying to help me out.

My Earth Angel wrote letters trying to find her friend who was with her in the California maternity home in 1972. We got many responses, and my birthmother was one of them. It took her many years, however, to allow me to have a relationship with her. I think she was getting her life together and needed to work out some stuff. I have had multiple reunions with my birthmother now, and I just traveled to Las Vegas last February to pay her and one of my sisters a surprise visit. We do this from time to time with the help of my aunt from California.

I must be very cautious with my adoptive mother since she can be sensitive. She supports my relationship with my birthmother; however, I can see deep down that it hurts her a little. She seems to want to make sure I will still be the same daughter. When I go visit my birth family, I call her daily to assure her that I'm still here for her. In the end, the relationship between my birthmom and adoptive mom is satisfying for me, and I'm glad that I did what I did. They both are thankful for each other and what they each did to bring me into this world. I turned out to be a good person with no real issues. I think it's important that I had my Earth Angel friend to help me along the way. She is very helpful in understanding this process since she is a birthmother as well.

My triad was completed when my two moms had lunch together in October 2006, and it was quite stressful for me. I guess it was just my worries about all the feelings involved and wondering if it would go okay. It did, and I feel the loop was closed so they could say thank you to each other. I currently have a birth aunt who would like to meet my adoptive mom, and I'm working on that. It will just take time to find an opportunity to get it done.

One thing that has always been important to me is a blanket I received from my birthmother when I was placed, and I have it to this day. I think knowing that she cared enough to send me with the blanket made me feel special. I would recommend to any birthmother to include a memento like that when you place your child. I always had that blanket growing up, and when I married, I had a snip of the blanket on my wedding dress. When I brought my two kids home from the hospital, they were wrapped in that blanket.

That blanket that my birthmother sent with me in 1972 meant so much. It gave me the ability to touch something from my birth family, and that was so helpful for me. In that same way, for my entire life, I was always looking for something physical, something I could touch, from my birth family. Before I met my birthmother, I had a friend happen to travel to the state where she lived, and I asked her to please bring something back for me. She brought me a leaf from a tree and a postcard, both of which I still have to this day. I had a coworker who was from my birthmother's state, and I was in heaven just talking to her. Once I got to meet my birth family, they gave me gifts, which I cherish. I have a dishtowel that my birthmother made, and I can't bring myself to use it. I want to have it in perfect condition and would never allow anything to happen to it. I also have a scrapbook of my journey, and I keep every letter and picture. Someday I would love to share it with my birth family. Much like a missing piece of the puzzle of my life, those objects hold a special place in my heart.

Adoption is complicated. There are positives as well as negatives. For example, on the negative side, I feel that my parenting is different due to my adoption. I have abandonment issues, so I have a hard time letting go of my adult children. I'm learning that they are adults now and I must let them live their own lives; however, it's hard for me. I also have some codependency issues that I feel are related to my adoption. I want to be there for them, and sometimes I go overboard. After I found my birthmother, I came to realize that she, too, is codependent, and I can see where I get it from. I go to meetings to help me with this issue, and I've discussed the things I've learned in the meetings with my birthmother.

Also, I find myself always trying to be good and do the right thing. That's okay, but I am fearful that I will be rejected if I am bad. I have a son with issues, and my codependency was a problem with him and my first marriage. I tried to fix all of my son's problems, which goes back to being good and fixing everything so I will make everyone happy. With the help of therapy, a loving husband, and Al-Anon, I have a pretty good grasp on the abandonment issues now. I'm learning in Al-Anon that I need to take care of me, and let my son take care of himself. That's a work in progress.

On the other side, there are many positive results because of my adoption. Obviously, my wonderful adoptive parents and family, and the fact that I had a loving home is one. Also, my adoption has helped me to relate in a special way to my nieces, who are from my second husband's family. They were raised by their grandparents, and from time to time their mother comes out for a visit and rocks the boat. The two different sets of parents are confusing to them. I feel like I have been able to help them when they have issues since my adoption situation is similar; I also have two different families that I want in my life. I have a strong relationship with one niece, and I know it's because of our similar experiences. I think they can relate to me with the confusion they experience in trying to please everyone and be respectful.

Of course, my relationship with my friend who helped me find my birthmother has been a very positive benefit—she is the reason for my success. She came into my life hoping to find her son, and I was hoping to find my birthmother. We both accomplished our goals and have built this long-term relationship along the way. We celebrate our friendship and still use each other for support when life gets difficult. I truly believe that she was placed into my life by God, and she is my Earth Angel. She travels to see me when she visits her son's family, and seeing her warms my heart and recharges my spirit.

Thank you for giving me this opportunity to share and help others on an adoption path. It has allowed me to take a deeper look at this issue so I can better understand my own thoughts and feelings. I have grown a lot through my experiences, and I do have some suggestions for others. One is to try to be as sensitive as you can to insecurities that your loved ones may have. I know my adoptive mom struggles a bit with my new relationship with my birthmom, so when I discuss my birthmother with my adoptive mother, I try not to refer to her as "Mom." I call her by her name. When I reference my relatives from my birth family, I refer to them as, for instance, Mary Jo's sister, not my aunt. I do see them as my family now; however, I don't want to hurt any feelings. My adoptive sister (adopted from another family) is also very emotionally vulnerable, and I have to use caution when discussing my birth family with her. She has not been as fortunate as me in finding her birthmother, and I sense jealousy.

This past Christmas, I had my adoptive family over to my house, and I felt the need to remove the pictures of my birth family from my refrigerator. It's almost as if I have a second life outside of my life. I spent Christmas Eve with my birthmother's sister this past year, and it was my first holiday with my birth family. I was honest with my adoptive mother, and she was happy for me. I also try to be sensitive to my birthmother's feelings and do things to let her know she is important to me. For example, she named me Mary Louise at birth, and when I send my birthmother cards, I add "ML" after my name.

I also wanted to mention the way the adoptee can get treated by the family of the adoptive parents, although I'm not sure my experience happens in all adoptions. My sister and I were both adopted from different birth families. We were raised in extended families that sometimes treated us as "not real blood." When our grandparents died and it was time to split up the personal belongings, we were told we were not blood family members and were denied certain items that they felt needed to be kept "in the family." We were very close to our grandparents and spent many holidays with them. We felt we were even closer to them than our other cousins living out of state. Such coldness was hurtful and hard to take at the time. I did get to keep a few cups, bowls, and tablecloths that we had used during our visits to my grandparents, and I will cherish those items for the rest of my life.

I also experienced this "not real blood" feeling when I filed for divorce from my first husband. My ex–mother-in-law decided to have a talk with my kids to discuss my adoption with them; they were four and six at the time, and I was not present. She basically said that she was their "true" grandmother, and my adoptive parents (their grandparents) were not really their true blood family members. This was pretty hard for me to take just after a divorce; however, I did go to see a counselor, and I overcame the insensitive cruelty. I think she was fearful of not seeing them so she was desperate to try anything to keep them in her life. From an adoptee perspective, these are wounding memories, and if someone could use this example to know what *not* to do, that would be great.

Another thing is, when it comes to deciding whether to search for your birth family, you have to realize you can't really live with "what could have been." Try to live with the understanding that "all you can do is try," or you will live with regret for not doing the search. I questioned whether my birthmother would reject me or my adoptive parents would be hurt. I had to do the search for myself, and, luckily, my adoptive family supported me. Also understand that in this process, everyone needs to deal with issues when they are ready, and sometimes you must wait. My birthmother wasn't at the right place when I first found her, but in time . . . in the *right time*, we had our reunion.

From an adoptee's perspective, something I would say to prospective adoptive parents is that I wish I did not have to live a second life and could feel comfortable discussing my birth family openly with my adoptive family. I think that allowing an adoptee to share the new connection openly is helpful. Sometimes I try to walk on eggshells to protect everyone—again, coming from my need to make everything all right, and this is something I need to work on for myself. I'm going to try to test the waters in the next few months to see how it goes and to see if it's just me or if my family really does get upset. I think a lot of it is me—the fear of being abandoned if I rock the boat.

I wish that I could know my birthfather. I have no hard feelings toward my birthmother; however, she never told my birthfather about me. Now forty-four years later I sometimes wish I could know more about him. At this point, it's not fair to contact him, and it would be hurtful to my birthmother, but that doesn't stop my longing to know him.

When I spend time with my birth family, I have learned that I must sit back and just absorb the family dynamics. I can't really step in and act like

I am a family member who has been there for the last forty-four years. There are some situations where I feel more comfortable and others where I just need to sit back and observe. There are some in my birth family who are welcoming me with open arms, and there are others who don't really want to know me. I can't push.

I think people make assumptions that adopted children are not wanted. I would challenge any assumption that no one wanted me. I was truly blessed to be placed with a family that longed for a child, and they loved me like their own. Later in life I found my birthmother, and now I have twice the love.

You cannot expect anyone to understand unless they have traveled the journey. I tell my story, and sometimes I must guard my feelings. I have just learned the hard way not to always share my story with everyone. I get a lot of people's opinions such as, "Your birthmom needs to tell you who your dad is," or "That must have hurt your adoptive parents." I know in my mind I did what I was comfortable with, and I would not have changed anything.

CHAPTER THIRTY-THREE

MOMENTS IN MY LIFE

Sharon Dahlberg

Sharon has three adult children and a three-year-old grandson. She's in a long-term, twenty-one-year relationship with her man. She is a real estate pro working on her creative bucket list in Orange County, California.

I am an adoptee, now sixty-two years old. My adoption occurred privately through a Los Angeles attorney. At three days old, I went home with adoptive parents, their first child. When I turned three, I had my first recollection: my birthday present was an adopted sister. I remember going to the hospital on my birthday to pick her up and bring her home. She was two days old. I guess I already knew at that time that I was adopted. I remember standing in the back seat of the car peering over the front seat to see my mom holding my baby sister. Those were the days before seatbelts or child car seats. We had a bag full of glass baby bottles that were rattling next to me on the car floorboard, sent home with us from the hospital staff.

In my early years, we attended functions with other adoptees at a place similar to the Society of Adoptive Children. They had Halloween parties and Christmas parties, and somewhere deep in a storage box, I have a few group pictures. We were told that there were many other children that had been adopted. My mother always made sure we knew about families that had adopted children as we grew up. It was presented as normal. We had a two-book set for children regarding adoption. One talked about animals being adopted and the second one about humans. There never was a time when I didn't know I was adopted. I was always comfortable with the idea, and being a compliant child, it was not an issue. It was a fact, and I had a loving, caring environment in which to grow up. It was no big deal to me.

When others asked "How do you feel about being adopted?" I would shrug my shoulders. I didn't seem to have the words to express that it was just normal. Nothing special. Now I know I was lucky that I had a great up-bringing in a loving environment. Adoption never was a negative.

Many years later on my adult birthdays, I wondered if my birthmother would think about me on that day she gave birth. I assumed that she did, as nine months is a long time to carry and think about a child. I also tell myself that placing a child for adoption has to be the greatest unselfish gesture of love. I still believe it to this day. Whatever her circumstances, I'm sure it was emotional. After having three children of my own, I know how special adoption is.

At times in my life I would overhear a conversation and interject my opinion. When I would hear people talking about how sad or frustrating it was to not get pregnant, I would say, "Has adoption been considered?" Boy, I remember some of the looks and responses I received: surprise and shock. I followed up with, "I am adopted, and it is a wonderful alternative to consider." I planted the seed, whether or not they were ready for the information.

I had a couple of friends who I heard were going to adopt. They adopted one girl, and then another one a few years later. Both babies. I decided to give my friends the adoption books I had grown up with. I wanted them to have this beautiful set of books to help them make the lives of their daughters as wonderful as mine had been.

I'm sure there were times when I was a little rebellious child or teen-ager, when I may have said things about adoption that I would regret if I remembered them. They weren't important, or I'm sure I would remember them clearly. At age fourteen, I was five feet, nine inches, blonde, Norwegian looking, and super skinny; my dad was five feet, eight inches and bald, and my mom was five feet, two inches with fair skin and black hair. Clearly, I didn't fit in or look like anyone in the family.

One of my greatest joys was when I had my children and they all looked like me. I never realized how much I wished I had looked like someone. Experiencing family resemblances turned out to be so important to me and has brought me great pride and joy. I probably have overdone it with photos because I think it is so significant to me. My children share body features and mannerisms, and I greatly enjoy the positive feelings I get from those similarities to this day.

Having no information about health issues that I may have inherited has brought concerns as I age. As my adoptive parents aged and passed, I knew that their health challenges wouldn't be mine. I am proactive in my health testing because I have no history. I also realize the importance of documenting my health history and my children's father's and his parents. This would be an essential piece of advice I would offer to birthparents: make sure your child has this data.

I quietly began to research my roots in my twenties since my sister had done so. My adoptive parents were hurt by her searching, so everything I did was private. I didn't want to hurt them because they *were* my parents. Classifying them as birthparents or adoptive parents didn't matter; they were just my parents, my mom and dad.

I began by requesting the state of California to provide me with what information they had. I received a sheet of paper with the mother's info on the left side and the father's info on the right. Basic info, no names, but age, hair color, hobbies, state of birth. It was fascinating, and I felt like I had "my papers," like a pedigree dog. I knew about my birthparents. I knew my heritage. I knew that I had two older sisters and that my parents couldn't afford another child—the reason for the adoption. My adoptive parents must have known some of this information because music and sewing were encouraged, and those were listed in the hobbies section.

My sister told me she had been given her legal adoption papers, so I asked my parents if they had any papers on my adoption. They said they didn't think so. I tried again at age twenty-nine, since I was getting married, and asked if they could check the safety deposit box since I needed my birth certificate anyway and wondered if there were any other relevant papers. I already had a copy of my birth certificate, but I thought this would be a good reason to have them check the box. My fiancé and I were having dinner after church at a restaurant with my parents, and they just handed a few envelopes to me. I opened them and quickly closed them when I realized what they were and tried to act nonchalant. Another moment in my life I remember extremely well.

I finally had their names, which meant I could begin my quiet search for my birthparents. Upon a closer look, I found information that differed from the state info and the adoption legal papers. The age of my birthmother was ten years different. Later, I also found divorce records that showed three children born after me, but the birth date of one child was too close to mine to be of the same mother. This stopped me cold, and I began to wonder.

Were my papers real? Or was I the child of a mistress, or even a plural wife, since my birthmom was from Utah? Or perhaps other children were actually adopted?

I have endless thoughts about the possibilities, and I haven't proceeded any further. My sister did some searching on my behalf and told me that both my birthparents have died, but I still haven't proceeded with requesting copies of death certificates. On my to-do list is to find out if I really do have two older sisters as the adoption papers state, and investigate the possibility of three younger siblings as found in the divorce records.

I let negative thoughts enter my search at times, which kept me hesitating to move forward. What if I find them and they are not good people? What if . . . ?

I should have forged ahead in my search to find and meet my parents. I do regret that. I'm now going to begin to search more diligently to find siblings. I've sent my DNA for ancestry testing to 23 and Me recently. My reports are consistent with what I received from the state of California many years ago. I have hopes that it might develop into something more informative. My life story is still unfolding.

Birthdays that end in a zero or a five remind me to pick up the search, realizing that the window of opportunity is passing. Back in the day, you used microfiche and "snail" mail to send off a letter to request a document, with a blank check "not to exceed x$," and you had to wait for six, eight, or twelve weeks or more for a response. I realize that the digital age brings easier ways to access information.

The reasons I searched were my curiosity and need for my health history. My sister has different recollections of our parenting and had different reasons for searching out her birth family. She also discovered sad news. Her mom died in childbirth a few children after her birth, her father committed suicide, and she had a sister that had cerebral palsy and was institutionalized. She searched and found that sister and saw her for a few years before she passed. She found a brother, and his family came to stay with her during some hard times, and I recall hearing they had to be asked to leave. She did find some other relatives with whom I believe she keeps in touch.

There are many things that are beautiful in life, if you focus on the positive . . . the bright side. There are always issues to bring you down, but an optimistic attitude helps you face those issues and find the silver lining. Giving a child the basics of life—food, shelter, clothing, and love plus guidance—helps them when they become adults, and that kind of providing for others feels right. In my opinion and experience, adoption is beautiful.

CHAPTER THIRTY-FOUR

LOOKING THROUGH
THE LENS

Perla Alvarez

Perla was adopted from Colombia at the age of six. She grew up in New Jersey and Naples, Florida. She is now twenty-four, and was recently married in New York City. She and her husband just took a travel sabbatical, with one destination being Colombia, and they have now moved to the Emirates.

My adoption story started later than most. I was adopted by a wonderful family living in Galloway, New Jersey, when I was six years old. I was beyond lucky; the chances of being adopted past the age of one drop drastically every year the child ages. Because I was six when I became part of my family, it was no secret to me, or anyone who knew my family, that I was adopted. Thinking back, I appreciate how liberating it was to know where I came from. I knew my story and, more importantly, I was so proud of having been chosen by my family. As I grew up, I openly and proudly told everyone that I was adopted, and my family encouraged my openness.

This story of my past and even my adoption process is an integral part of my identity. What I didn't realize until recently is how inherent to our family identity and family structure my adoption was and continues to be.

In any family dynamic, each person has their place. A typical, if cliché, structure could include the spoiled youngest child, the middle sibling who feels slightly neglected, the bossy oldest sibling, the strict mom, the dad that is a pushover, and so on. These family structures inform how families act and interact, regardless of whether we acknowledge them verbally or not.

Being a youngest, adopted daughter brought its own set of issues when figuring out my place in this family. To some degree, my family and I coded my place in the family as simply the adopted daughter. Not to say that I wasn't first and foremost a daughter, but at some point, I think we forgot to talk about how the adoption affected my sense of identity and place in the family, causing some tensions between everyone concerned.

Upon reflecting on my family and our early days together, I realize that a range of behaviors was viewed through a lens of adoption rather than through the lens of a nonadoptive family dynamic. Instead of seeing me as acting out and whining when I wasn't getting my way as a function of my being the youngest child, it was seen as an overreaction brought on as a result of my rough childhood. Whatever the case actually was, these perceptions and this lens of adoption through which we saw our family dynamic, our interactions, and our lives affected us and how we behaved around each other.

I also realize that this misperception wasn't entirely one-sided. Whenever I would get in trouble for things that any parent would reasonably be upset about, I would think that I was getting in trouble because I was adopted and not because I was acting inappropriately. It was a way for me to avoid responsibility for my actions. While in some ways, it made me feel better and ensured that I didn't have to deal with my own misconduct, there were some rather dark moments in which I truly felt excluded and alienated from my family because I was viewing my life through this adopted-child lens. I knew about my adoption, and even though it was a celebrated aspect of our family, the fact that I was adopted became a lens through which I experienced the challenges of growing up, even when they had nothing to do with being adopted.

The lens of adoption affected my sister as well. Recently, as we were having brunch, we spoke about some of her childhood frustrations about me getting to do whatever I wanted to do, while she had experienced more restrictions growing up. Did I really have fewer restrictions? It certainly never felt that way to me, but for my sister, it seemed like I was given more leeway *because* I was adopted and new to the family. But was it really because I was adopted? Many older siblings feel like the "spoiled" younger sibling gets a longer leash, but the fact that I was adopted added a level of tension and uncertainty, one that we didn't know how to discuss without hurting feelings.

Although my family spoke about my adoption openly, freely, and proudly, we didn't always address the way it affected our perceptions of our familial interactions. When I acted out, was it because of my difficult childhood or because I was a rowdy child? When I felt like my parents were treating me differently, was it because I was adopted or because every child has different needs? Even if we do not discuss it openly even now, the fact that I am adopted is always there in the way I perceive my family interactions.

My family dynamic, like every family dynamic, has its challenges, but the fact of my adoption is an inescapable lens for me and for my family. It's always been something we celebrated, but it's also been something that we try to evade when it could (admittedly easily) lead to hurt feelings.

Adoption is wonderful, and I am blessed to have been adopted after many years of going back and forth between foster care and an abusive home, but being adopted as a six-year-old with memories and a fully formed personality adds to the complexity of joining a family. It adds a layer of difficulty to the already difficult task of managing the kinds of relationships you might find in any household between multiple people with different tastes and sensibilities. There is an inherent impulse to talk about adoption exclusively as a beautiful completion of a family, and that is a good impulse. However, even as there are so many moments of unrivaled joy, there are also difficult moments, and those difficulties need to be talked about and analyzed. I often felt like if I brought up negative feelings about being an adopted child, I was being ungrateful for the wonderful family that had taken me in and built me a paradise.

If I could have done away with that guilt, and expressed those emotions, a far more productive conversation could have happened, as opposed to the one that I was having with myself. My fears and concerns could have been assuaged, and my parents and my sister would have been able to explain to me the impact my addition to the family was having on them as well.

CHAPTER THIRTY-FIVE

THE COLD SHOULDER

Catherine Heath

Catherine is sixty-one and lives in New Braunfels, Texas. She's been married to Steven for almost thirty-six years, and through their many years in the military, she's lived around the world. She now works in the dental field and has three grown children and two young granddaughters. She never knew her birthparents.

I was born in February 1956 in St. Petersburg, Florida. I had always known that I was adopted, and that I had been born to a mother who had been in a home for unwed mothers. I was adopted in June 1956 by two very sweet and loving people. I also have a brother, who was adopted two years after me. My father was a minister. My mother said that my father's profession made it easier for them to adopt.

I never really knew that being adopted was something different until I was teased in elementary school one day. A mean child had said to me that my parents didn't want me and had given me away. I had a friend's dear mother say to me, "You're a very lucky girl, actually; your parents chose you out of all the babies in the world." That's really when I learned that my family was different from most of my friends.

Through the years, the questions about my adoption would come up, and I saw that it troubled my mother, so we really didn't discuss it very much. I was curious, but the last thing I wanted to do was cause her any pain. My brother had no desire to locate his biological family. My adoptive mother passed away in 1991 from ovarian cancer. In 1997, my adoptive father brought up the subject with me and said, "I think we should look for your biological mother." He knew that I had always felt a need to find out what my story was.

It was really an easy process getting my non-identifying information from the adoption agency in Florida—extremely easy, when I think back on it. Computers were around, but you didn't have the access that you have today, so I had several people helping me. My husband's family, sisters-in-law, and even my father and his companion went on a road trip to obtain some information. One of the first things I learned from my adoption information was the county and city in which my biological mother had lived.

I mentioned before that my father was a minister in Florida, and the last town that we lived in Florida was Lake City. Coincidentally, that was the town in which my birthmother and her family lived. I had lived in Lake City when I was five years old and had even started first grade there. I learned from my adoption records that I had a half-brother five years older than me. At that time in Lake City, we believe there was one elementary school, so there is a high probability that I was attending the same elementary school as my bio-brother. And there was probably a good chance that my birthmother and my adopted mother could have been standing together, side-by-side, outside that school, picking up or dropping children off every day.

I was finally able to identify my birthmother and her family, but I was never able to identify my birthfather. From the information I obtained from the adoption agency, I learned that my birthmother had married right out of high school and had a son within the first few years of marriage. That marriage did not last, and she became a single mother.

She started a relationship with my biological father when he traveled throughout Florida working for the Farm Bureau of Florida. He was not from Lake City; he was from Orange County, near Orlando. They dated for several years and became engaged. Her family liked him, her son liked him, and they were happy. She found out that she was pregnant, and they decided to go ahead and get married sooner. She left her son in the care of her parents and took a train to meet my bio-dad in Daytona Beach.

When she stepped off the train, she was met by my birthfather, his current wife, and his child. You can imagine her shock. My birthfather had decided to stay with his wife for the sake of their child. He and his wife suggested that my birthmother go to a home for unwed mothers, and they would pay all expenses. After some consideration, and concern about being a single mother with two children, she decided that was the best thing to do. She met with him one more time during her pregnancy regarding finances, but I'm not certain that he was ever aware of my birth. My adoption records gave me a first name for him but no other personal information that I've been able to use to identify him. I think my birthmother was concerned that anything he had told her was not the truth.

After locating my birthmother's personal information, I decided the best way to reach her would be to write her a letter. Again, with my father's help and my brother-in-law, I was able to obtain her address. I also found out that she was married to a prominent high school coach in Lake City. I mailed a certified letter in December 1997 and waited with anticipation for a response.

When my adoptive father read my adoption information, he was struck by the fact that my birthmother said she did not want to hold me after my birth. She was afraid that if she held me, she may not be able to give me up. My father was certain that she would have been yearning to hold me all these years.

Unfortunately, that is not the way things went. I got a call. From the caller ID I could see that it was someone from Florida, and I answered. The first words on the other end of the line were, "This phone call is being recorded. I do not want you to contact me again, and I do not want you to be a part of my life."

I asked her if she could give me any medical history, and she said *no*, she could not help me with that, and she hung up. She sounded so cold and so angry. That had definitely not gone the way I had anticipated it would. I felt rejection and sadness on many levels. I had bought into the dream that my father had, that she was probably missing me all those years, but the reality hit very hard. I realized that I must have been the deepest, darkest secret of her life, and she was not ready to share that with anyone else! I had to respect that decision, even though it hurt. I had to respect it. After all, she had given me a life, a good life, and I had to be thankful for that.

Fast forward twenty years. My husband has retired from the military, and we're living in Texas. Two of our children are married; we're grandparents now, and our third child is in graduate school. I've definitely thought of my birthmother through the years with a pang of sadness. My precious father passed away a year and a half ago. Life is ever changing.

I was watching TV alone last April 8, and a show came on called *Long Lost Family*. I watched about five minutes and suddenly felt very compelled to google my birthmother's name. I had to go get my adoption file out, because I couldn't remember exactly what her name was. When I googled her name, her obituary immediately came up. She had died on April 6. Two days prior! Her service was going to be on April 10, two days after I saw the obituary.

It's amazing how much information you can find out about a person through their obituary. I found out that her husband had been dead for many years, also her sisters and her parents. She had three children. My older brother, five years older than me, and a younger sister and brother. I decided to send flowers to the cemetery and put my full name and address on them, in case the family was curious about who I was. This way they could contact me, or at least send a thank-you note. I've received no response as of this date.

So here I am . . . trying to figure out what to do next and how to do it. I want to contact my half-bio-siblings, and I've thought that I will probably contact them via old snail mail. With technology the way it is today, I've located all of them on Facebook. My daughter, Meredith, asked me what I wanted from them. I'm not really sure what that answer is, but I don't want to not try. I don't want to have regrets. I'll never meet my birthmom on this earth. That makes me sad and mad. What a loss!

CHAPTER THIRTY-SIX

LOST AND FOUND

Virginia Johnson

Virginia is a mother of two grown children and lives with her second husband in Needles, California. She recently reconnected with her sister, who was placed for adoption at the age of five.

There's a lot to my story, but I will try to keep this as short as possible. My mother, Bonnie, had four children: my brother, David, was born out of wedlock in 1961; I was born in 1965, approximately two years after my parents married; and my only full sister, Brenda, was born approximately two years later but unfortunately passed away right after her fifth birthday. My parents separated and divorced not long after my sister Brenda was born, and we moved back to Seattle, Washington, leaving my father in Bellingham, Washington.

When I was approximately six years old, my mother gave birth to my sister Jessica, also out of wedlock. Jessica's father was a violent and despicable man and beat my mother up several times before she finally kicked him out for good. At around the time Jessica was approximately four years old, I was living with my father and stepmother. During this time, my mother was drinking a lot and not coming home for days at a time, leaving my sister, Jessica, with our grandmother, who was ill-equipped, both physically and financially, to care for her. Someone called the authorities to report that Jessica was not being properly cared for, and my sister was subsequently placed in a foster home. I moved back with my mother not long after she was granted supervised visitations with Jessica; I was allowed to attend with her.

I remember taking a city bus to a facility; once there, we would go into a room that was, from what I remember, set up like a living room, and I believe it had a two-way mirror. I believe we were only allowed to visit with her for an hour, maybe two. Either way, it was too short, since I loved my sister very much. I have no idea how it came about, but I was actually allowed to go spend the weekend with Jessica and her foster family on two separate occasions. When I was at Jessica's foster home, I was a bit jealous of her because she was living in a beautiful home and had her own bedroom, filled with wonderful toys and a beautiful bedroom set. She had several friends that lived in the neighborhood; the one who lived right next door had a heated swimming pool that I got to enjoy the two weekends I spent there.

Then one day, completely out of the blue, I was told that Jessica's foster parents were going to adopt my baby sister in a closed adoption; Jessica and I were not going to be allowed to ever see or talk to each other ever again! This devastated me beyond belief. For the life of me, I could not understand how or why we couldn't continue to be sisters; it just did not make any sense to me! I was also told that her first name was going to be changed to Wendy, which, to this day, I have never understood why. I do remember my mother being very sad and crying a bit before the news of my sister was dropped on me; then after the adoption was finalized, I could hear Mother crying herself to sleep every night for a very long time.

My mother was also very depressed for a very long time. She wasn't the only one. I not only was hurt and depressed but also cried a lot myself. Although I had been a little jealous of what my sister had at her new home, I was relieved that she was able to escape our mother's alcoholism and everything else that came with it. I was very happy that she was in a safe home with a loving family. I loved my mother with all my heart, and I hate the thought of vilifying her, but facts are facts, and they cannot be downplayed or ignored. Because of Mother's alcoholism, I was put into situations that not only were dangerous but allowed me to be molested by several men, including Jessica's biological father.

I had a horrific childhood, some parts of which I have blocked from my memory, obviously for good reason. I went through many years of counseling and came out of my situation a better person. I take a lot of pride in being the best person I can be, and I believe I became a stronger person because of my experiences.

Please don't get me wrong: I do realize that there are children who have gone through much worse childhoods than mine, and I also know that I am not perfect. I've made more than my fair share of mistakes throughout my life. But I digress—back to my sister's adoption story.

After my sister was adopted, I always kept a picture of her with me at all times, but I kept it out of sight of my mother. Mother packed away *all* pictures and any reminders of Jessica, and we were not allowed to talk about her or mention her in any way, the thought of which still brings me to tears. I never forgot her, and I *never* stopped loving her!

Throughout my childhood, I moved back and forth between my parents a lot, and every time I moved back to Seattle with Mother, she had moved to a new apartment. When I started my sophomore year in high school, I had to take a city bus to and from school every day, and every day we would pass by a building with a sign that said something like "The Children's Society." Every day I would look very hard at that building, asking myself why it looked so familiar, and every day I would rack my brain trying to figure it out.

Then one day, on my way to school, it hit me: that was where we would go to visit Jessica for the supervised visitations! I knew that Jessica's name had been changed to Wendy, and I knew that her foster/adopted parent's last name was Harkema, so I decided to stop there on my way home from school. I went inside and was able to talk to a woman there, explaining what happened with my sister and expressing my great desire to find her. The woman there told me she would look into it and asked me to stop back the following day. The next day, the woman took me back to her office and told me that she had spoken to Jessica's/Wendy's adopted parents, and they agreed that I could see her but that it would have to be in a neutral place such as a restaurant. I was so excited!

I remember asking the lady if I had to tell my mother about it, and she told me that I didn't have to, but she thought it would be best for me to be honest with her. That turned out to be a huge mistake. When I told Mother about it, she hit the ceiling; she had never been so angry with me. She went into a tirade, screaming at me that I had no business doing that, asking me how could I do such a thing to her, and saying that I had never hurt her as much as at that moment.

The next day, I stopped back by the facility and informed the lady about what had happened and that I wouldn't be able to follow through with it. This is another decision I greatly regret! After becoming an adult, I would scour the phonebook looking for any "Harkemas" that lived in that area, still thinking that is where they lived. I tried for many years to find my sister, wanting to hire a private investigator but never being able to afford one. I cannot remember why I wasn't able to go back to the The Children's Society, but I believe it was no longer there.

Then, sometime after the social networking site "MySpace" was created, I joined it and started periodically looking for my sister. I would search for "Wendy Harkema" about once every other week or so, to no avail; I was never able to find any "Wendy Harkemas" on MySpace. Later, I joined Facebook, and once again, I would periodically search for a "Wendy Harkema," but every time I would search for my sister I found nothing.

Then in January 2010, when I was in California visiting family, I went on Facebook and once again did a search for my sister. This time, I found not only one "Wendy Harkema" but three! I looked at each profile, looking at each picture very closely, and when I saw one picture in particular, my heart started racing, and I got butterflies in my stomach and a huge lump in my throat. In this one profile picture, there was a woman sitting on a couch holding a baby, and a little girl was by her side. When I looked at the woman's face, I saw she was the spitting image of my mother.

I proceeded to send a message to each of the Wendys just in case, but I was sure that this one particular Wendy was my sister. Within fifteen minutes of sending the messages, I got a response back from the Wendy I believed to be my sister, saying "It's me, it's me, I AM THAT SISTER!!!!!" Within five to ten minutes, we were talking on the telephone, and I found out that the baby is my beautiful nephew, Draven, and the little girl is my beautiful niece, Skylah.

It's still hard for me to believe that I found my sister and that she will be in my life now for the rest of my days, and I couldn't be happier. I told Wendy I *never* forgot about her and I *never* stopped loving her! She says that she remembered me and our grandmother the most. I found out that when I was in high school and our grandmother had her stroke and was in a coma, Wendy was taken to the hospital to see her and to say her goodbyes.

Right after finding my sister, I had to give her the sad news that approximately five years prior to finding her, our mother had had a major stroke that left her unable to communicate verbally. My mother understood everything people said to her and around her and could answer yes and no questions, but her brain would not allow her to form coherent words. My sister considers her adopted mother to be her mom and always called our birthmother by her first name. Fortunately, my sister was able to visit with our mother a few times before she passed away.

One of my most treasured memories is when my mother got to meet her youngest grandson and granddaughter for the first time. I know it was very frustrating for my sister to only be able to ask our mother yes and no questions. My sister told me that she had always thought about the questions she wanted to ask her if she ever got the chance. After my mom's stroke, I found all the pictures and papers regarding my sister hidden away. I had held onto them, and then I passed them on to Wendy, and I believe that I was able to answer a few of my sister's questions on our mother's behalf.

For anyone out there thinking of giving up a child for adoption or thinking of adopting a child: first, please consider getting counseling to help guide your decisions. Take into consideration everything that it entails and how every decision you make will affect *everyone* involved, especially the child.

Don't ever give up; family is everything. If a loved one was taken out of your life because of an adoption, remember that with today's technology, there are many options to help you in your search. Unfortunately, not everyone will be successful, and for a long time I thought for sure I would never find my sister, but I never gave up, and thankfully I was wrong. I used to have terrible thoughts about "what-ifs": what if she got sick or was in a terrible accident and was no longer there for me to find? I really hated those what-ifs!

Thankfully policies have changed in regard to adoptions, and closed adoptions are no longer deemed necessary for all cases. I know that my sister went through feelings of abandonment, which wasn't fair to her. After I found my sister, she told me that when she was a teenager she believed that our biological mother had given her up because she didn't want or love her, which was the furthest thing from the truth. The truth is, our mother gave her up because she did love her, a great deal, and she wanted my sister to have a better home, loving parents, and a better chance at life.

I do wish that things could have been different. Of course, I wish that my siblings and I had not been born into a home with dysfunctional parents, and that maybe my sister and I could have grown up together. Second, I wish that, back when my sister was adopted, there had been a way to keep the adoption open, at least to the point that my sister and I could have continued to communicate with each other, even if just by writing to each other. I wish that back then, the "experts" would have understood that separating us as older children was detrimental to our mental well-being. Finally, I believe all of us kids should have gotten counseling—before, during, and after the adoption—to help us all to understand why this was happening and how to deal with it.

While I do believe a lot was done wrong in our case, I also feel that the adoption, and even my tough childhood, made me a stronger, better person. At a very young age, I decided that I would never make a child go through the kind of pain and turmoil that both my sister and I went through. Also, because of my dysfunctional upbringing, I decided at a young age that I was going to "break the chain" and make sure that my children grew up in a safe and happy home, and that while growing up, they would *never* be separated, for any reason. Although I tried to make my children's childhood as perfect as possible, such is life: things are never perfect. Unfortunately, my children's father and I divorced while they were still very young, and they had a hard time with that; but they were always well-cared for, very loved, well-provided for, and were always kept safe. I'm happy to report that both my children grew up to be very upstanding and successful adults. I couldn't be prouder of them!

Finding my sister after searching for her for approximately thirty years was one of the happiest days of my life and was almost too hard to believe at the time. One of the first things that I remember my sister saying to me right after I found her was "I finally have a real sister," which truly warmed my heart. It is going on seven years now since I found my sister, and I am very pleased with how close we have become. We lived near one another for a short time, and I got to know my sister, my niece, my nephew, and my brother-in-law, all of whom I am very close to now.

Unfortunately, we live several states away from each other once again, but we keep in constant touch with each other and visit whenever possible. One of the most important things I was able to tell my sister was how truly difficult it was for our mother to sign the adoption papers. I told her about how our mother cried herself to sleep and would just break out crying for no reason for many years after making what I believe to be the hardest decision of her life. I told my sister that our mother knew she would be in a safer, more stable environment if she gave her up for adoption, and she did it because she loved her.

CHAPTER THIRTY-SEVEN

A NATURAL
CONNECTION

Chris Wilson

Chris, sixty-one, is a nurse/attorney/bioethicist in Los Angeles. She has been married to her wife for twenty-three years, is active in her Reform synagogue, and still loves Irish music.

I am an adoptee. I learned this when I came home from school in the first grade and, having heard from a classmate her version of "how babies are made," I asked my mom if this was really true. She clarified the physical aspects within my ability to understand, but she added the story of the lady who loved me so much that when she knew she couldn't take care of me, she found my mom and dad to adopt me. Having known other adoptees who were not told the truth from the beginning, I am sincerely grateful that I grew up knowing about my adoption, having been told as soon as I asked the right questions. In fact, not only did I know I was adopted, my parents went a step further. Each year we celebrated my "Gotcha Day" with a family party. To this day, I still receive an adoption day card.

Knowing that I was adopted helped me to understand why I was very different in many ways from those who raised me. I believe that I am the product of 50 percent "nature" and 50 percent "nurture." From my birthmother, I got my rebellious streak, love of music, and intellectual curiosity. From my parents I learned discipline, tenacity, service, and compassion; they also nurtured my love of learning, reading, and the arts, particularly theater. Since both mom and birthmom were "cat ladies," there was no question that this would be my destiny as well.

When I was thirty-six, I decided to find my birthmother. I first asked my mom how she felt about this, and she said that, after this long, she didn't expect that it would change anything in our relationship. So, thanks to an online adoption bulletin board, I found an investigator who eventually located my birthmother—in Hawaii!

I had been told that my birthmom was Irish because "that's what it said on the papers." My parents, who were not Irish, celebrated their "Irish girl" as best they knew how, and I wondered sometimes if I was one of those Irish babies who was shipped to a US family by the nuns. Upon receiving her address, I wrote to my birthmother, and when I returned home one evening, there was a message from her on my answering machine, so I immediately returned her call. We spoke like two people who knew each other well—there was a feeling of family from that very first call.

When I asked about my Irish heritage, she paused and hesitatingly said, "Well . . . actually you are Jewish!"

She explained that when I was born, she knew I was going to be placed with a family who was not Jewish, and she did not want me to suffer from the anti-Semitism she herself had experienced. At that point in her life, she had an Irish stepfather and was at times using his last name; her explanation was simply, "Well, it seemed like the thing to do at the time." I assured her that, as a lawyer in a predominantly Jewish law firm, I was actually quite excited to share the news with my colleagues.

Our relationship continued, and I learned that she had been seventeen and on her own, and had become pregnant with me through a brief relationship with a significantly older man. She was headstrong and fiercely independent, just like me. That made sense, since things had been a little rocky between my adoptive parents and me due to my rebellious nature. It truly wasn't them—it was me.

For instance, I tested my adoptive parents when I decided to move out of the house at sixteen. I didn't leave all at once, just started staying away and moving things out a little at a time. One day, when I had my stereo system under my arm, my mom said, "Are you moving out?" and I replied, sheepishly, "I guess so."

I credit them for *not* forcing me to come home. A few months later, by Mother's Day, I had my mom over for dinner at my shared apartment and made spaghetti. Things got better from there.

The reality is that I had graduated from high school and was chomping at the bit to have an adult life. I worked as a nurse's aide on the weekends while I went to nursing school during the week. It was an example of a basic personality trait that came from my birthmom, who was also a rebel.

One of the side benefits of our reconnection is that I have been welcomed with open arms into her huge extended family. Although she is now gone, I am blessed to have known her and continue to be grateful for my connection to the other family members. I have learned much about the family tree, including the patriarch from Ukraine and matriarch from Belarus who came over from "the old country" at the turn of the twentieth century. There was even a published book about "Mama" and "Papa," and the author, my biological great aunt, greeted me with a copy on our first meeting, saying, "Welcome to the family. Here's your book!"

And what a family! There are actually two strong branches of this family tree, since "Papa" married twice. But it doesn't matter what branch you are from: if you are a cousin, you are a cousin, and that's that. Fortunately, one of the cousins lives nearby and has hosted lovely gatherings, events in which I have had the opportunity to meet many other members of this extraordinary family. What has also been wonderful is the interest that my mom has taken in my learning more about my family of origin. She met my birthmom shortly after I located her and has enjoyed a concert given by one of the cousins, who is a professional singer. Now in her mid-nineties, my mom has expressed that she is glad my life has been enriched by these amazing folks.

I have three words of advice for adoptive parents and that are: *tell the truth*. I am forever grateful that I was told of my adoption as soon as I asked about my birth. I have known others who found this out much later in life, and it forever changed their relationship with their adoptive parents. An adoptive parent is very likely to have a child whose personality is very different from theirs. I realize that this can happen with biological children, too, but in my experience, there are more similarities between parents and biological children than just physical features. Because of this inherent difference in cases of adoption, it's important to be upfront about the reason why. I know it sounds like a fairy tale, but really, in my case, the honesty avoided any major "issues."

Having "two moms" never even felt strange to me: I had two grandmothers, and multiple aunts, uncles, and cousins, so why not a mom and a birthmom? My primary motivation to find my birthmom was based upon what my mom told me—that she loved me very much and wanted me to have a better life. If this was true, how could I not seek her out to let her know that, yes, she chose good people and I turned out just fine. Well, of course, except for that teenage hippie rebellious streak that resulted in my leaving home at sixteen ... but I now know for certain that I came by that naturally.

CHAPTER THIRTY-EIGHT

UNCONDITIONAL FORGIVENESS

Johnnie Ware-Barnes

*Johnnie is seventy-six years old and a retired purchasing agent. She is origi-
nally from Shreveport, Louisiana, and now resides in Plano, Texas. She
and her husband, Earl, a chemist, were married thirty-four years before his
death in 1995. She has four adult children, four adult grandchildren, and one
great-granddaughter.*

My birthmother was a pregnant single teenager. She was told by her mother
to not bring me home after giving birth at the local hospital. According to
her, her mother's suggestions were to abandon the baby at the hospital or
leave the baby on the sidewalk.

Instead, my birthmother confided her story to a nurse, requesting her to
ask around to see if there was anyone she knew who wanted an infant. The
nurse knew that my adoptive mother-to-be wanted a child, so she explained
the dilemma to her: that this teenager was in trouble, as well as her newborn
infant.

My adoptive parents immediately went to the hospital to see me and visit
with my birthmother. My birthmother had only two requirements: 1) Do
you have electric? 2) Do you have an inside restroom? My adoptive parents
answered "yes" to each. This was important because my birthmother lived in
a rural parish in Louisiana and did not have either of these accommodations.
Although I go by Johnnie Ware-Barnes now, at birth I was named Mary
Lee Gordon, "Gordon" being my birthmother's last name. It's one of many
ironies that my husband's mother was named Mary Lee Barnes.

The legalities were dealt with, and we were discharged from the hospital,
but no family was there to pick up my birthmother, so my adoptive parents
took her to her aunt's house, and the three of us went to our home. I cannot
imagine the feelings my mother had exiting the car without her child—her

child riding off with strangers because she could not take me home. It would be almost twenty-seven years before she would lay eyes on me again.

In my opinion, being adopted means "I was chosen!" And as happy as I am that I was adopted, I must admit there were some mistakes made, and many lessons learned. For one, I believe my adoptive parents should have told me earlier that I was adopted. I was twenty-five years old, married, and had three children when they finally told me the truth. There had been whispers in our neighborhood when I was growing up, but I shook them off as rumors.

As an adoptee, my advice to others in this same position would be to meet your birthmother and birthfather if you are interested and they are willing to do so. I wanted to know from whom I originated. I wanted to know what they were like and whether I looked like them. My adoptive mother was very instrumental in connecting me with my birthmother. I am grateful to this day for her help, even though my connection with my birthmother was not always rosy. My adoptive parents were always there for me.

I experienced many issues with my birthmother once I found her, but I don't regret doing the search. Along the way, I witnessed my birthmother's lies more than once. Once I found her address, I sent her a certified letter, one only she could sign in order to receive it. The letter was mailed and received, and she signed the return card, but over two weeks passed with no response. I finally called her. She seemed surprised, which was not what I expected, since I knew she had gotten my letter. I also thought she seemed excited, but she blew it when she asked, "What color are you?" referring to my skin tone. I was a bit taken aback but also so glad to hear her voice, so I responded that I was "a caramel color," not mentioning how I felt about the question. Months later, I put two and two together that she had asked the question because she was going to try to pass me off as her present husband's daughter.

My birthmother continued with the lies, and she even tried to label my adoptive parents as kidnappers. She told stories about sending them money for me when I was in college, and so on. All lies. I think her stories stemmed from her resentment that they had reared me to be an independent lady with compassion for others. I did get a lot of negativity from my birthmother, and I believe if she had been more truthful, our relationship would have been better.

Even so, I tried to give her the benefit of the doubt. Two years straight I flew to her city and went with her to a Mother's Day Tea for mothers and daughters. Over the years, I told her that I loved her because she gave me life and placed me in the arms of loving adoptive parents. But one thing I would not tolerate was talking negative about my adoptive parents, because they had done nothing but save my life and give me a wonderful upbringing.

Unfortunately, my birthmother passed away in 2015. Before her passing, however, she met my adoptive father, along with my husband and our children. Now, both my adoptive mother and father are deceased as well. There is no point in hanging on to any negative feelings, but I did learn so much from my story.

My personal words of wisdom would be to adoptees who have found their birthmother or are considering the idea of finding her: stay focused on being the best friend you can be to your birthmother. Thank her for giving you life, and if you hold any ill feelings or if you think she should have kept you, try to find it in your heart to forgive her!

For me, I appreciate her courage to give me up for adoption to beautiful and loving parents. She followed her heart, and I have my life because of it! Also, to be chosen by adoptive parents that love you unconditionally is the best blessing in the entire world.

CHAPTER THIRTY-NINE

A LEARNING CURVE

Greyson Mitchell

Grey is forty-nine and from outside of Tacoma, Washington. He was adopted from birth. He is married to Cheri, who has adopted his son from a previous relationship, and he has adopted her two children.

I am an adoptee. I have always known that I was adopted. I was told since before I could remember that I was special because I was chosen. I think that was one of the best ways to handle being adopted. My adopted parents could have kept it from me because I'm white and so are they, and looks-wise I don't think I would have ever noticed. In fact, people who didn't know that I was adopted would say that I looked like my mom, and I would always respond with, "That's funny because I'm adopted."

When people would find out that I was adopted, the first thing they would ask is, "Do you want to find your real mom?" I always hated that term, "real mom," because I have a mom. I have *two*, in fact: one adoptive and one birthparent. My answer was always "no," because I honestly had no desire to meet her. In my mind, my birthmother was a fictional character. I knew a little of her story: older, already had several kids, and a waitress. Meeting her would have been like having the desire to meet Batman: not possible, because she really doesn't exist.

But then I witnessed the reunion of a birthmom with her son that she had adopted out. My girlfriend at the time had an aunt that had put up a son for adoption, and her son was about my age. I had met the aunt on several occasions, and I knew her as a real person, and at that point, my birthmom became a real person. I started to wonder about her, about my siblings, about the life that I would have had if I hadn't been adopted.

My girlfriend's mom had been the one to help her sister locate her son. We started a conversation about her helping me find my biological mom.

We pieced together some really important clues, like the fact that since I still lived in the town where the adoption occurred, my adoption papers should be in the local court system. (I was actually born two hours south of my hometown but adopted in the town where my adopted parents lived.) We started that conversation on a Thursday night, and by the following Tuesday night, there was a message on my answering machine from a woman named April, my birthmom. Long story short, we met. She and my two half-sisters came up to my hometown and met with me. I think there was a lot of staring and a lot of questions.

I first met my birthmom when I was twenty-two, and I'm now forty-nine. I was curious about her, and maybe my siblings, but I had no idea what was in store for me. People in my birth family started calling or coming up to me at work and saying, "I'm your uncle Bill." Well, I have an uncle Bill; he's my mom's brother. This guy is not my uncle Bill, and yet . . . he was. I was welcomed into this birth family (on both my birthmother's and birthfather's side) with open arms: weddings, showers (they even threw a baby shower for my wife), cousin luncheons, dinners, random phone calls, etc. All of them claiming to be my family: a cousin, a brother, an aunt, an uncle, etc. And yet every time I would hear someone exclaim who they were to me, I would shrink back a little. The reason was because I *have* a family— my adoptive family. It's small, but it's what I know to be family.

My story with my birthfather is very different, although his family reacted in a similar way. I had limited knowledge about my birth family, and I only knew that my birthfather had gone to college but was not in the picture. I think that was enough for me originally because I really only sought out my biological mother. It turned out that April had many connections to my birthfather's family. Her third husband was even his cousin. One person in particular was a man that most referred to as Uncle Bill. It's my understanding that when April was in the hospital giving birth to me, this Uncle Bill happened to be in the hospital for another reason. He put two and two together and realized that Hunter, my biological father, was the father of April's baby. It's also my understanding that Uncle Bill is a meddler and a gossip (more on that later). April told him that Hunter was not interested and that she was putting me up for adoption, and she begged him to keep this secret. Which I believe he sort of did until I resurfaced.

I am not absolutely sure of this, but I believe when my ex-girlfriend's mom was searching for April, she was going down a list of people that shared April's last name and lived in the city where I was born. In contacting these people, she found one that exclaimed that April was his aunt; I believe this is how Uncle Bill found out that I was looking for April. At that point, the word spread like wildfire. I did not know this until later.

When I met April, she told me that Hunter's response when she told him was to not tell anyone because it would ruin his standing in the Catholic Church. This also played into my choice to not pursue meeting him. But, with Uncle Bill spreading the news, people starting showing up, calling, and so on. I think they were so excited because Hunter never had any children of his own. He was married, however, and his wife had two sons from her previous marriage.

I became close with a cousin on Hunter's side of the family because we had a lot in common, and she happened to live in the next town over from me. She even asked me to play the piano at her wedding, and that's when I'm pretty sure I met everyone on that side except my biological father, who didn't live nearby. Now I was brought into family events on both sides of my birth family, and it was overpowering. About two years later, after my son was born, I moved back to my hometown, which was much farther from where everyone lived. This made it much easier to quietly just disappear from family functions and so on. I did stay in touch with the cousin, and somewhat with my two sisters and April, but I really wasn't trying to keep the relationships going.

Shortly before I moved back to my hometown, I received a call. This was pre–cell phones, pre-caller ID, so I answered the phone not knowing who was on the other line. The caller identified herself as Hunter's wife, who asked, "What do you want from us?"

I was immediately taken aback. I ended up telling her that I didn't want anything from her or Hunter. I never had any intention of seeking him out or meeting him. I told her I felt it had been made clear that he wasn't interested and that was fine. I informed her that I originally set out on this journey to meet only my biological mom, but I had no idea what I was in for. I didn't know how all these people found out about me or how to even really respond to their overwhelming but loving inclusion to the family.

As we talked, we started to piece some things together, and just about everything pointed back to Uncle Bill. So not only was he telling everyone about me and encouraging family to reach out to me, he was also chastising Hunter for not being one of those people to reach out to me. I guess he had gotten after him a couple of times, saying that he needed to reach out to his son and so on. Hunter and his wife assumed this was coming from me, but I assured her it was not.

A few other things that we cleared up was that I was a boy. When April told him she was pregnant, she also told him she thought I was a girl. (At this point in her life she had had four sons and two daughters.) She asked him if he wanted her to call him after I was born, and he said "No." So, she didn't, and she also never told him that I was a boy. For years, he assumed that he had a girl out there somewhere. When I showed up on the scene, a boy, he was skeptical. My opinion is that he was ashamed and just didn't want to deal with it, but that's just my two cents.

She and I talked for quite some time, and she realized that I wasn't trying to get away with anything, and I wasn't asking anyone for anything. She told me she thought I seemed like a nice person. She was going to talk to Hunter to see if he would at least talk to me on the phone. We made arrangements for her to call back, and she followed through and did call again. We spoke for a little bit, and she was pretty sure that when he got home, he would talk to me. I heard him come in, and then through the muffled voices I could hear her asking if he was ready. He wasn't. She got back on the phone and told me he just wasn't ready at this time. That was the last time I ever spoke to her, and I have not reached out, and neither has he.

I'd be lying if I said this wasn't hurtful. He rejected me twice, and I'm not one to put myself in a situation for a third rejection. My cousin says that her Uncle Hunter is her favorite uncle, and she has encouraged me to reach out to him several times. I've thought about it, and I even wrote out a letter at some point, but I just don't feel like it's worth it.

I can't say that a birthparent owes it to the child to meet. I would like to think that they should at least, in adoptive situations, provide medical history and genetic make-up (German, African, etc.), and maybe they do now, but in 1968 most information was based on income, race, and religious affiliation. I know this because one of April's requests was that the adoptive family *not* be Catholic.

It seems like most people that reach out to find an adoptive parent almost always start with the mom. I'm not aware of too many that seek the father first, but I would imagine there are a few. I think that when you set out on a journey to find a birthparent, you need to be open to the possibility of rejection. To assume that they're just waiting to meet you is just not realistic. The phrase "absentee father" is all too common, and this term is generally applied to men who have met and spent time with their children, so expecting a man that has never even seen you to respond positively is unrealistic. Maybe I'm jaded, but I really think that any man who wants to meet their birthchild is not the norm, and that man would be very special. Anyone would be lucky to have that kind of man in their life. Any man who doesn't want to meet their child . . . well, that child is better off not having that man in their life.

I am so thankful for adoption. My bio-sisters are in good places now, but growing up was tough on them, and on my four half-brothers. I think one of the most poignant moments after meeting them was a time when we all went out to celebrate our birthdays and my oldest sister said to her mom, "Mom, after hearing about Grey's life, I wish you had adopted me out." Ouch.

I know I had opportunities that just weren't possible or expected for my siblings, and I think that what my birthmom did was a huge sacrifice. She also provided something for a couple that tried for eight years to conceive and just couldn't.

I didn't tell my mother that I was planning on finding and meeting my birthmom, and when I told her that I had, she was very upset. In fact, it's been twenty-seven years since I met her, and we still don't talk about it. I'm not sure how I could have handled it differently, because if I had told her ahead of time, she would have made me feel guilty for wanting it, and it would have been difficult to go through with it at the time. My birthmom was almost forty-two when I was born, so I knew that I couldn't wait a really long time.

My mom was very hurt and didn't even speak to me for a few months after I told her that I had met my biological mom. Years later, as I was preparing to get married, she and I got into a fight, and she brought up the whole thing about me being adopted. I'm not sure she's ever gotten over her insecurities about it, even though I am all Mitchell (my adoptive family's name). When I talk about family—when I say mom, dad, grandma and grandpa, aunt, uncle—I'm talking about my adopted family. I have a hallway that is plastered with pictures of my family, my adopted family. My biological mom passed away a few years ago, and I hadn't seen her in the years prior. She wasn't the woman I called Mom. In fact, to this day I refer to her as April.

Many people seemed to believe that I would harbor a sense of rejection or feel angry at my birthmom for giving me away. I never did, though. I knew how much my mom wanted to be a mom, and knowing just the little bit that I did know about my biological mom led me to believe that her putting me up for adoption was a beautiful sacrifice. I'd like to challenge that notion that adopted kids feel abandoned and rejected—no, they are filling a need and a desire and are usually put in a place where they are loved and provided for in such a way that creates opportunities they may not have had otherwise.

One thing I would want to say about being adopted is that it means you are an anomaly. Growing up, knowing I was adopted, I was always aware that my adoptive family's history was not really my history. This family's DNA is not my DNA. I look at pictures of my mom's mom, and I can see how my cousin Aimee is her doppelgänger. There is a biological piece to the puzzle that I don't have. On my biological side, I don't have a history of life experiences with my blood relatives; therefore, a relationship is somewhat forced just because we're related. As I've mentioned, I have two sisters and four brothers, but I was raised as an only child. I say the word "sister," but honestly, they feel more like people I once worked with, and with whom I now sort of keep in touch. But I see the relationship that my sisters and brothers have with each other, and it's different from what I have with them. They share blood, and they share experiences. I can't be blood related to my family, and I can't go back and share life, those formative years, with my birth family. Anomaly.

I think the one thing I would have liked to have handled differently was the overwhelming response of the biological family. I eventually excused myself from everything; it was too much, too fast. I kept in touch with the cousin who lived near, and that was about it. I lost touch with my birthmom and had really lost touch with just about everyone. In the last few years I have reconnected with my sisters (thank you, Facebook) and keep up with the younger of the two pretty regularly (the older one won't do Facebook). The younger one put together a family reunion last summer, and I went and met some "relatives." It was nice and laid back.

I'm not sure how I could have handled it differently. To them, I was just one long-lost nephew, cousin, etc. But to me, it felt like they were thousands of strangers staking claim on some branch of a family tree with which I wasn't familiar. I guess I just wish I would have known the "can of relatives" I was about to open and would have been better prepared.

I love watching the show *Long Lost Family*, but the one thing that I wish they did better is showing the complicated follow-up. The meeting is easy; it's what follows afterward that is hard. The relationships are unpredictable, and I imagine that ones that are easy to maintain and grow are few and far between. I could be wrong, and I am very interested to find out what others have to say. Maybe it was just my situation that left me overwhelmed and backing off. I did miss out on the last few years of April's life, and I think I would have liked more information about her: what her life was like and how she persevered through everything. Was she happy? Did she have any regrets? Motherly advice perhaps . . . ?

Doing my search gained me an appreciation for what my life was, and how it could've been drastically different. Like I said before, my siblings had a rough go of it; my birthmom didn't always make good choices in husbands, and I guess there was abuse. Both my sisters had babies before they were out of their teens; in fact, the younger sister also put a child up for adoption and has since met him. I assume if my birthmother had kept me, my life would be much different today.

I do have one other connection to adoption. When I was twenty-five, my girlfriend got pregnant. She wasn't interested in having a baby or sticking around, but she did not have an abortion, which I fully supported. I decided that I was going to keep the baby and that I would do whatever it took to raise my son, even if I remained single. When I was first told about the pregnancy, I considered the adoption route my girlfriend wanted for about a minute. While the timing may not have been ideal, I felt that I was in a good place for taking on this responsibility. And yes, I can honestly say that being adopted myself totally played into my wanting to keep him. He was the only human being that would be blood related *and* have a history with me. That being said, it really made me realize what a mom who puts a baby up for adoption must go through. That has to be the most difficult decision a woman ever makes, and yet, it's truly a selfless and beautiful thing.

When my son was eight, I did get married. It was very important to my wife that we all become one family, and we proceeded with her adopting my son, and me adopting her children. So, while it's not quite the typical adoption story, it is another story about adoption.

Family is very essential to my wife and me. Our desire to have all of us be one family and create a legacy of putting family first is incredibly important to us. So even though my son's mom was not in the picture and we never had to work out a parenting plan or visitation, having any family member with a different last name made us feel incomplete. Having her adopt my son, and me adopt her two children, was a step in creating a complete family.

This next paragraph is from my wife.

Our children are part of the fabric that makes us who we are, influences how we behave, and molds our worldview. I could not love Grey without loving Jack, just as he could not really love me without loving Leo and Lila. And while emotions can be separate from legal issues such as this, it was extremely important to me that my words, deeds, and actions all conveyed to Jack that I was 100 percent committed to him becoming the man he wanted to become. I wanted him to know that he was an equal heir to all I have to offer, and that he was as much my child as Leo and Lila. The adoption process is just a symbol of that desire.

I have two last bits of advice for those involved in adoption. For adoptees, this is your story; you get to narrate it in the way that you feel is best. If you have a desire to seek out your birthparents, then do so. But if the desire isn't there, don't feel guilty about it. If you've lived a good life, feel blessed to be who and where you are. It's okay to keep it that way.

And finally, love is love, and it knows no boundaries. Not only was I an only child, but I was an only grandchild on my dad's side. I have nothing but amazing and fond memories of those grandparents, and not sharing DNA never made one bit of difference. I think now, as a stepparent and a step-grandparent (though I never use those terms), I don't think about my three grandsons as not being a part of my DNA. They are my family and my grandsons. Period.

CHAPTER FORTY

MY MOTHER, MY HERO

Theresa Larivee

Theresa is fifty-one years old and from Los Angeles, California. She is the production manager for Rock against MS, an animal energy healer, and the owner of Tranquil Touch Equine Sports Therapy Massage.

I was adopted in Germany in 1965 by Frank and Edith Larivee. My father, Frank, was in the Air Force and was stationed there. My German biological mother was single. From what I understand, my birthmother met my parents. My parents were looking to adopt, and they adopted me legally through the courts in Germany. At the time, Germany had a cooling-off period of one year for birthmothers to confirm their decisions. During that time, I lived in an orphanage. After one year, my adopted parents could foster me and then start the process to adopt me. We lived in Germany until my adoption was final. We came to the United States for a couple years, and then we moved back to Germany. I now live in Los Angeles.

I have never not known I was adopted. I've known since I can remember. My adoptive mother was amazing. She wanted me to know everything about being German, my culture, and who I was. She had such a beautiful heart. Any questions I asked about my biomom, she answered the best she could. I do not know if the story she told me is true, but she always made me feel special. She always let me know how much my birthmother loved me and how generous and loving she was to bring such a meaningful gift into my mother's life.

I really don't have any strong feelings about being adopted. It's all I have known. I don't mean that in a cold, non-feeling, ungrateful way. Quite the opposite, actually. I am so thankful to my biomom for picking the right family for me.

I feel if my adopted mother were alive, her answer would be more emotional. Adoption meant more to her than me. I was her blessing. I was so loved by her. She longed for a child, and adoption was her answer. To see how special adoption was for my mother probably means more to me than me being adopted, if that makes sense. I just knew that was where I was supposed to be.

Although my parents met my biomother, I never have, and I would love to meet her. Adoptions in Germany are open, so I have all my birthmom personal information: her name, birthday, where she is from. I know in 1967 she married a man named Wright and moved to the United States. I have my adoption papers and my original birth certificate.

I'm afraid she might not be alive anymore, and I fear that her family does not know of me. I would never want to hurt her or her family. I guess I don't know how to approach her since I don't want to cause her any problems. I hoped she would find me and that would erase all my fears. I've always wanted her to know how thankful I am for all she did for me. I know my mother would also want her to know how appreciative she was. God answered all my mom's prayers when my birthmother came into her life. I wish I could let her know how much she meant to us.

There is not one thing that I wish my parents had done differently. I don't want to come across as boring or a waste of your time, but my parents did an amazing job, including through the good, bad, and teenager years. They did everything they could to help me know who I was. My story is amazing, and it was my mother who made it so beautiful, and who presented my birthmother in such a special way. I never felt abandoned or unwanted.

Another example of how beautiful my mom was: she always told me how pretty I was, and how I looked and walked just like my birthmom. That takes a special woman to tell their adopted child something like that.

I know people who have a lot of issues because they were adopted, but I cannot relate to that. It mostly stems from how their parents dealt with adoption. For example, I have cousins who were adopted, but our adoptions were treated very differently. They were not told about it as they were growing up, and I see how not telling them early on hurt them and left them confused. It's really about the people who adopted you, and who they chose to be as parents. It's about how they make you feel, whether you're adopted or not.

Don't get me wrong. I have dealt with negativity. After my mother passed away, my father remarried. Luckily, I was in my thirties when he remarried. His new wife does not believe in adoption. She believes adopted children are someone's trash. She constantly put me down for being adopted, but I never let her affect me. She is a pathetic person, and those are her issues, not mine. I was old enough to know that. Sadly, if I was a child, or not raised by such a strong woman, it could have affected me very differently.

There are always going to be hateful, negative people who find a reason to put you down. If they are using the fact that you are adopted to do that, then shame on them. I've never been a person to even tolerate something like that. I loved the story my mother told me, and I held that close to my heart. To have a birthmother who was strong enough to want something better for me, and an adopted mom strong enough to put all her fears aside and answer every question, was such a blessing. It was my destiny to be strong, too.

If I were to give adoptees any advice, I would say that everyone deals with adoption differently. It's all about your parents. My parents never kept anything from me. I would say to adoptive parents, always let your child know they were adopted. Learn about their birthmother. Don't be scared to answer questions. Be kind with your answers. Let them know they are loved by their birthmother. It takes a special woman to give up her child for the good of the child. It is an extremely selfless act.

Everything about my adoption was positive in the way I was treated, loved, and raised. I feel the way my parents dealt with everything was much different from most, especially in the way they never took my questions personally or thought I was being disrespectful. They were smart enough to know it's normal for children to be curious about who they are. They wanted me to be proud of who I am.

I am proud. I am a German Jew (birthmom), French Canadian-American (Dad), and Mexican-American (Mom). With my adoption came many cultures. I am my own melting pot.

CHAPTER FORTY-ONE

I LOVE VALENTINE'S DAY

Angela Paxton

Angela is a twenty-two-year educator and adoption advocate from McKinney, Texas, who is running for Texas state senator in November 2018. She was adopted as an infant and met her birthmother as an adult. She and her husband, Texas Attorney General Ken Paxton, have been married thirty years and have four children.

I've always loved Valentine's Day. I know I'm not alone; it's special to many people for many different reasons. Some celebrate proposals, some anniversaries; to most it is the simple opportunity to say "I love you" to someone dear. But for me, Valentine's Day—this day of celebrating love—is my birthday, and it has always seemed profoundly fitting. You see, I am an adopted child, and Valentine's Day is the story of my life.

I never remember being told I was adopted. I just knew, the same way other children know they are natural children of their parents. And I knew it was a special thing. I grew up knowing that I was chosen. I knew that my birthmother had been an unmarried college student, and I lived in gratitude for her noble choice to give me a life in a family with a loving mother and a father. My younger brother was adopted two years after me.

I was born in New Braunfels, but I grew up in Rendon—a small, still-unincorporated Texas town south of Fort Worth. My mom, Anita, and my dad, Wayne, and my brother, Corey, went to church every Sunday morning, Sunday night, and Wednesday night. My parents attended (and sometimes coached) every volleyball, basketball, and softball game I ever played, were on the front row for every piano recital and church solo, and used their yearly vacation time to voluntarily chaperone my youth-group mission trips. I grew up with friends who loved me no matter what and challenged me to be my best and follow God with all my heart. I graduated third in my class at Mansfield High School and went to Baylor University on a scholarship.

There I realized I really liked math, began taking my love of music seriously, and made lifelong friends. My senior year at Baylor—and just in time, I might add—I fell in love with the student body president, Ken Paxton. We married the following year on the only open weekend of Baylor football season and finished out our honeymoon at Baylor Homecoming.

We began married life in Houston, where I pursued a master's degree in education, and then we moved to Charlottesville, Virginia, where Ken received his law degree. After three years, we returned to Texas. Ken began his law career, and I taught school until we began our family. Tucker, Abby, and Mattie were all born in Dallas. Two days after Mattie was born, we moved to McKinney to help start a church, and Katie was born two years later.

August of 2002 found us approaching the first of Ken's elections to five terms in the Texas House of Representatives and a term in the Texas Senate. Our children were three, five, seven, and nine. Ken and I were both on the verge of our fortieth birthdays. Ken had just launched into solo law practice, and I was engaged in our church's women's ministry and sang on the worship team. Life was exciting and busy and about as unpredictable as it had ever been. But it was about to become even more so.

That August, an unexpected letter arrived among all of the election-related mail addressed to Ken. It was a certified letter addressed to me. Not recognizing the return address, I opened the envelope and read the letter, which began:

> Dear Angela Suzanne Paxton,
> I am a birthmother searching for my first child who was born February 14, 1963 in New Braunfels, Texas. . . .

It wasn't that I had never been curious. But I had long ago decided to be comfortable with the mystery inherent in being an adopted child. My father had once confided with me my mother's secret fear that my brother and I might not see her as our "real" mother. I had no desire to contribute to that fear by seeking out my birthparents. Her peace of mind in that regard weighed in more heavily than curiosity ever could.

But I had always longed to tell my birthmother thank you. In fact, in 2000 I had written a song to my unknown birthmother and called it "A Thank You Song (for Linda)." I'm not sure why I gave her a name in my notes, but I did.

So, you can only imagine my surprise when I saw how the letter concluded:

> I hopefully wait to hear from you.
>
> Sincerely,
>
> Linda

This is part of the letter I received.

> I am a birthmother searching for my first child who was born February 14, 1963 in New Braunfels, Texas. She was picked up from the hospital several days later and the adoption took place in Fort Worth. I was a college student at TCU in Fort Worth and my parents insisted that I allow my daughter to be adopted. If you are she, you may not have been told that you were adopted.
>
> Once I married and started having a family, I wanted to try to find out if my first child was at least being well taken care of. In the 1970s I called the attorney in Fort Worth . . . who handled the adoption and gave him my address and phone number in case my daughter or her family ever tried to find me. I found out that because Texas adoption records are sealed, I was not able to do much more. [The attorney] has since deceased. However, the doctor who delivered my child is still alive and I have talked with him off and on through the years because I wanted to be locatable. . . . I also finally found out about the Texas Dept. of Health Adoption Registry where birthparents and adopted persons can register and the Department will connect the two parties. They also offer pre-meeting counseling.
>
> My greatest hope has been that her young years were in a loving family and that she grew to adulthood as an emotionally, mentally and

spiritually healthy person. It is possible that this is not what happened.

Finally, with the assistance of a Fort Worth attorney and a detective . . . we narrowed my search down to two women and you are one of them. If you do not know if you were adopted, you can call . . . the Texas Dept. of Health Adoption Registry . . . and [they] can look up your original birth record and tell you one way or the other.

If you want to know me and hopefully meet me to talk, I offer my references . . . so that you can verify my story. I hope that you will extend me the courtesy of some response, either yay or nay to my question, just for my own peace of mind. I hope this does not cause you to be distressed. I am not only in search of the truth but also a relationship of some kind, if that is possible.

I was shocked, thrilled, and joyful. But before I could make a decision, I knew I had to talk to my adoptive mom. I sent Linda an email in response, part of which is included here:

Dear Linda,

Thank you so much for your letter. I don't get many certified letters, so I was a little surprised even before I opened it! And of course, after I did open it, I was even more surprised. But I want you to know that it was a very welcome surprise.

I think I may very well be the person you are looking for. Indeed, I am adopted, my birthday is February 14, 1963, and I was born in New Braunfels. My adoption was finalized in Tarrant County. And the one bit of personal information I've been told about my birthmother is that she was a TCU student. . . .

If it is true that you are my birthmother, I am so happy to have the opportunity to finally say this to you: I have always had the utmost respect for you, and you gave me the most wonderful life any child could have imagined. I did grow up in a loving home. I always knew I was adopted, and I have always felt very special because of it. My parents were Christians, and I came to the Lord when I was eight. I am healthy, happily married, and have children of my own. I would not trade my life for anyone's . . . and I thank you for that life, because you gave it to me.

It's important to me to talk to my mother face-to-face before I proceed with a face-to-face meeting with you, but I think I would like that very much. I hope you understand and that you will be patient with me in this (you've certainly been patient so far!). But I didn't want you to have to wait any longer for at least a response to your wonderful letter.

Please know that I am far from distressed by your letter. I am happy for it. . . .

God's blessings be upon you, and again, thank you so much for all you have done for me.

Sincerely,

Angela

A few weeks later, with my mom's blessing, I met Linda face to face. I sang the song I had written for her, to her. We cried. We laughed. My children welcomed a new grandmother into their lives. "Grand-Birthmother" was the title our son, Tucker, bequeathed to her. Ken acquired a second mother-in-law. At the age of thirty-nine, I met four brothers and sisters I had never known, along with aunts and uncles and cousins. They told me, "We have been praying that the Lord would bring you back to us." And I met my grandmother, Mattie Rena, and Ken and I marveled together that five years before we knew her, we had named our third child Mattie—after her!

Although my mother had encouraged me to meet my birth family, she privately struggled. For two years, she resisted the invitation to meet Linda, my birthmother and her feared "competition." Linda even sent her the following letter:

Dear Anita,

I thought that you and I might have had an opportunity to meet by now, but since we haven't, I sincerely hope you will accept this note to you as from the deepest part of my heart. I still hope that I will be able to see you sometime soon to thank you in person for taking such good care of Angela.

Thank you for adopting her. Thank you for giving her such a beautiful name. I can tell that she has been and always will be your angel. You and your husband did a marvelous job of being parents and she has certainly developed into an outstanding, talented woman. I am especially grateful to you that you took her to church early on and introduced her to her Lord Jesus Christ. It sounds like she has had a very real relationship with Him throughout her life. . . .

She went through her picture albums with me. . . . The pictures of her as a baby with you and your husband holding her are so sweet and gentle. And she loves you very dearly and truly appreciates all that you have done for her. . . . You are a wonderful mother.

When I first met her in August, I wasn't sure what our relationship would be like, but she has been kind, gracious, and accepting of me—more than I ever could have hoped for. Her attitude toward life is in large part the result of your influence on her.

I have so much to thank you for. And I do pray God's blessings will continue to abide in your life.

Please accept my very warmest regards,

Linda Kluthe

And then suddenly, my mom announced, "I'm ready to meet Linda."

And so it was that in the spring of 2004, in a hotel room at a women's retreat, I witnessed something I never dreamed I would see. I watched my birthmother present my mother with a dozen red roses, kneel before her, and say, "Thank you. You gave Angela what I never could have given her. You gave her a life." And then I watched my mom, who had been unable to conceive a child, reply through tears, "No, thank you—you gave her what I never could have: you gave her life." And we all cried smiling tears as one woman's lifelong fear melted into a miraculous friendship.

Adoption has been such a blessing to me. The one primary piece of advice I would give others, no matter if it is to an adoptee, a birthparent, or adoptive family, is to be open and be compassionate. These are matters of the heart, and seeing things from each other's point of view is so important.

There are so many wonderful ways I've benefited in my adoption experience. I have witnessed healing I never expected to see. When my birth-grandmother—the woman who made the decision that I would be adopted—accepted me into her life with open arms, her daughter—my birthmother—felt accepted again, healing a deep, though hidden, pain of rejection. And my adopted mother, after so many years of fear, was set free. In fact, when her health began declining and she came to live with us for five years, it was my birthmother—and her friend—who stayed with her for ten days so our family could go on a vacation.

I have grown up with a deep sense of being loved and accepted by my adopted parents, by God, and by the birthmom who placed me for adoption in order to take care of me. Truly, being adopted has been one of my favorite aspects of who I am.

I have grown up with a deep sense of purpose: I was given the chance to live! I am very aware that I might not have had this chance given the circumstances of my conception. I am here for a reason. Life is a sacred opportunity to make a positive difference in the world, and I want to do that in big and small ways every day.

The brave sacrifices of others gave me the life I have been blessed to live. When I held my firstborn for the first time, I realized in an entirely new way the depth of sacrifice of my birthmom. In that spirit, I too want to be a fearless giver, even when it is hard, risky, or scary. I want my life to be a thank you to God, my adopted parents, and my birthmom.

One of the best things my adopted parents did was to teach me I was adopted from the very beginning. I literally don't remember the first time it was a topic—there was no special occasion, just a natural understanding. I wish I could tell you how they did that (both of my adopted parents have passed away). They always framed it positively, that they chose me and were so thankful for me. They framed my birthmom's choice to choose adoption for me as a loving, beautiful, and noble thing for a young woman in her circumstances to do so that she could look out for my best interest. They were honest with me about what they did and did not know about the circumstances of my adoption, including some of their own insecurities as adopted parents, and shared these sorts of things with me at what seems to me to have been age-appropriate times.

And that's why I've always loved Valentine's Day. It's not only my birthday; it truly is the story of my life. Psalm 16:6 says, "The boundary lines have fallen for me in pleasant places; surely I have a delightful inheritance." Indeed, I have lived in love all of my life because the goodness of God put two very special women in my life: one who gave life to me, and one who gave me a life.

CHOOSING HOPE

Lorri Antosz Benson

All these stories made an impression on me. I hope they did on you as well. One thing strikes me . . . although these words of wisdom based on experience are meant to be helpful to those traveling on an adoption journey, I believe they are valuable for the broader reaches of all kinds of families. Families are different today. They are made up of stepparents and stepsiblings, and half-brothers and half-sisters. Some have two dads, or two moms. These stories contain truths that are valuable for all blended families, and really, for all parents.

For some potential contributors, the prospect of going public with their story either was too difficult or didn't sit well with other relationships in their lives. As I said in Chapter One, it can be complicated. There were two stories with similar themes that fell into this category, but I at least wanted to share their essence here because I feel like they capture the spirit of adoption.

Both were parents who had adopted sons from troubled birth families; both had extreme challenges while raising them. One child struggled with alcohol dependence, and one had mental illness and drug abuse issues. Both sons were given the best possible childhoods, and as issues were revealed, both families did everything they could to help. In one case, the adoptive mother feared for her family's safety; in the other, she feared for her son's life. In both cases, their troubled young adult sons eventually had children, and their parental rights were severed. Their drug-addicted babies faced foster care. After two decades of pouring out love, going to kids' games, paying for lessons, doctors, medicines and rehab, after sleepless nights, as babies and teenagers . . . after all the worry and anxiety when their child disappeared into a world of substance abuse, both of these parents, now grandparents, have chosen the same thing. They each have adopted their adopted son's baby.

They know the risks; they know the chances. They've lived it. They know they could be facing another twenty years of the same thing. But both chose adoption. Why? Because they felt every child deserves the best chance possible at a happy childhood and a productive life. They told me that each child deserves a loving family, and who better to provide such a family than someone who has already dealt with the worst-case scenario? Here's what I was told: "We know his genetics, and a lot of people couldn't handle that. We know we can, because we've done it. We can give him the best, and that's the attitude you have to have if you're going to adopt. Even a biological child can have problems you don't expect. Your child is your child. This baby brings joy to our house and deserves a chance. So did my son. And I love them both."

What a testimony for adoption! In both of these cases, they dealt with an adoption nightmare. They saw it through to their child's adulthood, and then chose adoption again, without hesitation. Adoption didn't fail them. They haven't lost hope—in fact, quite the opposite. They've chosen to hope again.

To me, the moral of these story is that each human being is unique and here for a reason. We all deserve a chance. There are no guarantees in life, but there are options. And for birthparents, adoptees, adoptive parents, and even adoptive grandparents, adoption is an amazing, life-changing, soul-stretching option. The stories in this book, and their writers, prove that.

ACKNOWLEDGMENTS

I want to thank all those who contributed their personal stories, feelings, emotions, and words of wisdom. For some, going back through time brought back wonderful recollections and even served to initiate conversations with loved ones, but I know this wasn't the easiest assignment for others. Adoption is an emotional, complex process . . . different for everyone. The feelings and experiences can be very complicated, and can be tied up with painful memories. I'm amazed at the honesty and openness that this project has brought out in people.

These contributors put their hearts and souls into this project. Many told me it was cathartic for them to go back through their recollections and come up with lessons learned to help others, lessons that express the things that were done right or wrong during their experience. After reading these very personal stories, I am convinced that this book will be a really important resource for those entering or already in the adoption world. I sincerely hope so.

Thank you to all those at Familius, especially Christopher Robbins, who had the vision to go beyond my memoir and create a collection of adoption books. Thanks to Leah Welker for her support, and her detailed and thorough editing process.

I'm indebted to David Miles, Kate Farrell, and the editing and design team for their work in making this a beautiful book, inside and out.

I would like to give my eternal thanks to my family: Halli, Taylor, Taryn, Keith, and Steve for their support, technical and website help, and words of inspiration and love throughout this project. Special thanks to Taryn for **always** taking time to be my writer's eyes. Your opinions are always spot on! And Steve, who could not be a more supportive and loving partner, and who has the patience of a saint with my one a.m. writing spurts, I live in gratitude for your encouragement, and for the day you walked into my life.

Also included in my family thank you's: Kate, Anne, and Mary Ellen: for helping to get this book right, and for being an important part of my family.

You too, Alex and Daniel! Anne, you will always be St. Anne in my book, and Katie, God bless your need to know! You are the perfect blend of nature and nurture! Sending a thank you to Temple in heaven, too—you and Anne were angels long before you became one in the afterlife. You were just the parents for my Aimee/Katie that I hoped and prayed you would be.

Finally, a special shout-out to my grandnuggets: Riley, Leo, Annabel, Owen, and Oliver. Just because I love them and they're so darn cute. They are the proof that no matter how it is formed, family is the best part of life's tapestry.

ADOPTING HOPE

INDEX

ABOUT THE AUTHOR

Lorri Antosz Benson is an award-winning television producer, writer, author and former nationally syndicated columnist. Most notably, she worked for *Donahue*, the acclaimed show hosted by the legendary Phil Donahue, for fifteen years, eight of which were spent as senior producer. Lorri received two Emmy Awards and ten Emmy nominations for her work with *Donahue*, and was awarded the American Women in Radio and Television Commendation several times.

She went on to write a nationally syndicated column for eleven years called Talk the Talk, a behind-the-scenes look at the world of talk television. During that period, she also spent two years as the executive producer of *Golden Lifestyles*, a regional talk show in southwest Florida.

Lorri's first book, *Distorted*, was a memoir co-authored with her daughter Taryn, which delved into Taryn's struggle with an eating disorder and the effect on the family. They were featured on many national broadcasts, including the *Today Show* and the *Montel Williams Show*.

Her second book, *To Have and Not To Hold*, was the start of her three-book series on adoption, and covered the placing of her first child, Aimee, for closed adoption, and the subsequent development of a flourishing relationship with her and her family, with a focus on the connection between the two mothers.

Lorri's work has led her to become a family advocate, and a speaker/expert on eating disorders, adoption, and resources for parents. She is the founder of Family Matters, her family-advocacy brand. She serves on the Parent, Family & Friends Network steering committeefor the National Eating Disorder Association, and is also on the board of Harvest Home, a Los Angeles-based organization which shelters and assists pregnant homeless women.

Lorri also maintains a blog for empty nesters, Feathering My Empty Nest at www.FeatheringMyEmptyNest.tumblr.com. She and her husband,

Steve, reside in Santa Monica, CA. They have four children, including Lorri's birthdaughter, and five grandchildren.

www.LorriAntoszBenson.com

ABOUT FAMILIUS

VISIT OUR WEBSITE: WWW.FAMILIUS.COM

JOIN OUR FAMILY

There are lots of ways to connect with us! Subscribe to our newsletters at www.familius.com to receive uplifting daily inspiration, essays from our Pater Familius, a free ebook every month, and the first word on special discounts and Familius news.

GET BULK DISCOUNTS

If you feel a few friends and family might benefit from what you've read, let us know and we'll be happy to provide you with quantity discounts. Simply email us at orders@familius.com.

CONNECT

- ✦ Facebook: www.facebook.com/paterfamilius
- ✦ Twitter: @familiustalk, @paterfamilius1
- ✦ Pinterest: www.pinterest.com/familius
- ✦ Instagram: @familiustalk

FAMILIUS

The most important work you ever do will be within the walls of your own home.

CPSIA information can be obtained
at www.ICGtesting.com
Printed in the USA
FSHW02n0917240518

9 781641 70036